Advance Praise for *Stuccoville: Life*

"This is really a beautiful book: wise, kind, generous and sometimes heartbreaking. My heart is better and stronger because I had the chance to read it."
—Steve Yarbrough, author of *The Unmade World* and *The End of California*
https://www.steveyarbrough.net

"Combining a novelist's command of character and plot with a memoirist's instincts and a poet's command of language, *Stuccoville: Life Without a Net* shines as Radke's debut. Unflinchingly honest, suspenseful, humorous, and at times heartbreaking, this book is a testament to a son's undying love for his mother. Radke's story is shaped by loss and illness, but also by moments of undeniable grace."
—Steven Church, author of *I'm Just Getting to the Disturbing Part: On Work, Fear, and Fatherhood*, editor of *The Normal School: A Literary Magazine*.

"*Stuccoville: Life Without a Net* explores the profoundly interdependent relationship between a boy and his mother, whose chronic and increasingly debilitating illness shapes both of their lives. Chuck Radke has written a compelling story of complicated familial love and commitment—a story of survival and acceptance."
—Corrinne Clegg Hales, author of *To Make It Right*

"Kafka said that a book must be the axe for the frozen sea within us. Chuck Radke's stirring, at times heartbreaking memoir is such an axe. When I finished reading, I wanted to stand up and cheer the author's unflinching honesty and filial devotion. Weeks later, I'm still seeing the world through its clarifying lens. This exuberant and harrowing story of difficult lives, of sacrifice and incapacity, is rendered with wit, charm, and intelligence. There's not a false step taken. There's not a sentimental moment. Just grit, grace, and gratitude."
—John Dufresne, author of *Requiem, Mass.* and *Love Warps the Mind a Little*
http://johndufresne.com/

Stuccoville

Stuccoville
Life Without a Net

Charles Lewis Radke

E. L. Marker
Salt Lake City

E. L. Marker, an imprint of WiDō Publishing
Salt Lake City, Utah
www.widopublishing.com

This book is a work of nonfiction. It is a product of the author's memory, which is flawed. It is also the product of hundreds of artifacts left to the author by his mother. Several of the names and personal details have been changed. Others have not. In almost every instance, the author worked in earnest for accuracy, except in places where fabrication became necessary, which has been noted.

Cover Design by Steven Novak
Book design by Marny K. Parkin
Fig leaf image from "Oak Leaf Vectors" by Vecteezy / dumbmichael

ISBN: 978-1-947966-43-7

For My Mother

Our days may come to seventy years,
or eighty, if our strength endures;
yet the best of them are but trouble and sorrow,
for they quickly pass, and we fly away.

—Psalm 90:10

"What's it about? Every book worth a damn is about emotions and love and death and pain. It's about words. It's
about a man dealing with life. Okay?"

—J. R. Moehringer, *The Tender Bar*

Prologue

The Wolf, I'm Afraid

"I saw Dr. Hoytt for the first time since October. He thought my face pretty round. Said it would probably be under 10 mg of medicine before it might be noticeable."

—Miss Barbara Lewis,
letter to her parents, December 14, 1959

WHEN I WAS GROWING UP, MY MOTHER MADE IT CLEAR that there were a number of things I would have to do on my own. Jigsaw puzzles, for one. I would have to do jigsaw puzzles on my own. She might look over my shoulder and suggest possibilities, but when it came to actually notching a piece into place, it was up to me. Because her health was poor and she was overcome with worry, she parented by diversion, feeding me activities requiring nothing more from her than good timing. When the allure of one amusement began to wane for me, she was ready with another. Tired of Lincoln Logs? Here's a deck of cards. Here's an Etch-A-Sketch. Here's Stretch Armstrong. And when all that was done? *Here's a book.*

Because I was a boy with a long attention span, this strategy worked well for her. I could be kept occupied for large blocks of time before growing bored, which gave her the space she needed to chain-smoke Virginia Slim menthols and await revelations and healing that never came.

Four decades later, when presented with the results of a workplace skills inventory, I was not surprised to find that I thrive on autonomy. Given the choice between a collaborative group project and rolling around on a carpet of thumbtacks, I choose thumbtacks.

"That sounds like you," Karen said. "*Autonomous*. A real lone wolf."

"To each his own," I said.

For Karen—a friendly, social woman who teaches children and has spent a dozen years in the same book club—community is vital to living well. She has committed us this year to entertaining more, and she has told me I should be more involved with other humans, maybe join a Bible study or a book club. I told her book clubs would be fine if everyone would just sit quietly and *read*.

"Those are called libraries," she said.

As a boy—before I was old enough to attend school—my mother and I connected through tattered board-books and *Highlights* magazines in physicians' waiting rooms. As long as I could turn the pages, she was happy to read, and she did so with altered pitches and inflections and a convincing basso profundo each time a menacing giant threatened a village. "Fee, fi, fo fummy, I smell a boy and boys are yummy! Now get that boy into my tummy!" Words transformed my mother in ways nothing else could; she became characters capable of courageous acts and feats of derring-do. She flourished with possibility, becoming demure or regal or wicked, depending on the story, depending on the context in which the tales played out. She was not, at least for those moments, a woman abandoned and buckling under lupus, which had been turning her immune system against her organs since she was sixteen. The disease gnawed at her connective tissues, leaving her joints in a state of bone-on-bone. It attacked her fingers first. Think of a wolf ravaging a carcass. Flannery O'Connor, who suffered the same fate, wrote of her disease, "The wolf, I'm afraid, is inside tearing up the place." The doctor who diagnosed my mother in 1959 gave her a fighting chance to live to thirty; she was twenty-one at the time. O'Connor, diagnosed at twenty-five, made it to thirty-nine. The same doctor who diagnosed my mother warned her against ever having children. She would leave them motherless at a young age, he told her.

She married my father three years later and had me anyway.

Because of her illness, my mother barely graduated high school. Her entire senior year was spent bedridden, her teachers kind enough to accept late, partially finished assignments. She never went to college. Other than children's books, all I ever saw my mother read were pill bottles, which I usually opened for her. This gave me a nascent clarity about how things would work between us, especially once my father left. From the time I could use my fingers until I went away for college, my relationship with my mother was one of mutual aid. She did what she could, I did what I could, and this went on for years until, at last, she could do nothing more. By the time I returned to Fresno for good, our mutually beneficial relationship had become one-sided.

Despite the attention and general goodwill I encountered as a boy from doctors and nurses and receptionists—people who saw me as often as they saw my mother—I resented my father deeply for leaving, for passing off my mother's care to me just before my eighth birthday. Of course, he didn't say that. He never sat me down and spoke the words to me—"Son, I am leaving, and it is time for you to care for your sick mother." Yes, she was sick when he left, but he could not have predicted how much worse things would get for her or, later in his life, for him as well. This does not excuse him. He was acting on impulse then, running from one thing to something else that seemed more promising. That's how I explained it to my own children when they asked why, unlike their cousins, they didn't have two grandpas.

"What are *greener pastures*?" they asked.

I told them it's when something else looks better to you than what you have. "Then you find out when you get there," I said, "that the *something else* isn't all that great."

They are older now, my children, and they know more of the whole story. But when they were younger, they couldn't know, or they couldn't understand, how it was possible that a father could leave his children. All I could tell them was that at some point in his life, their other grandpa decided to disappear. This concerned them. If he could decide to disappear, could I?

"Don't worry," I said. "I am not going to disappear."

What would have made less sense to them, but which is just as true, is this: I am, but *I am not*, my father's son.

My mother, though, that's a different story. Her lupus was not just the defining feature of her life, it became the formative experience of mine, one synonymous with pain and worry and, during my adolescence, deep, abiding shame. Her poor health was my most sensitive secret, and I was terrified that if other kids found out, they might find me equally defective or worse, unlikable. Consequently, along with the prednisone to which she'd become addicted, we were skilled at keeping my mother's deficiencies hidden. When the director of a play asked Mom to sew my costume, I spoke up before she could answer: "We don't have a sewing machine."

Who was I kidding? Everyone back then had a sewing machine. Ours was in the coat closet next to the TV trays. I was obviously lying, but it was a lie to prevent suffering. A lie of the noblest sort, I felt. We did have a sewing machine, but my mother couldn't operate it any better than she could the controls of a passenger jet. Her fingers, by that time, were mostly swan-necked and functionless. She hid them in sweater pockets or beneath a purse. For photographs, she concealed them with a lap dog. And when utility became necessary, as it was with driving, we worked it out. She turned the steering wheel and depressed the clutch. From the passenger seat, I managed the stick shift. Sure, there were moments of grinding, bickering gears, but we always got where we needed to go, and when I turned sixteen, all the driving fell to me.

Long before I could put it into words, then, I had the sense that I was living in reverse. Hospitals and pharmacies and doctors' offices were for old people, not for kids, but I had spent enough time in them to have favorite chairs, favorite books, and favorite nurses who gave me stickers and candy, who gave my cheeks a squeeze. They said, "I wish I could take you home with me." I loved my mother, but I couldn't help but be intrigued by such a fantasy, especially if there was a man involved, and other children, because the two things I wanted most in the world were a father and siblings. When I was older and knew those wishes would never come true, I turned my longing to love. I would be a husband.

Then, since I couldn't have a father, I would be one of those, too. I would be the best husband and father ever because I would look to my own father, then do the opposite. That seemed a surefire formula, easy to accomplish, even though I had already learned that life is not so tidy. I would have to puzzle through it. I would have to figure it out. Though my mother might suggest possibilities, putting it all together was on me. But before I could do that—before I could reckon with life as a husband, then father—I had to learn to be a son.

1

There's Money in Paper Bags!

"Probably has had lupus or something before she was sixteen years old, at that time she lived in Illinois and they told
her she had rheumatic fever. Managed without Prednisone
until 1971. Since then, she has been back on it. She just kind
of aches and hurts all over."

—I.G.T., MD, Progress Notes,
January 20, 1975

IN SEPTEMBER OF 1973, AROUND MY FIFTH BIRTHDAY, WE
moved to Tigard, Oregon, from Los Angeles. My parents had both
worked in Hollywood, where they met at the ad agency Erwin Wasey.
It was in the Lee Tower on Wilshire Boulevard's Miracle Mile, southern California's first real skyscraper. Dad was a copywriter in charge of
an in-house recording studio. Years later, on the book jacket of his self-
published novel, he credited himself with having written over "500 copy
ads and TV commercials beginning in the mid-1960s." One of those was
a twenty-second, black-and-white Carnation Coffee-mate spot featuring a mustachioed man in a chef's hat. "Here's a man who loves good
coffee," the ad began. "And he's discovered a coffee creamer that lets him
enjoy his coffee even more." It featured key dietary facts (non-dairy, only
eleven calories per level teaspoon) and ended the way it began: "Enjoy
your coffee even more. Switch to Coffee-mate."

Enjoy. Switch. The copywriter's formula, at its most basic. You want to enjoy life? Switch from one thing to something else. Coffee creamer, cotton briefs, canned peaches. My father dealt every day in words designed to convey the message that mankind's capacity for happiness is limited only by his willingness to change. Every time he wrote something like "Enjoy your coffee even more," my father must have heard "Enjoy your life even more." For him, "Switch to Coffee-mate" became "Switch to another city, another state, a whole new life." Enjoy. Switch. Eventually, he swallowed his own hook. Since there could be no happiness without change, my father left Hollywood and—at least this first time he left— he took my mom and me with him.

My dad's parents, Leo and Margaret, had a place in Oregon with a view of Mount Hood. The canopy of green trees stretched for miles. Their picture window overlooked the Willamette River and the tall, leaky smokestack of the Portland Cement plant. There was a giant kiln at the base of the smokestack full of hot limestone and clay, something Grandpa Leo called "clinker." He seemed to enjoy saying that word to me, and I liked saying it back. Clinker, clinker, clinker. It was happy-sounding. He told me how it worked: Clinker mixed with gypsum to make cement, the basic ingredient in concrete, mortar, and stucco. These were all solid, tangible things the country needed. Men built stuff with them. Even though he didn't work at Portland Cement, Grandpa Leo was proud of the plant for what it made, for its proximity to him, and for the type of men it employed: solid, working-class guys he'd share off-color jokes with at the State Street Barber Shop or over Reubens and whiskey sours at Gubanc's Pub (*What do you call a smart blonde? A Golden Retriever*).

Clinker. Clinker. Clinker. I repeated it to myself as I built my own version of the Portland Cement plant from wooden blocks on a card table in my grandparents' living room. I don't remember why I was there, or how often. What has imprinted itself is the image of my grandmother standing over an ironing board starching Grandpa Leo's dress shirts and handkerchiefs. She ironed while she watched *Perry Mason* reruns on television, swooning over Raymond Burr, his dark suits and barrel chest and gravelly voice. She always forgot herself, her iron hissing plaintively during those last few minutes of the program when Perry thundered away, then broke down his fragile witness en route to courtroom triumph.

My grandfather was a broker who supplied brown paper bags to grocery stores in northwest Oregon. He was a prototype of masculinity, like a NASA engineer or federal agent: deep lines in his face, clean-shaven, horn-rimmed eyeglasses, graying hair in a crewcut. He wore suits and ties and polished shoes to call on grocery store managers, driving his Buick to Thriftways in Tualatin, West Linn, McMinnville, and The Dalles. His business card had an imprint of a regal-maned lion in silhouette. It was his symbol: Leo the Lion. He had huge, paw-like hands and a firm grip. His handshake was his contract, the only thing he needed to close deals in suburban Oregon, and God help the paper bag salesman who tried to undercut his relationships.

There was a thought that once my father got settled in the area, he might take on some of my grandfather's accounts so the paper bag business could stay in the family. "There's money in paper bags!" Leo said. Maybe my father—despite his fluency in ad-speak—completely missed the metaphor. Maybe he literally believed he would bring money home by the paper bagful. And it wouldn't stop with Dad. Leo's vision was a paper bag dynasty that would trickle down to me, an idea my grandmother wouldn't stand for. She thought I should be an attorney.

"Don't get into sales," she always said. "You're smart enough to be a lawyer." I have to be honest. I fancied the idea of being just like Perry Mason, of getting to the bottom of seemingly unfathomable mysteries and defeating the hapless Hamilton Burgers of the world. This dream wasn't without foundation. Already, I'd been reading *The Hardy Boys* and puzzling through whodunits like a real gumshoe, so I believed what my grandmother said of me. I was smart and capable and could do anything I wanted. But when you're five, the dough hasn't quite risen yet; I would have believed anything anyone said of me, good or bad. Words stuck. My grandmother's idea was that I was too good for paper bags. She thought I was better than the vocation my grandfather had settled into, one he was really good at, but one she believed didn't require much in the way of smarts. I think this hurt him. Of course, he would never have said so. Instead, he made jokes: "The only difference between a dead dog in the road and a dead lawyer in the same road," he would say, "were the skid marks in front of the dog."

I also remember that my grandfather was never satisfied when it came to my appearance. When my hair was uncombed or I went without a belt, it made him sour. "What boy doesn't wear a belt?" he would say. He'd look at my mother when he said this. In his mind, it was her job and she was failing. Never mind that aching fingers made it difficult for her to button a blouse. This would have to be overcome, for a substandard appearance led to poverty of the spirit, which then drove men to philandering and overconsumption and flimsy careers in television advertising. Every one of society's ills could be backward-mapped to slovenliness and poor childhood grooming. "Barbara," he'd say, "put a belt on that boy."

Then there was the dirt. I had a bad habit of licking a dry patch beneath my lower lip, which brought about a subdermal grime Grandpa Leo was forever trying to erase with a handkerchief. My eyes were dry, too, and I would wet my fingers on my tongue then moisten my lids, which left crescents of dirt over my cheekbones. My grandmother made sure to rub the pink back into my face and slather me in ointment before Grandpa Leo returned from sales calls. My parents made no such effort. In front of them, when he'd see I was dirty or unkempt, Grandpa Leo teased that I could grow potatoes under my fingernails and behind my ears. He said things like this feeling sure it would drive my parents to higher standards for child rearing. For holes in my jeans: "Your knees are gonna catch cold." For pants that were too short: "When's the flood, Noah?" Wrinkled shirts? "Did you sleep in that?" And his favorite, for mussed hair: "A bird build a nest in there?" All of these jabs were his way of giving me definition in the hope I would be bright enough to reinvent myself. Instead, they just made me self-conscious.

I don't know what my father did for work in Oregon, but it had no connection with who he wanted to be. It was simply a means to an end that paid the rent on our Spartan apartment in Tigard and kept food in our cupboards. Leo said this was the noblest pursuit of all. He didn't believe that a man had to love his job. There was a reason it was called *work*, after all.

My father didn't buy into this, nor did he buy into paper bags. Because Dad felt a man *could* love his job, the passing of the paper bag baton never happened. We lived in Oregon for just six months, partly because of Grandpa Leo's meddling and how it made my parents feel. There didn't seem to be much either of them could do right. But the bigger thing was this: My father had a love affair with California he just couldn't shake. She may have been big and phony and too glamorous for a guy from Idaho, but he believed she held open a spot in her overcrowded heart for him. It was the least he could do to return.

In February of 1974, we left. My father drove ahead of us to rent an apartment and start a job selling ad spots for local television near Fresno, California. It wasn't Los Angeles, where he really wanted to be, and it wasn't writing, which he really wanted to do, but at least he was in a place far from his father's scrutiny and control. He left Tigard in a Chevy Vega wagon with nothing more than a suitcase and three core beliefs: It was always sunny in California; the next thing was always the best thing; and, contrary to what Leo told him, there *was* such a thing as fathers who cared too much.

My mother and I followed a few days later in a 1969 Volkswagen Beetle that broke down in Shasta and stranded us overnight in the snow. I don't remember this; my mother told me I was sleeping, that the tow truck driver was kind enough to lift me into his rig while snowflakes dusted our smoldering car. I remember only one thing about the drive back to California. On the interstate, shortly after leaving Tigard, affixed to a chrome bumper on a long sedan, there was this sticker: "Welcome to Oregon. Now go home."

2

This Is How I Came to Be Charles

Witness: I had the hysterectomy during the time they sold the hotel and I didn't have a job to go back to.

Counsel: And when was that?

Witness: June of '74.

Counsel: Okay. And am I correct in assuming after you recovered from the hysterectomy you weren't able to work?

Witness: I wasn't able to work for a period of six months.

Counsel: And then what did you do?

Witness: I wanted to stay home for a little longer, but my ex-husband told me to go get a job.

—Workers' Compensation Appeals Board,
December 12, 1983

WE MOVED INTO AN APARTMENT COMPLEX CALLED MONterey Pines. Our unit had two bedrooms, a small kitchen, and one bathroom the three of us shared. There was a living area with a green sofa, a black vinyl recliner, and a beat-up buccaneer's coffee table with copper flashing and matching rivets, which Mom said must have been salvaged from a shipwreck. These were things we brought with us from Oregon, second-hand furniture my grandparents had stored in the event we ever needed it. Privately, my mother wished it had all fallen from the moving van. Nothing matched. She did her best to decorate and make things homey, but it was as though we lived in a flea market.

Our carpet was gold shag. We had gold-speckled Formica counters, gold-deco vinyl floor squares, and dark brown cabinets with gold knobs in the kitchen. Gold was the theme. I suppose it made people like us feel wealthy and pampered like Elvis or Zsa Zsa Gabor. Our appliances, though, were avocado green, the same color as my mother's sail-shaped ashtray, which had notches for a dozen cigarettes. It was an ashtray for entertaining, but the only one who ever used it was Mom. She smoked a pack of Virginia Slim menthols a day, which she could do without bending her fingers. She kept the ashtray in the center of the shipwreck coffee table, and she sometimes fell asleep on the sofa with a cigarette still burning in one of its notches. We had a small dinette set for four, but most times it was just me and Mom; my father liked to eat sitting in his recliner in front of the TV. Every night after the evening news, he had me turn up the volume on the Bicentennial Minute, when celebrities and politicians told stories of our nation's birth two hundred years ago to the day. My father loved them for their drama and irony and shameless patriotism. Each installment, in a nod to Walter Cronkite, ended the same way: "And that's the way it *was*."

Our apartment had a fenced-in front patio with a concrete walkway that split two plots of dirt. On one of them, my parents put a glass-topped patio table and two outdoor chairs. On the other, I rolled a Tonka dump truck in my underwear. My mother may have thrown down some potted plants here and there, but she never bothered much with landscaping. During the hot Fresno summer, plants withered to twigs anyway.

In our living room stood a tall oak entertainment center with a turntable and a stack of albums, but I only remember my father listening to one: Don McLean's *American Pie*. He played the title song over and over. This wasn't something he played as background music while he puttered around the apartment. He listened to that song the way it was meant to be listened to, without distractions. He shushed me when I was in the room and waited until the song was over to answer my questions.

"A levee stops the flood," he once said.

The song was a cleansing for him, a kind of religious act, an immersion. He pulled up a chair from our dinette to be close to the speakers, the volume and the turntable, to the needle he handled so gently. He leaned forward in that chair with his elbows on his knees and his hands steepled over the bridge of his nose, eyes closed. His lips whispered the words, "The lovers cried, and the poets dreamed." My father may not have had God, but he did have Don McLean, and each time the song ended, he sat back and sighed. It seemed to fill him, but at the same time, it was as though he had lost a part of himself that he could never get back.

There were two churches and two schools on our block. Across the street from our apartment was the Catholic parish, St. Anthony of Padua. I would learn later that Anthony was the patron saint of lost and stolen things. The sanctuary at St. Anthony's had a tall concrete spire topped by a gold cross visible from our apartment. I could see it from my parents' bedroom window, from the oval of Bermuda grass where I threw a football with the boys in the complex, from the pool where we swam, and the sizzling concrete deck where we laid our towels and warmed our wet backs. Wherever I went within Monterey Pines, wherever I ventured in the neighborhood, the cross followed me. It felt like I was under the ever-watchful eye of God.

The St. Anthony Catholic school was on the same manicured grounds as the parish, situated farther west. At the end of the block sat the public school, Carroll H. Baird Elementary, where I went for part of kindergarten and all of first grade. Mornings when my mother walked me to school, I watched the St. Anthony kids climb from the back seats of sparkling cars in the circle drive to be greeted warmly by a nun in a rustling habit. The boys wore pressed white shirts and dark slacks. The girls all dressed in plaid skirts and knee-highs, their small feet tucked into shiny black Mary Janes. Some had white ribbons tying back long ponytails. None of these kids looked lost or stolen. They looked clean and well cared-for, as impeccably tended to as the boxwood hedges, the red rose bushes in neat rows, the luxurious pines standing nobly around the buildings, the black tops and green playing fields that seemed to stretch for miles.

At the end of the block, on our side of the street, was the Mormon church. It had a white steeple. My father's family on Margaret's side was full of Mormons, Danes who boarded the *S.S. Monarch of the Seas* from Liverpool in 1861 and spent nine weeks at sea. They traveled by boxcar from New York to St. Louis, then by ox team over the treacherous plains of Missouri and Kansas on their way to Utah and ultimately, to Boise, Idaho, where my father was raised. Three girls who would have been my great-great aunts died of typhoid on the trip, the last of whom, the baby Hanne, had to be left along the trail. Her parents wrapped her in a blanket, placed her in a shallow grave, and covered it with whatever stones they could find. I imagine the trail to have been full of these tiny monuments.

My most direct ancestors set out from Denmark with five children but arrived with just two, both boys. One of them was my great-great grandfather, Carl Christian. He and his wife, a Welsh beauty named Caroline, had ten kids, my dad's grandpa Charles among them.

This is how I came to be Charles. My name is his.

One Saturday morning, the telephone jangled. Mom was in bed with "the aches and pains." That's what she called them. She hobbled through her mornings with cigarettes and coffee and said she was fighting off "the aches and pains." That morning, my father was eating a piece of toast. He answered the phone, mumbled a few things, then slammed down the receiver.

"Get dressed," he said. "That was your principal."

I was in my pj's on the floor, glued to a cartoon. I didn't respond, so my father nudged me in the ribs with his toe. He wore sky blue slacks and white shoes with gold pilgrim buckles. "Get up," he said. "He wants to see you, and I need to be there." I didn't jump to my feet right away. I moaned and stretched out on the gold shag, then rolled onto my back. I looked up at my father. He wore a belt that matched his shoes and a white short-sleeved shirt with the top two buttons undone. He was clean-shaven and smelled like Aqua Velva.

"Now!" he said. "He wants us there right away!"

I wasn't too keen on getting dressed and I hadn't quite processed what he'd told me. When I still didn't get up, he nudged me more sharply. "Get moving," he said. "Whatever you did, it must have been bad if your principal wants to see you on a Saturday morning." I got dressed. I got moving.

My father marched me along the sidewalk from Monterey Pines to Baird. We passed the statue of St. Anthony tucked into a concrete alcove in front of the parish. As we did, my father gave me a nudge from behind. "Move it," he said, so I double-timed it. Up ahead, the school parking lot was full, and there were children milling around outside the cafeteria with their parents. They were laughing. As we drew nearer, I smelled buttered popcorn. It seemed like a happy time in the cafeteria, but it did not figure to be so happy for me. I had the crazy notion that I would be beaten in public while onlookers ate popcorn.

"This way," my father said. We turned and walked toward the cafeteria and suddenly, my father's mood lightened. He tousled my hair, which was an odd gesture because my father wasn't given to affection of any kind.

When we got to the cafeteria door, a teacher I recognized handed me a bag of popcorn. "Here you go, sweetie," she said. "Popcorn for breakfast." There were chairs lined up in rows. She handed my father a bag of popcorn, too. "Sit anywhere," she said to him.

The principal, Mr. Ebersole, went by "Mr. E." He stood at the front of the cafeteria, leaning against the stage. He was chortling with another man, not at all appearing as though he were preparing to beat me. He stood with his arms folded over his broad stomach, fat and slow-moving in ill-fitting clothes. His face was swollen and pink, and his cheeks and neck folds were lacquered with aftershave. Sometimes, just sitting at my desk in the morning, I'd smell my father's Aqua Velva and look up to see

Mr. E. moving like a glacier through our classroom. That Saturday, there were children running free around the cafeteria. Parents chatted breezily with one another, drinking coffee from Styrofoam cups.

There was a projector in the middle of the cafeteria loaded with a large film reel. As we took our seats, my father slapped my knee. He grinned and laughed at his own joke. Laughed so hard, he cried. Wiped away a tear with his knuckle. He must have said something like "Gotcha!" or "Surprise!" but at that moment, I heard nothing. I could only see, and what became clear was that my father had not brought me to my own public paddling. It was, instead, a special Saturday movie festival for Carroll H. Baird students and their parents: two hours' worth of Laurel and Hardy short films.

The projector ratcheted its way through *The Music Box*, in which Ollie and Stan attempt to move a piano up a flight of stairs. I remember the children squealing each time the piano crate went careening down. I also remember being suspicious about laughter. I wanted to laugh, but sensed that there was something wrong with it. For me, there was nothing funny about pratfalls and bewilderment and failure. There was nothing funny about a man slapping another man upside the head so hard as to knock his bowler to the ground. What did other kids see that I was missing?

I remember something else, too, and this was something too clear to miss. Had my father tried to put his arm over my shoulder or take my hand, as I saw other dads doing with their kids that Saturday morning, my first impulse would have been aversion. Rather than edge closer, rather than rest my head in the slope of his shoulder, I would have edged away. I would have moved just out of his reach.

My father, though, did not put me to that test. We sat next to each other, not touching, staring straight ahead like two strangers on a train.

Over forty years later, I still remain puzzled over the ruse. Why intentionally lead your six-year-old son to believe he'd done something heinous enough to be paddled on a Saturday? Why not just say, "I have a surprise for you, Chuckie. I've got a fun morning planned for just the two of us."

What would have been so wrong with that?

3

Everything Wrong in His World
Somehow Started With Me

"Barbara has had kind of a strange feeling low down in her abdomen, kind of doubled her over. This seems to be happening quite often now lately."

—I.G.T., MD, Progress Notes,
January 20, 1975

SOMETIME LATER THAT SAME SCHOOL YEAR, IN THE SPRING of 1975, our class was lined up after recess. I was jockeying for position in line with a mean kid who pushed me to the ground. He sprawled me out over the hopscotch squares and then did a Muhammad Ali jig over my body.

"Float like a butterfly, sting like a bee," he sang, punching at air and shuffling his sneakers, one giant production that sent the other children into a caterwauling meanness.

I knew what my father would have said to me at that moment: "Get up and don't be a pantywaist." That was one of his favorite words, *pantywaist*, used with a kind of disgust reserved for men who exhibited anything other than the most masculine of qualities. *Pantywaist*. He also used it on me every time I whined about a skinned knee. "C'mon, ya' pantywaist," he'd tease. "Do I need to get a bucket for the blood?" He always said this last thing in a pouty, baby-talk voice. Grandpa Leo used to say it, too, in the same manner. "Do I need to get a bucket for the blood?"

So, even if it meant getting pushed down again, I got up. And then I did about the worst thing a kid can do by way of retaliation. A kind of kid rage came over me that took control of my body and shut down my brain. I don't know how I came by it, but there was a yellow pencil that I held like a knife. I raised it over my head, then plunged it into that mean kid's ear hole. It's not what I was aiming for; I think he just saw what bad intent I was up to and turned his head so I wouldn't drive that pencil through the top of his skull. My finding his ear hole was sheer accident, like dropping a marble into the top of a milk bottle, but once I did, the mean kid crumpled to the ground at my feet, pressing both hands to the side of his head.

Silence. Then howling. "My brain!" the mean kid cried. "He poked a hole in my brain!" In fact, I had not poked a hole in the mean kid's brain. Even in my rage, I saw one thing clearly: The pencil entered eraser-end first. At worst, I gave his eardrum a good scratching.

Our teacher, Mrs. Waterman, hobbled over. She was fat, and we were insensitive, so naturally we called her Mrs. Watermelon. She stopped and stared down at the mean kid, who lay on his side; the pencil had rolled away. There was no blood or brain plasma oozing from his ear. The mean kid was all spectacle. Mrs. Waterman looked appalled anyway. "Who *did* this?" she said. The other kids stood quietly, pointing fingers at me. Mrs. Waterman glared and trembled. She grabbed me by the earlobe and twisted until my head cocked to one side. "You're coming with me," she said. She left the mean kid on the ground, squirming on the hopscotch squares, and dragged me by the ear through the gauntlet of my classmates, all of whom in their mindless, collective stupidity could come up with just one thing to say: "Oooooooooh." When they once again found their voices, I heard whispers behind me: "He's going to the principal's office," they said. "He's gonna be whipped!"

Mr. E.'s office door stood open and Mrs. Waterman hauled me inside like a suitcase. My earlobe burned as she dropped me into a metal chair, which I tumbled over. She turned and shut the door, hard. Pictures shuddered on the wall. I scrambled into my seat. There was a small, square window in the door, but it was covered with a piece of black construction paper. I sat facing Mr. E.'s desk. He sat across from me, and Mrs. Waterman situated herself in a chair next to him. She wore a floral print dress and as she settled, she modestly brought the hem down over her tree stump ankles then smoothed the pleats across her broad lap. Her wide bottom rolled over each side of her chair in fat pillows. She looked like an overstuffed recliner.

There were windows in the office, but they were tinted on the outside. I could see out, but no one could see in, though not for lack of trying. The flotilla of children who'd witnessed my crime converged on the windows and pressed their faces against the glass. Other teachers shooed them away, but I could hear them asking questions. "What's gonna happen to him? Is he gonna *die*?"

Murmurs passed between my teacher and the principal. I sat quietly, my earlobe throbbing.

Mr. E. cleared his throat. "Sit up straight, young man," he said. I did as I was told. I sat up straight. He popped a stick of gum in his small mouth and Mrs. Waterman folded her arms over her shapeless bosom. "Joan?" he said.

Her breathing slowed, then she spoke. "This young man just jammed a pencil into another boy's ear!" There was sure to be damage, she told him. Parents would need to be called.

Mr. E. continued to stare at me. Everything he did was slow and calculated. He chewed his gum like an elephant eats hay. "Is this true?" he said. "Is what she said about you true?" I nodded and said it was. I had jammed a pencil in another boy's ear.

"But he pushed me first," I pleaded. "He pushed me down." I began to pull my pant leg up so I could show some evidence of injury, a bruise or raspberry or anything that could demonstrate that the other boy acted first and earned every bit of what was coming to him. Mr. E. anticipated this. He waved his huge, meaty hand toward my face like a stop sign. I persisted anyway. "But it was the eraser end," I said.

Mrs. Waterman interrupted. "Doesn't matter," she said. "You can still rupture an eardrum." She was smug and scarlet-cheeked as she wagged her finger at me; a bracelet dangled from her baggy wrist.

Mr. E. then reached into a drawer and withdrew a wooden paddle. It had red rubber bands stretched tight around it. Holes the diameter of a pencil were drilled at random spots through the wood.

Mr. E. placed the paddle on the desk between us. I couldn't take my eyes from it.

"Do you know what this is?" Mr. E. asked. I nodded. I felt the tears well up in my eyes but held them back. I knew that crying wouldn't help me. I had to think of something else. There was a clear path to the closed door, and I was pretty sure I could have reached it and escaped before either adult could stop me. Mrs. Waterman must have seen me appraise the distance between my chair and the door. She stood and re-positioned herself so there was no longer an escape route. I sat still and gathered my fists in knots. I gritted my teeth until my jaw ached. I knew I'd have to sit there and take whatever I had coming.

Mr. E. stood up. The chair springs sighed as he rose. I watched him consider me, watched his hand balance over the wooden paddle. He picked it up and gave his palm a firm slap.

"Joan," he said. "I'll take it from here." Mrs. Waterman stood and left.

I don't know what he said next. I am sure there were words, for how else would I have wound up on my knees with my jeans and white undies bunched at my ankles? I remember feeling the shame of being hunkered over a chair, half-naked on the floor. I remember that shame giving way to ribbons of searing pain each time he struck me. I remember the *whap whap whap* sound against my skin. Mr. E. flailed recklessly as though everything wrong in his world somehow started with me. I couldn't see him, of course. But I've had more than forty years to imagine his pink face and narrow black eyes, the banded wooden paddle which, in his huge hand, must have weighed little more than a flyswatter.

There would have been other words, too, something that prompted me to rise from the floor. I remember pulling up my underwear and jeans, how my flesh stung when it brushed against denim, the heat radiating down the backs of my legs, then something like an acid lump burning in my throat. I couldn't swallow. I couldn't find air to fill my lungs. And I remember feeling at that moment, as I stood in Mr. E.'s office in the enormity of him, that I had been set apart somehow. I remember feeling like I could never walk amongst other kids again without them staring at me, without them whispering. I thought this suffering was singly assigned to me, but I would find out fourteen years later that it was not.

While sorting mail in my college fraternity house, I came across a letter from my mother. She had written me a couple letters a month since I'd been away, the usual la-dee-das and goings-on from Fresno, missives prepared on an electric typewriter with an italics Daisy wheel, since writing by hand had become too slow and painful for her. She could hunt-and-peck more easily using a contraption she'd fashioned from a small foam ball, a pencil, and a pink rubber eraser she'd popped on its end. She used this anytime buttons needed pushing: remote control, microwave, telephone, and her typewriter. She navigated the keyboard one excruciating letter at a time, but always took care at the end to scribble "Mom" in ballpoint pen.

I tore open the envelope and read her letter. She wrote that she'd trained her cockapoo Reggie to tinkle in the bathtub and that my Uncle Jack bought an aluminum fishing boat. Neatly folded along with the letter was an article from the *Fresno Bee* about Mr. E: "Mr. Loren Ebersole," I read, "has been arrested for molesting children." The cops showed up in his office after a film processor discovered pictures of young, partially clothed girls he'd turned in for developing. There was also this: "Police found numerous slides and videotapes at his home with more of his former students partially clothed." Was I among them? His attorney asked for leniency because prison gangs were drawing lots to see who would kill him when he arrived. At his sentencing, he begged forgiveness of the families and said there was a good chance he would not come out of prison alive.

He said, "This will ring in my head and my heart for the rest of my life." Mine too, Mr. E.

4

Jackrabbits, Ground Squirrels, Field Mice, and the Hawks That Ate Them

"She's awfully anxious to lose weight. Went to some funny weight losing clinic that was going to give her HGC, but they wouldn't accept her because of her carcinoma, thank goodness! Will suggest she try Weight Watchers."

—I.G.T., MD, Progress Notes, November 7, 1975

My parents left Monterey Pines and bought a house, a brand-new place that set them back $17,500. They got to choose the color, which after some conversation on the matter turned out to be yellow. My dad got a VA loan to pay for it, one benefit of his service in the United States Army, where he served as an advisor. To me, he once said he was a radioman, so I always pictured him wearing headphones in a dusty tent. He spent three full weeks in Vietnam and once told his sister Ginny that he saw a man get shot as he ran along a barbed wire fence.

I found out about this after he died, in my effort to dredge up shrapnel on him and draw connections between the two of us. I scared up some things I wish I hadn't, such as the fact that after he left us he didn't give my mother one penny of child support to help raise me, even though a judge ordered him to do so. That might have helped a lot with our situation, which at times was pretty dire. We once ate tomato and mayonnaise sandwiches for dinner because it was the only food I could find in the house and my mother, collapsed on the sofa, had no energy or money to do anything else. She tried to make something fun of it anyway, dispatching me like a soldier to the kitchen on a kind of food scavenger hunt. I marched back with a loaf of bread, one tomato, and a jar of mayonnaise, and she said we'd make the best tomato and mayonnaise sandwiches ever. This led us to our life motto, which she coined after our meal, her pat response to the question, "Barb, how are you doing?" to which she'd say, "We're doing the best we can with what we've got."

When life gives you a tomato and bread and mayonnaise, you make a sandwich.

The house Dad bought was one of about two-hundred single-story ranch homes, a stucco and wood-shingled oasis nestled within a vast fig orchard and situated alongside the Santa Fe Railroad. About a dozen of these houses backed up to an unfenced ponding basin, a place where small, unsupervised children gathered to throw pieces of white bread to urban geese.

These new houses with modern kitchens were called "Trend Homes," though I'm not sure the development of a middle-class colony next to a working railroad and a municipal pond was the latest wrinkle in the real estate market at the time. Rather, these homes were in keeping with a trend that has persisted in Fresno for decades: growth outward, never upward. It became famously known in our city as urban sprawl, and it has never stopped, not in the many decades I have been here. In our case, we were pushed as far to the edge of the Santa Fe tracks as we could get without going over them. The freight trains ran at all hours, always blowing their whistles as they passed. From inside our house, we heard every clack of steel wheel to rail. We felt those trains surge through our foundation, and our pictures never hung quite right. Maybe the only upside was that our neighborhood, as the sun set in summer, smelled of citronella and DEET, fragrant defenses against the mosquitos that swept in from the ponding basin at dusk.

Dad called it "Stuccoville."

Our neighborhood was truly the end of the line. You had to drive west until Bullard Avenue became a narrow country road. Until home-owners arrived, the only living creatures were jackrabbits, ground squir-rels, field mice, and the hawks that ate them. There were small, flitting birds, but they never seemed to last long because the neighborhood cats gnawed them into clumps of feathers. Summer afternoons in Stuccoville brought suffocating dust that rolled in from the orchards like a fog and drained all color from the land and sky. And since the tar was fresh and the trees were saplings, during the Fresno summer we immolated in our urban island with nothing to protect us from the cruel sun except our wood shingled rooftops and our asthmatic air conditioners, which, like us, choked on orchard dust.

On the north side of Bullard, just a few hundred yards from our house, stood long, neat rows of fig trees, which at one time covered most of Fresno's city limits. They arrived as cuttings and seeds, left in the earth by mission-building Spaniards looking to colonize the Pacific Coast and convert Native Americans into devoted Christians and Spanish citizens. But the fig trees of my youth reach back in time even further, to the Gar-den of Eden, where Adam and Eve are said to have sewn garments from fig leaves to hide their nakedness. Fig trees grew in the Promised Land, in the gardens of ancient kings, where just one of them was a symbol of wealth and prosperity. Fig trees meant full tables and households that lacked nothing, and from our front doorstep, we could see acres of them. By such a measure, then, we should have lived a life of comfort and ease.

But there is a counter-narrative, one that cannot be ignored: On the day Jesus left Bethany, just before he entered the temple courts and over-turned the tables of moneychangers and the benches of those selling doves, he sought nourishment from a fig tree, then rebuked it when he found nothing but leaves. "May no one ever eat from you again," he said. And there, before his disciples, the fig tree withered and died.

The land where I grew up, then, was as holy as it was cursed.

Dad lived in this house for just fourteen months. The only day I remember him being there was his last. A month before my eighth birthday, in August of 1976, we were sitting in the driveway in the Buick Skyhawk he would drive away in. We were quiet, and then his eyes narrowed on some imagined horizon. I tried to track with him, but all I could see was the garage door. He put his hand on my knee and gave it a pat. Then he broke into verse:

> *The summer—no sweeter was ever;*
> *The sunshiny hills all athrill;*
> *The grayling aleap in the river,*
> *The bighorn asleep on the hill.*
> *The strong life that never knows harness;*
> *The wilds where the caribou call;*
> *The freedom, the freshness, the farness—*
> *O God! how I'm stuck on it all.*

In the front seat of a Buick parked in the driveway of our yellow house, he quoted the fifth stanza of Robert Service's "The Spell of the Yukon," as if that would somehow explain his leaving. "Life that never knows harness." That was my father. He had met someone else, a woman named Patty, and she was thin and pretty with long legs and dark, straight hair. I would see her only once, after she and my father settled in their new rental house and had me over to dinner on a Sunday afternoon. I remember her hair and overlarge sunglasses and the satiny feel of her sleeve on my cheek as she reached around me to remove a paper dinner plate. My dad had grilled hot dogs, and we ate outside in the backyard.

Years later, after my father was diagnosed with MS, my grandmother Margaret told me it was a good thing my parents couldn't work it out. "They could not have taken care of each other, what with them both being so sick," she said. I have always drawn from that idea that Margaret felt Mom was partially to blame for the divorce, that it was more than just my father getting bored and falling out of love.

Mom never really knew. She said Dad just came home from work one day and told her matter-of-factly that he was leaving, a pronouncement she didn't fight. In fact, she giggled. This doesn't surprise me; they both hated conflict and it is easy for me to accept that this scene played out like a simple business transaction. Mom told him, "I get the house." He shrugged his shoulders and said, "Okay."

Within the hour, I was sitting with my dad in that Buick as he recited Robert Service. When he was done, he said, "See ya, pal," and that was it. I got out. I closed the door and he backed out of the driveway, his Sky-hawk packed with all of the things he would need to start a new life with a thinner, prettier woman who craved adventure and wide-open spaces and didn't want anything to do with me.

5

The Beautiful Brenda Cuttin

"Her husband has moved out and filed bankruptcy and everything has kind of blown to pieces on her. Gone back up to 15 mg of Prednisone a day [...] I really wish this lady would get off this stuff."

—I.G.T., MD, Progress Notes,
August 10, 1976

WITHOUT A FATHER, I FELT VERY PERIPHERAL AS A KID. I was sure that everyone but me had a dad, which was a distressing way to live. My mother knew this and did her best to help me feel like a normal boy. A month after my father left, Mom took me to Ringling Brothers in Selland Arena. She had given me the tickets in a birthday card that morning. "Surprise!" she said. "Instead of a birthday party, I'm throwing you a circus." Mom was clever like that.

The day of the circus was September 8, 1976, a Wednesday, the actual day I turned eight. To commemorate the occasion, Dad sent me a post-card from the National Bison Range in Montana. It was a close-up of a shaggy-headed bison staring indifferently in the direction of a camera. On the back of the postcard, he wrote that he was in Montana "on business," but even I knew this was a massive load of bison crap; he was with Patty. I know this because I heard Mom talking with her mom about it on the phone. This marked the beginning of a long period of juvenile loathing for my father, something to which I felt entitled, and something I believe my mother—though she would never have said so—felt some satisfaction over.

Our seats at the circus were as high as the arena would allow. The climb to our row winded my mother. She paused once and took hold of a seat back to catch her breath. This caught the attention of some folks, whose faces twisted up in a look of concern. My mother made a joke of it. "Whew," she said. "Are we there yet?" The ascent must have seemed endless to her, but she was determined to make it. She told me to go up and find our seats, as much to let her get another moment of rest as to give her a target. She was pretty chubby at the time, an affliction she called "heavy-set," her bloated face a product of the steroids she took to treat her lupus flares. Her weight was up to 176 pounds.

There were other factors, too: poor habits, a broken marriage, worry over money. Even before my father left, we were barely making it, eating meals from greasy bags and drinking a lot of Pepsi. My mother was still smoking too much because, she said, it helped keep her weight down.

When she finally got to our seats, she plopped down next to me, breathless. "What a view," she said. "You can see everything from here."

On the car ride there, Mom told me we were *splurging,* a word I would come to know meant spending money we didn't actually have on things she felt we deserved. Life had not gone well lately and extravagance in the form of ice cream sundaes or extra packs of baseball cards was her chief means of self-preservation. It was also her way of trying to make me feel as though I wasn't being deprived of anything, even if that meant spending foolishly, the way she did one night at the Big Fresno Fair when I had been riding a hot streak on the midway at the pinball horse races. I was achingly close to the top prize when we ran out of cash, but rather than give me a lesson in contentment and self-restraint, my mother wrote a check for another twenty dollars to keep me in the contest. I wound up falling just short anyway, but I still took home a beautiful bronze quarter-horse the size of a toaster, which sat like a trophy on my dresser all the way through high school.

Splurging also meant that my mother was too tired to cook, so we'd fall into our Chevy Vega wagon and head to the Burger King drive-thru for a couple of Whopper Juniors and some fries and a large soda, which she'd let me take a couple hits from on the way home. On nights she did cook, it was mostly frozen beef pies she could pop in the oven for thirty minutes, or a hamburger casserole that we'd eat off of for a few days. There was lots of white bread in our house, and she wasn't opposed to slapping some bologna and American cheese together with some chips and slaw for something she called "sandwich night." Meals were generally quick, wordless affairs, neither of us ever all that hungry, neither of us really knowing what to say to fill the silence, which at times felt oppressive to me. It was a weight that could only be unburdened by television, so the two of us watched a lot of sitcoms to pass the time until bed, Mom usually falling asleep on the couch with one arm draped over her forehead, the other hanging down to the floor, an open bottle of Bufferin on the shipwreck coffee table.

That night at the circus, she splurged on Cracker Jack and a swirled lollipop the size of my face. She got us some root beers, too, along with a mustard dog for the main course. It was my birthday dinner, after all, and she told me to get whatever I wanted. "Shoot the moon," she said, and since I was only eight and didn't know how bad things were for us, I took her up on it.

From somewhere on the arena floor, the ringmaster said it was time for the act we had all been waiting for. We sat down and my mother gave my leg a squeeze. "Ooh," she said, "this is exciting." The house lights dimmed, then clowns and caged animals vanished into darkness below. The crowd hushed to a murmur, and there was an unsettling pause before the ringmaster's disembodied voice promised an aerial act so death-defying and spine-tingling, it would leave us on the edges of our seats. Anticipation blossomed all around me. My mother and I sat up straighter. We peered into the darkness, and in a moment—after someone turned on the spotlight—we saw them: a sandy-haired man in a tasseled white jumpsuit straddled a motorcycle perched on a wire and below the man, on a trapeze connected to his motorbike, was the Beautiful Brenda Cuttin.

That's what the ringmaster called her. She wore a white sequined leotard and sat suspended elegantly on her trapeze, her porcelain legs crossed and toes pointed. At first, I thought the man was Evel Knievel. The ring-master introduced him as the Great Elvin Bale. From our vantage, they were eye-level, yet they seemed impossibly far away, like twinkling stars.

I looked over to my mother, who gazed at them dreamily. Tears welled in her eyes. "Isn't she lovely?" she whispered. I nodded and she took my hand.

The Great Elvin Bale revved his motorbike, kicked it into gear, and rolled along the wire with the Beautiful Brenda Cuttin glimmering and floating on her trapeze below him. She swung back and forth like a girl in a park. Then Bale stopped in the middle of the wire; he waved and revved his motorbike again. Something was about to happen. We knew this because something always happens after a stuntman revs his motor-bike. Cuttin put one hand over her mouth as though in a state of great surprise.

Bale then stood on his foot-pegs and thrust both arms in the air and we roared. No hands! He wriggled his hips dramatically and pretended to lose his balance. He tipped his motorbike to one side, then the other, then he brought it back to center. His arms were still raised over his head. Below him, Cuttin wobbled. Once steady, she wagged her finger at him. *Shame on you, Elvin.* Nothing like near tragedy to excite a crowd. We whooped it up for the Great Elvin Bale and the Beautiful Brenda Cuttin. I shoveled some Cracker Jack in my mouth, unable to take my eyes from the spectacle.

"Would you look at that!" my mother said. "I can't even imagine." From somewhere near us, a man let out a whistle.

Brenda Cuttin started swinging with more energy then, pumping her legs to go higher. Bale had settled back into his saddle and grabbed hold of his handlebars. Cuttin leaned back and laid her body flat, like a plank, one leg out straight, the other bent at the knee. She was looking up at Elvin Bale. He waved to her as she swayed beneath him, and she waved back. Then, as she seemed to find a place of perfect ease, she brought her second leg in and hooked both knees around the bar. She was still hold-ing the swing with two hands.

There was a drumroll. The spotlight left Elvin Bale altogether, settling its focus solely on Brenda Cuttin. Then, in one of those sudden movements that cause people to jump and grab hold of one another, Brenda Cuttin flung her head back and let go of her swing. There was a massive, audible gasp. The ringmaster was right. We were literally on the edges of our seats. My mother threw both her arms around my shoulders.

Brenda Cuttin's plan all along, it seemed, had been to let her momentum swing her around far enough to release her knees, and—for just an instant—float freely in space before snatching the bar again with her hands. Release, rotate, and catch, like a gymnast on the parallel bars. Instead, Brenda Cuttin cried out. It was a cry that lasted only a moment, then stopped. Her hands groped at the air, at the bar that swung just out of reach, and her body plunged to the ground. From our seats up high, my mother and I watched Brenda Cuttin pinwheel downward, away from Elvin Bale, the spotlight operator following her descent and revealing to all of us the unnerving, tragic truth: The Great Elvin Bale and the Beautiful Brenda Cuttin performed their spine-tingling, death-defying act without the safety of a net. There was nothing to catch her except an unforgiving sawdust-covered floor. Her body cracked against concrete from a height of sixty feet.

A cloud of sawdust flowered up around her. The thousands of us there fell silent. I looked at my mother, then back to Brenda Cuttin splayed out on the ground, her limbs at grotesque angles. Clowns rushed to her side, knelt, then huddled around her body as the spotlight shut down. At the same time, the house lights came up to reveal costumed performers and prop hands shuffling about the floor. I watched two men maneuver a ladder up to Elvin Bale, who was dangling upside down from his motorcycle.

My mother clamped her hands over my eyes. "Oh, Chuckie," she sobbed. "That poor woman's never getting up."

As Brenda Cuttin's body was carted from the arena floor, my mother took my hand and led me down the stairs. The walk down was just as difficult as the walk up for my mother, her joints stiff from sitting so long. I followed her labyrinthine path through the throng pushing through doors that stood open to the parking lot. From there, my mother mumbled letters of the alphabet, looking for the section where she'd parked our Vega. It did not take long to find it, parked beneath a tall lamp post, bathed in dingy, yellow light. She opened the passenger-side door and I climbed in. Once I was buckled and secure, she settled herself in behind the wheel. Her hands were shaking. There was a moment of just sitting as my mother stared vacantly through the windshield at the downtown Fresno skyline, at lights in building windows, at the rotating time and temperature clock atop the Guarantee Bank building. She lit a cigarette and held it out the window as we drove home.

That night, I was still awake in bed as Mom sat in the front room watching the eleven o'clock news. I crept out there and nuzzled next to her on the couch. She was right, of course: Brenda Cuttin never got up. Her last moments alive were spent at a circus in Fresno, California, on the very day I turned eight. What we learned from the newscaster was that she had a heart condition at the time of her accident, and that she likely had some kind of seizure while swinging on the trapeze. One doctor speculated she died while falling, which could explain why she screamed, then stopped, before she hit the floor. She was thirty-eight years old and had two kids. And then there was this: It was Brenda Cuttin's first week with the show; she was a replacement for another performer, a woman named Paula Cleveland, who had just left the circus to have a baby.

Mom held me there on the couch. The last thing I remember was her whitewashed face in the television's glow. I grew drowsy watching her, my head on her shoulder, my eyes on her murmuring lips, which whispered, like a lullaby, "We just never know. We just never know."

6

People With
Perfect Smiles and Impeccable Hair

"She has been able to keep up her job and manage her son and her household and get her weight down to 135 lbs. She takes 15 mg. of Prednisone a day and I think she is just addicted to this. She thinks she will not have enough pep and energy to keep going if she stops."

—I.G.T., MD, Progress Notes,
November 8, 1977

MY MOTHER KEPT A CEDAR HOPE CHEST AT THE FOOT OF her bed full of artifacts and letters and important medical papers, some of it locked in metal boxes. One day after school I was home alone, rummaging through her private things. She had gotten a job as a clerk-typist for the Fresno Unified School District, so she didn't get home until about four-thirty. I used a spare house key under a flowerpot to let myself in. I rode my bike to and from Figarden Elementary, which—like our neighborhood—was surrounded by orchards. I rode through fig trees both ways.

When it was built in 1952, Figarden was a small country school meant to serve what was then the rural west side. Farmers' kids, mostly, but also those belonging to farmworkers, boys and girls with last names like Diaz and Gomez and Navarro. In the next twenty-five years, thanks to urban sprawl, there came to be others, kids like me from Stuccoville, but also kids from a place I knew only as "north of Herndon," white kids whose dads were lawyers and university professors and financial analysts. Some of these kids belonged to ranchers and cotton farmers who worked all over the Valley and traveled in Cessnas, which they parked in personal airplane hangars next to their sprawling houses. The boys wore Nike and Levi's and Izod. I didn't pay much attention to the girls, who at that time were still strange to me. I just knew that any kid with a green alligator over his heart was privileged. I was so self-conscious of my Toughskins, poor-kid jeans from Sears, that during one of those afternoons alone, I found a seam ripper from a sewing kit Mom never used and removed the big *X*'s stitched into the back pockets. Had I been skilled enough to do so, I'd have re-stitched the Levi's batwing logo in an effort to add value, albeit counterfeit, to a life I considered insufficient.

My back pockets, for years, were blank.

I don't know what I had hoped to find, but I disassembled Mom's hope chest until the evidence of her life before I came along lay in disorder on the bedroom carpet. There were the expected things: a wedding album, baby books, sepia photos of expressionless people whose lives were in some way connected to mine. But there were also black and white glossy photographs of people who seemed not quite so dull, people with perfect smiles and impeccable hair, people who autographed their pictures in black ink along with cheerful messages. These were people I'd never heard of: Ricky Nelson ("With Love"), David Nelson ("Best Wishes"), Richard Chamberlain ("Best Regards"), and Eleanor Powell, who seemed very fond of my mother, calling her a "charming young lady" and wishing her "a world of good luck." Who were these polished, successful people and where were they now?

I made sure I put everything back just the way Mom had it, but when she got home, she called me into her bedroom and asked me what I had been looking for. Somehow, she knew that things were out of place.

I said I wasn't looking for anything special, just looking because I was bored.

"What did you find?" she asked. I pointed to an autographed team photo of the 1950 St. Louis Cardinals resting atop an old copy of a tabloid newspaper, *The Hollywood Reporter.*

"Let me show you something," Mom said.

At the time I was born, Dad managed accounts at KCOP and Mom was an industrial relations secretary at Paramount Studios. To commemorate my birth, Mom took out a small, thumb-sized ad, which appeared on the bottom left corner of page twenty in the paper. It was a simple statement of my particulars (Charles Lewis, 7 pounds, 6 ounces) followed by the names of my parents, Ken and Barbara Lynn Radke, and their bottom-of-the-rung status in Hollywood. My birth notice ran alongside other advertisements of similar inconsequence: one for the "correction of foreign & regional accents," one for the "largest new collection of men's imported boots and shoes in the area," and one that appears to have a clever typo: "DRINKING PPROBLEM?? Taper off at Loran Hospital under medical supervision." A guy might have to sober up before he *ddialled* the *ttelephone.* I shared the pages of the *Reporter* that day with some of Hollywood's biggest stars: Bob Hope, Mia Farrow, Vic Damone, Raquel Welch.

Mom told me about her life in Hollywood, about her front desk job at the Beverly Hilton in 1959, about how she got paid twelve dollars a day, six days a week, seven a.m. to three-thirty, but she had "lived in a dream."

"Oh, the movie stars!" she said. "The place was crawling with them."

But the one she really wanted to see was Frank Sinatra. The night *Porgy & Bess* premiered on the West Coast, Mom went to the after-party at the Hilton. She was off that night but went to gawk. "Eight hundred celebrities came to the dinner," she said. Her eyes sparkled as she remembered. "Then the Beverly Hilton publicist asked me to help the photographer take pictures in the ballroom. Next thing I knew, I was holding a light on Frank Sinatra as the photographer took movies of him!"

My mother, for a few minutes of her life, held a bright light on Frank Sinatra.

There was more. She talked about Natalie Wood and Bob Wagner. About Spencer Tracey, and seeing Harry Belafonte at the Greek Theater,

a "live stage show under the stars." She told me about Elvis Presley and
how she saw him every day up close when he was filming a movie called
Blue Hawaii. "I was as close to Elvis as I am to you right now." About seeing Wayne Newton in the Hollywood Bowl, and her first boss, George
Gobel, whose company produced *Leave it to Beaver.* Nine days after I
was born, she danced with my father on the *Lawrence Welk Show.* She
had the ticket stub from that evening, right there in her thin fingers. She
told me about Michael Landon, "You know, the guy who plays Charles
Ingalls on *Little House on the Prairie*?" One day, dressed as Joe Cartwright, he shook my finger while she prammed me around Paramount
and introduced me to a bunch of TV stars.

I began to look at her differently that day. She wasn't just a woman in
failing health doing the best she could with what she had. She was the
owner for a short while of a life people envied, of days marked by happy
accidents most folks only dreamed about. As a nine-year-old kid holding that copy of the *Reporter*, I remember feeling thrilled. My name was
in a Hollywood newspaper and I had already brushed up against fame.
Michael Landon had held my finger in his hand. My mother knew Elvis
Presley, the biggest celebrity in the whole world. And there were all those
autographs in that cedar chest of so many rich, famous people whose
names meant nothing to me at the time other than the value they'd
added to Mom's life and, by extension, to mine. I could lay claim to that
value because I belonged to her.

Mom lit a cigarette and blew smoke through the side of her mouth.
"It was a lifetime ago," she said. She closed her eyes and kept them shut for
a moment, as though she were looking back to that life.

"Anyway," she said, opening her eyes. "That's neither here nor there."
That was a favorite expression of Mom's. *Neither here nor there.* It meant
that something wasn't important. What she was saying at that moment
was that her life before me wasn't important, but I thought it was. At
nine years old, I thought it was terribly, urgently important. The reason
I thought this was I believed in its nearness to us. I believed we could
still touch it and be within its orbit and that it was a space we could still
inhabit. For my mother, though, it was a non-space. My mother could

see just how far removed we were from that old life of hers. My mother could see through the veneer to the absolute. Joe Cartwright wasn't Joe Cartwright at all. He was just a man who went by Michael Landon in real life, who before that had yet another name, Eugene Maurice Orowitz, not Michael Landon, not Joe Cartwright, just Eugene, a man who played the role of another man, and another man, and yet another man after that. And this man who was many different men took hold of my finger for a moment, then let it go. I never touched this man again, because he and all of the men he was—Eugene, Michael, Joe, Charles Ingalls—are gone. They were there for a moment, then not. And this last thing I did understand, this thing about being there, then not. This last thing, I had seen. Like my mother, I had seen it quite clearly.

7

I Want to Be a Child Star

"She has gotten awful gloomy and down and just not able to make herself do anything. Weight up to 180 lb."

—I.G.T., MD, Progress Notes,
March 12, 1978

IN THE SUMMER OF 1978, WE DROVE TO LA TO VISIT MY grandmother Marzelle and my uncle Jack. They lived in a second-floor apartment on South Serrano in Koreatown. The front of the building was landscaped in sparkling white rocks out of which sprung tall, thin palms that leaned to one side. There was a bronze starburst attached to the front of the building and in the center, the address number, 702. Their carport was just off the street and there was enough room on the concrete skirt to park one car behind another. When we arrived, Mom pulled in behind Jack's car, her front bumper nuzzling the rear of his green Datsun. At the time, he was an instructor for a driving school, and the car he used for work had two steering wheels, one for the student driver and one for the teacher on the passenger side. There were also two brake pedals. One of the things I'd been told we might do was go for a ride in this car. Jack might let me ride shotgun while I commanded the second wheel. It was boxy and covered in a fine layer of dust, nothing as grand as Mom made it sound, but all I wanted to see were the two steering wheels. I'd never heard of such a thing.

Uncle Jack got drunk almost every day. On the days he had student drivers, he waited until nighttime. At his most animated, he was a complainer: about his Korean neighbors and the persistent odor of steamed cabbage; about toilet paper hung backwards so it fed under, not over, the roll; about long sedans that encroached on sidewalks when parked. He was six-foot-three and everything except his stomach, where all the beer went, was thin as straw. His posture was poor from having to contort his body to fit inside the Datsun, which bore hair oil stains on both sides of its vinyl interior roof. He ate little and struggled with an unruly esophagus that made swallowing solid foods difficult. At the dinner table, his face would twist into a look of consternation and he'd excuse himself to the bathroom, leaving his balled-up paper napkin on his chair. Marzelle would say, "Oh, he's choking again," and she'd take a sorrowful drag from the cigarette she kept smoldering in an ashtray on the corner of the table where we ate. We'd listen to Jack cough up whatever he'd gotten down, then the toilet flush, then his bedroom door click shut behind him.

One day during our visit, I was watching roller derby from Jack's chair. It was orange with a bath towel over the headrest, put there to soak up his hair oil. For all her shortcomings—and by this I really just mean the daily drunkenness and cigarette puffing—Marzelle kept tidy living quarters, all except for Jack's room in the back, where he collected the sediment of his life. He walked into the front room wearing pajama bottoms and no shirt. It was early afternoon and we hadn't seen him all day. We had already eaten lunch, cream cheese on crackers and red velvet cake washed back with 7-Up straight from the can.

"Hey lazybones," Marzelle said. She sat, purposefully knitting. I looked up at my uncle. He yawned and stood beside his chair, rocking on his heels and scratching himself, an oily black forelock descending over the bridge of his nose. He didn't say anything. Apart from the excitement of the roller derby on television, the room was quiet. There was something expected of me; I could sense as much. But I didn't know what that something was.

"Honey, you're in Jack's chair," Mom said.

I took in his stubbly face and bloodshot eyes, his hangdog head bobbing on his neck, the way people look when they're sitting up and fighting sleep at the same time. He wasn't really looking at me. Instead, his half-mast eyes were looking through me to his chair, to his urgent need for comfort. I said, "Oh, sorry," and moved to the floor so he could take his rightful place. He sat slowly and laid his head back on the bath towel, put his feet up on the ottoman, and closed his eyes. He put one hand on his distended belly, the other to the side of his head where he started working circles into his temple as though he might just rub hard enough to scare out whatever was bringing about the hurt inside. The night before, I'd slept on the roll-away bed with a bar running under my back and heard him wearing a path between his bedroom and the refrigerator and then to the toilet and back to his bedroom. He'd had a student driver during the day, so his slide into drunkenness began later and lasted well into the night.

"Jack," Mom said. "Maybe you could take your nephew on that car ride today?"

I whipped around and shook my head at her. I didn't want to go anywhere with my uncle. He smelled like he was rotting from the inside out.

Mom said, "Or, not. It's up to you." She lit a cigarette, then told Marzelle she wanted to get me out to Paramount to see her old stomping grounds. She said some of the gang might still be around and wouldn't that be a hoot, to see some old pals and show off her handsome son.

Jack sat in the chair still working on his head. His lips moved like he was talking to someone in there. Marzelle told him she could start some coffee. "Maybe that might get you going," she said. "You just sit there and watch the roller derby, and I'll get that coffee on. Barbie will want some coffee, too." Marzelle put aside her knitting and moved herself to the kitchen. On the armrest of her chair, a Lucky Strike smoldered in an ashtray. She waved at the smoke in front of her the way windshield wipers clear rain. "Get that coffee started," she said, but more to herself than anyone else in the room. She needed a reminder now and again about things she set out to do. She was the type to get places and wonder why she was there.

Mom patted the sofa cushion next to her. She wanted me to come over. I got off the floor and sat on the couch, under the long picture window where cars went by on the street below. The window was open and car exhaust seeped inside. I was wearing a black T-shirt with the *Grease* movie logo silk-screened on the front. I pulled at my frayed cutoffs and looked down my legs at my toes. Marzelle had always said how big they were. "You have such big toes," as though having big toes were some kind of talent.

Jack was on the other side of the room. Every so often, his sunken chest would rise, then fall. That was the only thing that made him look anything close to being alive. His face was red and the sacs below his eyes were swollen. His beard stubble was black and gray. Despite being so skinny, he had this kind of puffiness about him, like if you pricked him with a straight pin he'd hiss softly and deflate.

Marzelle came in from the kitchen and sat down. The coffee was on, she said. The nutty smell of brewing coffee mingled with car fumes and cigarette smoke. She took a sip from her beer, which she'd been nursing for some time, probably because she had company and she didn't want to get too blurry while we were there. Mom said something to her and Marzelle said something back, then she picked at her teeth with a knitting needle. I kept my eyes on the roller derby, where the guys calling the match were going bonkers over Skinny Minnie Miller. Her teammates had whiplashed her to the head of the pack, and because she was wearing a special helmet, that meant the T-Birds just scored. The roller derby was fast-moving, but the skaters just went round and round a small track, and the only excitement was when someone got rammed into a rail and their momentum carried their padded bodies over the edge, onto the floor. They always flew into a kind of theatrical agony before climbing back into the ring. Marzelle said they were going *ass over teakettle*, then she'd clamp her hand over her mouth and her big eyes would get even bigger because she realized she'd said a-double-s in the presence of a nine-year-old.

The conversation Mom and Marzelle carried on somehow came around to me, and there was talk of Paramount Studios and actors and some folks Mom used to know. I thought about the people in Mom's hope chest, those glistening stars, and I imagined them seeing us at Paramount, then embracing Mom with their perfect arms, kissing her cheek with their perfect lips, smiling upon me with their perfect teeth. "We've been waiting for you," they would say, and just like that, I would be a star.

I thought it was as simple as that. I was sure Mom knew people who would see the value in me. It was a total invention on my part, a buried fantasy that came bubbling up. I wanted to be a child star. So, I said it casually aloud to make it real. "I want to be a child star."

Mom and Marzelle both laughed out loud. Marzelle was laughing so hard tears streamed down her cheeks. They thought I had *made a funny*. That's what Marzelle always said when I told a silly joke. "You made a funny."

"Where did you come up with *that* idea?" Mom said. She was tearing up, too, just like Marzelle, the two of them laughing and crying.

Marzelle couldn't get any words to cross her lips, that's how funny she thought I was. She hunkered over wheezing, holding her knitting needle like a pitchfork, and I had this thought that she might keel over right there at my feet, but not before she stabbed herself in the eyeball. She suffered from something she called an "overactive thyroid," a side effect of which was that her eyeballs bulged almost fully out of their sockets. On the other side of the room, Jack shifted in his orange chair. He didn't think I was so funny, but he did have it inside his cottony head that I was off my rocker. "Psshh," he said. "You've got quite the imagination."

A minute passed. Marzelle was catching her breath and saying "Oh, goodness," Mom was dabbing at her eyes, and Jack had a smirk on his face. Each, in their own way, seemed to think I was mixed-up and silly and maybe I should go into stand-up comedy instead of acting. I felt exposed, like someone had pulled my pants down on a playground. My guts got all twisted and heat rose from my neck to my cheeks. I felt pounding behind my eyes, then came the hot tears, and the next thing I knew I had jumped from the sofa and bolted out the door.

I ran down the concrete stairs and out the back of the building along the busy street, shoeless and not yet ten years old, mad at everyone who thought I was a crackpot with stupid, unreachable dreams.

I don't know why I took this so hard but I did, and at that moment, I had officially become a runaway and the only thing filling the valley of my skull was that I wanted to make them all sorry, even Mom.

After that initial burst of adrenaline pushed me out the door, I found myself on the sidewalk barefoot, hungry, amidst strangers. The sun was slipping lower and my blackened feet were stinging from heat blisters and small cuts. More than once, my heel picked up a jagged little rock, so I walked on the balls of my feet. Korean shop-owners took note of me with odd grins as they swept.

Every so often I stopped along the sidewalk to rest. I leaned against hydrants or the backs of bus stop benches. Once I even found a chair under an awning and I watched people scissor by. Many of the small women carried colorful umbrellas. I felt bad about running off and causing trouble. I was sure my mother was panicked and I wanted everything to be back the way it was.

Finally, in the near distance, I saw a fountain. It spouted tall, arching streams of clear water from its center. I walked toward it, and as I got closer I saw that the waterspouts fell into a glimmering pool. It was just on the other side of a circle driveway and nestled between tall white office buildings trimmed with flower beds and green hedges. I needed to cross Wilshire Boulevard to get there. I waited with others for the walk signal and simply moved when they moved, carried along by them.

I made it to the edge of the fountain and stepped inside. There was a sense of cool relief between my toes, then a cold needling along the bottoms of my feet and into my ankles. I sat on the fountain's edge and cupped my hands to bring water from the pool to my face and neck. Beneath the water, pennies sparkled. Then, in front of me, a police squad car pulled into the circle drive. Mom was in the passenger seat and she had the door thrown open before the car came to a complete stop. I had never seen her run before. I know she wanted to close the distance between us quickly, and she was doing the best she could. Her pale, swollen face told me everything I'd ever need to know about gratitude.

The following year, in April of 1979, Ricky Schroder appeared as Jon Voight's son in *The Champ*. A month before, I'd been the most teased boy at Figarden Elementary School thanks to Rickie Lee Jones and the song *Chuck E's in Love*. Kids poked fun at me: "Who are you in love with, Chuckie?" It was good sport for others on the playground to pair me with girls who had dandruff and ate their own boogers.

Ricky Schroder changed all that. *The Champ* came out just four days before Ricky's ninth birthday, so he was almost my age. I had about eighteen months on him. I remember seeing the movie trailer on television and listening to adults all around me talk about how moving and amazing a performance it was for such a young boy. People talked about how this little kid had been in show business for a while. His parents had taken him to photo shoots before he could walk. By the time he turned six, he had appeared in dozens of catalogues and print ads, exactly the kind of work my father helped produce at Erwin Wasey before he chucked the whole thing and left Hollywood. The words "child star" became synonymous with Ricky Schroder. He was adored. He was internationally famous. His face was everywhere.

And this made me crazy. Ricky Schroder was inhabiting the life I wanted, the one I thought I could have had if only my parents had done for me what his parents had done for him. The worst part of all, Ricky Schroder looked like me. Or, since he was the child star, *I* looked like *him*. For months, Alpha Beta checkout clerks said "You look just like Ricky Schroder." Fast-food workers, neighbors in Stuccoville, yard duty teachers, kids at school, even my own mother, all said I looked like Ricky Schroder. Marzelle called one night for the sole purpose of bringing this up. So did Leo and Margaret, who had begun flying me to Portland in the summer where we'd play golf and Scrabble and they'd buy all of my school clothes. Even there, at Lake Oswego Municipal, the golf pro had to look twice at me. Margaret's co-workers at the Oregon Bank said the likeness was uncanny. But it wasn't, really. I have studied the photographs and we shared a dirty blond hairstyle and maybe the same cheeks, but beyond that, nothing. I had dark, narrow eyes like my father. Ricky's were wide open, alert to opportunity, magnetic. Still, it happened everywhere I went, a few times a week, for more than a year: "Anyone ever say you look just like. . .?"

Ricky Schroder. I'll admit, it was fun at first. Looking like a child star was almost as good as being one because it gave me the attention I craved. My rise to fake stardom was as meteoric as Ricky's was to the real thing. Fifth-grade girls squabbled over me. They flirted. On the school playground, two soft hands would cover my eyes, and they would stay there until I could guess who it was. I remember blossoming girls pressing against my back, their breath on my neck, fingers on my cheekbones. Their hands were clammy, and I loved that musty nearness. "Guess who?" they'd giggle, but they were otherwise quiet so as not to reveal themselves. I loved the mystery of it all and I was rewarded for mistakes. The more incorrect guesses I took—*Julie? Robin? Cindy?*—the longer they held on.

When at last I guessed right, I took their hands in mine and twisted out from under their embrace, letting our grasp linger. We'd stand for just a moment like a young couple at the altar. Then, the moment was over. Invariably, they ran away squealing with their friends, and I played it cool with my own: *Stupid girls.* But I didn't mean it. I loved the attention. I loved, too, the folded notes on binder paper, the affectionate words written on them, the tiny hearts in ballpoint pen. It was all evidence that to people other than Mom, I meant something, even if it was a hollow something, even if it was a masquerade.

It was around this time—fifth grade, maybe sixth—that a boy named Tommy got fed up with me. He didn't like the attention I was getting as Ricky Schroder's twin. Tommy was an eleven or twelve-year-old boy and, because he was under the influence of a ballistic pituitary, he had facial hair, much of it on his sweaty upper lip. In the warm weather months, he wore tank tops that showed off his considerable armpit hair. His body was muscular and oversized compared to the rest of us, who could do nothing but ogle him as if he were some sort of midway fascination. I don't remember him being a nice kid, but maybe I didn't understand him. Maybe he didn't understand himself, either, this disorienting time-lapse growth and hormone tsunami the rest of us wouldn't navigate for another year or two. I remember his deep voice, his Mormon-ness, his wardrobe: Brigham Young T-shirts and athletic shorts. But these very public declarations of his faith didn't stop him from bedeviling smaller boys—every other boy at Figarden—with headlocks, noogies, Indian burns, and what were indecorously known as "titty twisters." Tommy had fingers like a pipe wrench and could summon a purple bruise on a boy's nipple within seconds. You did your best to stay out of his way, but in a small country school like ours, that wasn't possible for long. Only those who never went outside or those with afflictions—there was a fragile kid named Gary with a hole in his heart, a condition that made his skin blue—were able to avoid Tommy.

The rest of us were fair game.

I don't know what I did. Probably nothing. Or maybe I just began to think too highly of myself, but at that time, I'm not sure how such a thing was possible. I may have been popular for a short while thanks to Ricky Schroder, and that may have given me just enough self-confidence to seem arrogant, but I still hauled around a wagonload of insecurity. If I could invite Tommy to sit with me here today, maybe he could explain what led him to do what he did, but I doubt it. More likely, he would say he doesn't remember the day he picked me up in the middle of the playground at Figarden Elementary, flipped me over so my blond hair dragged along the grass, said Ricky Schroder was a *faggot* and so was I, then hauled me to the boys' restroom where he dumped me head-first into a trash can.

If he could remember this, he might explain it away as precocious puberty, an overload of testosterone that he couldn't handle. He might apologize. He also might say that he could have nabbed anyone that day; I just happened to be close by. Or maybe I was his target all along, that I had no reason to be so proud, that I had let this Ricky Schroder look-alike sham go to my head. But again, his torment of me has prob-ably moved itself far from that place in his brain that retains such things. Likely, so has Figarden Elementary School in Fresno, California.

Tommy left Fresno the following year and moved to some town in Texas. He said everything was bigger there. He even had a shirt that said so: "Everything's bigger in Texas." He swapped it for his BYU shirts and wore it with pride in the days before he left our tiny country school, an emblem to remind us that he was big and the rest of us were small. He was off to a place big enough to hold every bit of him—his deep voice, his body hair, his sweaty upper lip—all the things that made him Tommy, this boy in a man's body, this boy who dumped me in a trash can, this boy who hated Ricky Schroder.

8

Here I Was,
With All Kinds of Badness in My Heart

"She is feeling pretty much undone lately. Her job ends in three weeks. She doesn't know what she is going to do. She is gloomy and she is hooked on steroids. I suppose we had better be sure she doesn't have an ulcer."

—I.G.T., MD, Progress Notes,
September 5, 1979

THERE WAS AN OLD WOMAN WHO LIVED A MILE OR TWO outside of Stuccoville. She had made a home in a rundown rail-side café, just over the tracks from an abandoned, steel-sided warehouse. At one time, the café served fresh sandwiches and Cokes. I knew this because there was a bullet-riddled Coca-Cola sign jutting out over the door, and hanging below that, another sign in faded black script: "Fresh Sandwiches." Its windows were covered in tar paper.

I saw the old woman once. I was eleven, and we were living in our second house in Stuccoville, a rental on Malsbary Street, after Mom sold our first place out of spite and necessity. After work one day, a woman named Vera dropped Mom at home because someone had hotwired the Vega and left an empty parking space at the district office. We were now in need of a new car, and we had no money to buy one. Mom was upbeat about this, though. The Vega smelled like Dad, and whoever had it would smell like him, too. She felt the same way about the yellow house, so she sold the place, bought a new 1978 Toyota Corolla hatchback, and launched us into a series of apartments and rental houses, a ride that would continue for more than three decades.

I was with my friends, James and Jeffrey, and we'd ridden our bikes along a worn dirt path that ran next to the railroad tracks and, a bit further along, the abandoned warehouse. It was a hot, dusty day, probably August of 1980. Mom was recovering from toe surgery in July and kept her bandaged foot propped on an ottoman. She was getting around all right with a cane, but she found it difficult to do much. We hadn't started school yet, so for weeks James, Jeffrey, and I rode bikes through the orchard and tried to shoot rabbits and squirrels and birds with Jeffrey's BB gun.

Jeffrey's real dad wasn't around, but his mom, Jane, had a boyfriend named Ed, who every kid in the neighborhood called "Uncle Ed." He always had candy for the children, and we collected around his white Oldsmobile when he parked on the curb in front of Jeffrey's house. I remember the car; it gleamed on the outside with fresh wax and shiny, spoked hubcaps. The inside was white and there were clear plastic floor mats. Ed stayed the night with Jane quite a bit, until one day he just wound up living there for good. Those were the kinds of furtive adult indiscretions that we kids didn't need to understand, but we did learn to accept. People like Ed just appeared in fancy cars offering candy and the next thing you knew, they were there to stay. It happened the other way around, too: The people you'd grown used to seeing would just up and disappear, leaving you with only a fading afterimage, a Polaroid in reverse.

Ed sold real estate and every time I saw him around Jeffrey's house, he brought to mind the chummy little fellow with the black top hat and white handlebar mustache from Monopoly. I imagined that selling real estate was a lot like the game, and that Ed added houses and hotels to his properties, then waited for other folks to land on them and fork-over money by the bucketful. Ed had white hair, a slim build, and a salon tan. He smoked thin cigars with plastic filter tips that clicked against his teeth and made a subtle whistling noise when he sucked smoke through them. He always greeted me by saying, "What's new, Chuckaroo?"

I had never seen a one-hundred-dollar bill until I met Ed. I didn't even know they existed. One day when Jeffrey asked for money for the ice-cream truck, Ed opened his wallet and riffled through four or five of them before he settled on a ten spot, which he handed over to Jeffrey with no expectation of change. "Here you go, boys," he said. "Buy your-selves a few Fudgesicles." This was a kind of unreal fantasy to me: several one-hundred-dollar bills, all appearing before my eyes at the same time. Ed flashed them so casually, as if he could drop them in a well somewhere and never notice. It was the first time I had seen that much money and it made my life, by comparison, seem inferior. Jeffrey pocketed eight bucks in change when it was all said and done, the two of us standing there with our rocket-pops. I thought Jeffrey was the luckiest and richest boy in the world.

James was a Filipino kid, and I'd never known what a Filipino was until I met him and his family. He had black hair with a center-part that ran thick and straight over his ears to his shoulders. He had narrow, tough-looking eyes and said he knew Kung Fu. He also ate foods I'd never heard of like oxtail stew and pork knuckles. Anyone who ate pork knuckles had to be tough, I thought. There were better names for these foods, which James trilled through in his native tongue: *adobo, humba, batchoy.* His breath always smelled of vinegar and lime.

James's dad was a cook in a restaurant somewhere. Whenever I'd see him, he was wearing a sauce-stained white apron tied around his waist. It was James's mom I saw the most. She was a stout, round woman with short, graying hair who stood at the stove all day preparing exotic, aromatic meals for her husband and four kids. The smells from her kitchen wafted through Stuccoville: slow-cooking chicken and beef, garlic, ginger, soy. James's mom had trouble pronouncing words with "th" in them. When she called down the street for James's younger sister Kathy, it came out "Kat-TAY!" For James, she dropped the vowels entirely: "Jmz."

That summer, we three boys set out every morning on our bikes when it was still cool enough to breathe. The Toughskins I'd worn during the school year had become frayed cutoffs. I wore vented football jerseys with stars and big numbers. My Keds' sneakers were grubby, and I pulled my striped tube socks to my knees.

The day we found the warehouse, it hovered in the distance. "Look," James said. "It's a city."

"Don't be a moron," Jeffrey said. "It's a mirage."

We stopped our bikes and peered through the wavy heat like John Wayne spotting Injuns on the horizon. We probably should have turned around and headed back, but it wasn't hot enough yet. Plus, in the middle distance, we could see the railway signal was green, which meant at any moment a freight train would rumble by. We'd need to fill our pockets with stones from the track ballast to hurl at the boxcars as they passed.

We collected our stones and rode toward the city mirage. As we drew closer, we saw that it was neither city nor mirage. We saw, as it materialized on the horizon, a boarded-up building next to a small train depot. All around, there was cracked, crumbling asphalt, discarded sofas, urine-stained mattresses, and televisions with screens broken out. We rode our bikes over the asphalt, over crushed cans with fading beer logos and silver pull tabs, over prickly milkweed growing up through the cracks.

The building itself was metal-sided and rusty. We rode up to a window, which still had a full pane of glass in the frame. We got off our bikes and took turns standing on a cinderblock to peer inside, but we couldn't see a thing through the grimy, webby glass. The freight train we'd been waiting for blew its whistle and thundered along behind us, too far behind, it turned out, to hit it with any of the sharp-edge ballast stones that cut through the hip pockets of our cutoffs. It blew its whistle again when we turned away from the warehouse window and waved at the engineer.

I don't know whose idea it was to do what we did next. I'd like to think it wasn't mine, but there's a very good chance it was. I'd been reading the Hardy Boys going on six years, and from them I'd learned that mystery lurked around every corner; an old warehouse always had something to hide. But the Hardy Boys weren't vandals. They never would have pulled ballast stones from their pockets and chucked them through a warehouse window just so they could see what was inside. We did. And the end result was a shattered window with one jagged tooth of glass hanging from the splintered pane.

James said, "Uh-oh."

Jeffrey was the first one to stand on the cinderblock. "You guys have to see this," he said.

I don't know what I was expecting—maybe a bunch of coffins or unlimited access to our own bumper cars—but when it was my turn on the cinderblock, I was disappointed.

"Ovens?"

"Yeah," Jeffrey said. "I bet they're all stolen."

Inside the warehouse were rows and rows of washers, dryers, refrigerators, and ovens, all wrapped in clear plastic, stacked on pallets. Had we been taller or more agile, we may have scaled the metal wall and heaved ourselves through the window to investigate, Hardy Boys-style. Maybe Jeffrey was onto something. Maybe we had stumbled upon some kind of organized crime ring where a bunch of organized criminals were stealing people's refrigerators then reselling them on the appliance black market. That's what we wanted to believe, rather than something much less farfetched: that the warehouse we'd just vandalized wasn't, in fact, out of commission, and every one of those appliances belonged to the local Sears about ten miles away, kept there because they wouldn't all fit in the store. Had we walked around the other side of that warehouse, we would have seen the big roll-up door and the Sears sign, a clean, concrete tarmac where trucks backed in to drop off and haul away, and next to that a sign on a steel pole announcing that trespassers would be prosecuted to the fullest extent of the law.

Instead of investigating further, we gave up. Climbing through the window to look over a bunch of dumb appliances became uninteresting, especially considering all of the broken glass we'd created to make that opening possible.

That's when we looked around for other possibilities and when we saw, beyond the depot building, a wood-sided shack with a rusty tin roof: *Coca-Cola. Fresh Sandwiches.* Jackpot. The appliance warehouse was old news.

The signs hung over the front door; if we jumped, we could slap "Fresh Sandwiches," which groaned on rusting hooks. The café itself was made of planks and brick and the earth surrounding it was cracked. Every window was blacked out. There was a low, metal link fence enclosing what looked to have been, at one time, a small yard. The gate hung open on one hinge, and a chain attached to the base of a dead tree snaked through weeds and anthills, all that remained of a tethered mongrel. Next to the tree, an old whirlybird sprinkler stiff with calcium was affixed to a split hose. Nothing of use had grown here for years. Nothing, that is, except for fig trees, which stood in neat lines behind the place, where people used to eat and drink and talk about the weather and the price of pork bellies. It was clear to us that there was no way, none whatsoever, that anyone was inside. This place was ours for the taking.

My imagination marveled over what might be behind that café door. I pictured a brassy cash register on the bar, drawer open and fat with bills. I didn't just picture this; it became a reality to me. I just knew that inside the café at the end of that empty road was a boatload of money that would change my life. I would grab fistfuls of it and shove it in my Toughskins, then ride home through the fig orchard, newly rich, wondering what I would do with it all; my mind had already gone there. First thing, an honest-to-goodness dirt bike to replace the street ride I'd been getting teased about, a denim-colored Wrangler with a banana seat and a sissy bar. It wasn't cool for a boy to ride a bike with a *sissy* bar, and every time some other boy gave me the business about it, I wanted to put him in a headlock and sock him in the nose over and over until I heard the cartilage break and I saw blood in his eyes. I was ready to be that kind of person if it paid enough. But maybe that badness would go away if I had a sleek new bike with knobby tires and a real saddle, shiny sprockets, and chain that didn't fall off.

That's probably why I went to the door first. The first one in would get the money, and I knew Mom and I needed it. She spent a lot of time laid up in bed wearing her bathrobe, sometimes sitting upright with her back to the headboard looking for all the world like a hospital patient.

She had a bedside tray Marzelle had set her up with and on it there was a small battery of pill bottles, a plastic water pitcher, a cup, and an ashtray. Sometimes she'd call me over just to wrap her arms around me and sniffle her drippy nose into my hair. She had a telephone next to the bed, and at night, I listened through the walls as she talked to Marzelle in LA, saying things that had implications for me, words like *Medicare* and *welfare* and *layaway* and *fresh start*. She'd always cut the calls short by saying "I'd better go. This is your nickel." I felt awful that Mom didn't even have a nickel to call her mother.

So, I went to the door first.

I didn't know enough to be afraid. It seemed simple: Open the door, walk in, take what I could. Easy. The sun was behind us and the door-knob was hot, but it turned, and I felt the latch slip away from the frame. The door began to open, but then got hung up by a safety chain.

"It's locked," James said. "We better go."

Jeffrey said the same thing. "Yeah, let's go."

They both started to back away.

I told them they were chicken. They could go if they wanted, but I wasn't leaving until I got inside. James had a working dad, siblings, and a mom who cooked big meals. Jeffrey had Uncle Ed and his wallet full of C-notes. By comparison, I had nothing. This was bigger for me, so I could not be a chicken.

My arm was thin enough to pass through the opening, all the way to my shoulder, and I was able to reach up and try to wriggle the lock free. I'd seen this contraption before. Just slide the traveler through a narrow groove to the end where it widened, and the chain would release. I felt it moving, but not far enough, so I stretched a bit more, swiveling my torso in and around and up. All I needed was just one, more, fraction.

I was working away on that chain, getting so close, I thought, when I felt fingers wrap around my wrist, followed by words I'll never forget: "Whatcha' doin', Sonny?" When I hear it play back in my mind—*What-cha' doin', Sonny?*—it always sounds frail and small, just the slightest whistle on the *S* as though spoken through toothless gums.

I screamed. So did James and Jeffrey. I tried to free myself, but this woman's bony fingers had a hold of me, had my forearm pinned to the back of the door with the full weight of her. "Whatcha' doin', Sonny?" I peered into the dark innards of that café and what peered back were the eyes of someone who wouldn't be bullied. I saw her small, pursed mouth and a few dark whiskers on her stubborn chin. By now, my shoulder was caught, too, because she had thrown her body against the door. I was in a vise and she continued to stare me down. Behind me, I heard James and Jeffrey scattering away. I heard them call to me, "Come on!" but it was no use. My feet were moving but my body would go nowhere. I couldn't pull myself away. Her grip tightened and I felt her fingernails cut into the underside of my wrist.

Suddenly, she let me go. She unwrapped her fingers, pulled open the door, and I ran. James and Jeffrey were up ahead. My lousy bike lay on its side in the dust. I lifted it from the ground and got myself a running start. The pedal cranks were moving faster than my feet, but once I caught up with them, I stood and pumped my legs as fast as they would go. I watched my friends pass over the tracks, then turn around the depot building toward the busted-up warehouse where we could pick up the path that brought us there. I wasn't far behind by now; the tracks were just ahead of me with no trains in sight. There would be no need for me to slow down, not until I got all the way home, breathless, choking down water from the garden hose.

I bumped over the rails, took my turn around the depot building, then stopped short when I saw James and Jeffrey standing next to their bikes, now in the possession of a tall man in front of a white pickup and another man in a sheriff's uniform, flat-brimmed cowboy hat and dark brown shirt with a gold five-pointed badge.

"There's the other one," the sheriff said.

He was right. I was the other one.

The sheriff drove us back to Stuccoville. We'd spent an hour or so in his custody, along with the man who turned out to be the foreman of the warehouse, there because the freight train engineer we'd waved to had radioed him about two blond boys and another one with black hair messing around on the property. This brought the foreman from his house, who then radioed the sheriff, which then led to the sheriff coming out to take the foreman's statement about the vandalism. That's what the two men were doing when James and Jeffrey rode up like two house flies into a spiderweb. Seconds later, I rode into the same web.

The foreman was pretty wound up about the whole thing and went on about how he was going to have the sheriff march us right down to juvenile hall and lock us up behind bars with other punk kids who damaged people's property. And those boys in "juvie" wouldn't be nice to us, either. "You'd better be ready for a butt-whooping of the kind you'd never seen in your young lives," he said. Those boys in juvie ate pretty boys like us for lunch.

The foreman jammed his index finger into my chest hard enough to knock me backward. "Do you hear me?" he yelled. "Do you hear what I am saying to you?" I'd been standing there with my head down, and the sheriff just let him carry on like that until he poked me again and got right up to the edge of his self-restraint.

"Okay, Bill," the sheriff said. "That's enough now."

Bill the foreman turned away from us, then wheeled back. "Your parents," he said, wagging that finger again. "Haven't your parents taught you *anything* about respect?"

One of us sniffled. It was Jeffrey, I think, but it may have been me. It didn't take much to make me cry. I was sensitive and broke down easily. I was trying to emerge from this, along with other deficiencies like my fear of being laughed at and my worry over money. James, though, he bristled. Our shoulders were touching, and I could feel his neck and upper back stiffen, his rage passing into me. Maybe it was his Kung Fu training, but his face had gone icy, his eyes narrow and his lips pursed. He raised his chin as though he were warming his face in the sun. He breathed deep through his nose and his nostrils flared.

Whatever it was that James had in him, I wanted it.

We were lucky. Uncle Ed was the first grown-up on the scene when the sheriff pulled into Stuccoville. Somehow, the sheriff had gotten Bill the foreman to return our bikes to the neighborhood in the back of his pickup. He drove in behind us. Jeffrey, James, and I rode in the back of the sheriff's car, shoulder to shoulder, our sweaty legs sticking to the vinyl. There was a metal grate separating the front seat from the back, and the doors where we sat had no handles, so you couldn't free yourself from inside. The sheriff didn't cuff us; he said old Bill had done enough scaring for the day. We weren't bad boys, he said. We reminded him of himself when he was our age, and look at him now. Maybe one day one of us would be a sheriff, too.

In the end, the foreman agreed to a cash payment for his trouble, which Uncle Ed paid on the spot. There would be no need for juvenile court, and Ed wouldn't accept money from my mother. It was Ed who explained the whole thing to her, about how we were just kids being kids, and there was no need to worry over paying him. He said we would wash and wax his Oldsmobile and polish his hubcaps to work it off. Mom sat listening from a folding metal chair on our front step.

Uncle Ed must have known that our families struggled, or at least he knew my mother did, what with not having a man around and with her being sick and now walking with a cane and her foot all wrapped up. Those kinds of things got around Stuccoville. The grown-ups knew whose homes were broken and whose teenagers were smoking pot and hanging around with the wrong people. They knew which fathers drank too much, who was struggling to find work, and whose kids had a hard time reading. Sometimes, they got involved in helpful, quiet ways; meals showed up because someone accidentally doubled the recipe and it would go to waste otherwise. "Please, take it," they'd say. Other times, neighborhood boys working on Cub Scout service patches converged on a single mom's weed-choked yard, expecting nothing but a signature in a workbook in return. Engine oil got changed for a cold beer.

When Ed finished, Mom tried to push herself into a standing position. Her cane wobbled. Don't get up, he said; there was no need. He patted her on the shoulder and walked toward his house, the one he shared with Jane, the one he called home at the time. After he'd gone, I sat with my mother in the heavy quiet. My bike lay on its side in the grass. With my foot, I spun the front tire in slow circles. It was hot and my face was throbbing and all I really wanted was a glass of ice water and to lie down for a while.

Mom said nothing at first. She just stared out into the wavy heat of our neighborhood as though it might come back with some answers if she waited long enough. She could sense how beaten down I was, and she didn't even know about the woman in the café. There was fatigue in her bloated, moon-like face. She asked, "What am I going to do with you?" and I hung my head and told her I would be good. I promised. I knew what she must have been feeling then. She was over her head and didn't know where she could find the strength to keep it all together. And here I was, with all kinds of badness in my heart, smashing warehouse windows and trying to break into the homes of old ladies.

"Come on," she said. "Let's get you cooled off." And then, as I helped her to her feet, there was this: "Thank you for helping an old lady."

9

Lust, Maybe, but Not Violence

"She has been feeling terrible. She cut her leg with a razor when she was shaving and it bled for 20 minutes. She is supposed to see Dr. K. next week about having her Morton's toe operated on."

—I.G.T., MD, Progress Notes,
June 24, 1980

ABOUT A WEEK AFTER THE INCIDENT AT THE WAREHOUSE, Jeffrey was over at my house, and we let slip about breaking into the café. "You should have seen your face," Jeffrey said. I asked him how he could see my face if his back was to me and he was running away like a big chicken.

"Jeffrey," Mom said. "Time for you to go."

So now I was a vandal and a would-be thief and, worst of all, I was a boy who kept secrets. Determined to fix me before I wound up in juvie, where Bill the foreman said pretty boys like me got eaten for lunch, Mom resorted to an extreme, desperate measure.

"We are going to church," she said.

It was September of 1980, and I had just turned twelve. Every Sunday for a good month or so, we sat in padded red pews as the jelly-jawed preacher told us how to live a life pleasing to God. To stave off boredom, I took a sketch pad in which I drew pictures of the saints who gazed down on us from the stained glass. Beside me, Mom scratched out sermon notes. She stopped writing and looked to the pulpit when something moved her. I could always tell when the preacher delivered some bit of wisdom that hit home. She'd nod and whisper yes, and every so often I'd catch her looking over at me as if she'd just heard something she might use to help me find direction. To give her the impression I was listening, I'd give her a nod and stretch my eyebrows into little peaks to show her we were on the same page.

One Sunday, after a sermon on giving, the red velvet offering bag made its way down our row. Mom slipped a card inside and passed the wooden baton handle to me. I took it, then made a show of sticking my hand inside and removing some of the bills. I thought I was being funny, but Mom didn't laugh. The woman next to me didn't, either. She got all furrowed and stared down her long nose into my face. Mom's cheeks went scarlet and she gave my hand a slap. It raised enough of a ruckus that others around us shot a look our way. My mother met their disapproval with a shamefaced grin.

After the service was over, Mom couldn't get out of the sanctuary fast enough. She had never been one to outpace me, especially when it came to leaving church, but that day she did. First thing when she got to the car, she looked over both shoulders to see if anyone was watching her.

"I can't believe you did that," she said.

I told her I heard it straight from the preacher's own mouth: "God wants us to share in His riches." Again, I thought I was being funny, and again, Mom did not laugh.

"That's not what he meant," Mom said. She started the car, and I pushed in the dashboard lighter, which popped in a matter of seconds. I took it from the socket and held the bright orange coils to the menthol resting between my mother's lips. She took a deep drag until the end of the cigarette glowed. Then she held it out the open window, down low against the side of the door. She said she wasn't sure we could show our faces there again, which was actually just fine with me. I slipped the dashboard lighter back into its socket.

We'd been back home not more than half a day when Mom answered a knock at our door. Right there on the front step were two sunny, apple-cheeked folks from the church we'd fled that morning. They'd seen the card Mom had dropped in the offering bag, the one where she checked the box saying she'd like to be contacted by someone from the church to talk things over.

"You folks don't waste any time," Mom said, and she stepped aside to let them in.

There was a woman about Mom's age and a young man who looked like he could be my older brother. He had straw-colored hair like mine, combed neatly away from his gleaming forehead. The woman introduced him as Scott and said he was the guy who organized activities for the children. He took one step in my direction and held out his right hand. In his left, he cradled a small leather Bible. I remember stepping back and feeling weak-kneed for a moment. I thought Scott had it in his mind to give me a talking-to about the money I'd pretended to steal from the offering bag.

"Tell him your name," my mother said. I told Scott my name. His hand was still hanging there in the space between us. "Shake his hand," my mother said. She said this from the side of her mouth, through gritted teeth, then followed that with a flat laugh. I could tell there was going to be a talk about this later, about the protocol for greeting guests to our home.

The woman sat at the kitchen table with my mother for a good long while that Sunday afternoon, and I sat on one end of our sofa while Scott sat side-saddle on the other end. His left leg was on the floor and he had his right hiked up in a triangle. While Scott small-talked me, I kept my mother and the woman in the corner of my eye. At one point, she reached across the table and placed her hands on my mother's. There came a moment when this woman and my mother bowed their heads and closed their eyes. The woman whispered while my mother nodded her head and said, "yes, yes, yes." Whatever was happening at our table seemed to be of great importance.

Even though I was worried about my mother and what the woman at our table was doing to her, I was interested in Scott. I liked him. He asked me all kinds of questions and seemed genuinely interested in finding out about me. His warmth seemed full and total, and I imagined that this was what it must be like to have an older brother. Lately, more than ever, I had been longing for siblings. Every kid I knew had them. I wanted so badly to say the words *my brother* or *my sister* and have those words attach themselves to a real person. I wanted to know what it meant to have a sibling rivalry. It was a strange longing, this desire to simply say, "My brother plays baseball," or "My sister has to get braces," and know there was a boy or girl filling that space of mutual history.

Scott asked me what my favorite sport was.

"Baseball," I said.

"I knew it. If you gave me one guess, I'd have said baseball. You play?"

"Yep," I said.

"I could tell. You look like a real ballplayer." He said I looked like a pitcher.

I told him no, mostly third base. Sometimes, catcher.

"Whoa, boy." This seemed to really astound him. He puckered his lips in a whistle. "Catcher? Well, that's something else. You must be really good to be a catcher."

"I guess I'm all right," I told him.

Scott moved from the arm of the sofa to the actual cushion and asked if I had any interest in going to youth group. He said they played mushball, which was like baseball only much softer. I was familiar with mushball. I told Scott we played it at school, that it was like playing with a pillow. You could swing your hardest and just might get the ball past the pitcher.

"We have other sports, too. Flag football, basketball, volleyball. You know we have our own gym?"

I said I didn't know that. I told him that Mom and I had only gone into the big church building a couple of times. We hadn't looked at much else.

"Well, then, I need to show you around, don't I?" he said. "I need to bring you out to our ball field. It's right there on the church grounds."

"Yeah, I guess," I said.

"That's great." He reached down the couch and gave my knee a slap. "It's all set then. Next Sunday I'll come find you. I'll take you up to meet some of the other boys and after the service, we can play a game."

He also told me about an event coming up in a few weeks, on a Friday night. It was a sleepover at the church, a movie night, a good chance for me to meet a few kids. He said this so Mom could hear it, like he meant for it to reach both of us at the same time. Mom was all finished with the woman at the table. Her eyes were wet. She said a movie night at the church sounded like a lot of fun. She said this as she dabbed at her eyes with a tissue. "Doesn't it sound like a lot of fun?" she asked. I shrugged. It didn't, but I said it did anyway because my mother had seemed to find relief from her talk with the woman at the table, and I didn't want to spoil it.

There were hugs and handshakes and the two of them—this woman and Scott—left our house as the sun floated over the colorless haze. Mom and I watched them get in their car. Scott was on the passenger side. He cranked down his window.

"See you next week, slugger," he said.

I waved back and said, "See ya," but not loud enough for anyone but my mother to really hear.

Everyone had arranged their bedrolls neatly, boys in the back half of the room, girls near the front, with a heavy concentration of pillows and sleeping bags at the midline. There were a couple dozen kids all around the same age, sixth and seventh and eighth grade, and we played games that afternoon on the field, something for us to blow off steam—sack races, dodgeball, things like that—before we settled in for the movie. I am sure there was food, most likely pizza, and Scott told our mothers to send us with a couple of dollars, because in the morning we would all walk down the road to Winchell's Donut House and have maple bars and jelly-filled for breakfast. Mom gave me two dollars for my wallet, which I sealed in the billfold slot under Velcro. I was in a persistent anxious state, so I checked and double-checked over the course of the afternoon and evening to make sure everything was where it should have been. It felt like an enormous responsibility and I wanted to do a fine job with it. I put my wallet in my back pocket. At some point, as I got ready for bed, I slipped it inside my pillowcase for safekeeping.

It grew dark outside. Some parts of the room were eerie and black. Earlier in the evening, without anyone knowing it, an eighth-grade boy and his girlfriend arranged themselves in a dark place and they were lying next to one another, kissing. How long this had been going on is anyone's guess, but there were soon whispers and giggles and murmurs passing through the room. I remember the boy well. He was Scott's little brother, a blond kid named Stevie.

What had grown into an entertainment for others became a source of distress for me. I wanted the kissing to stop, and I was both irritated and confused by the fact that it was happening in the first place, right there in front of everyone, in a church, where we were supposed to think about God and follow the rules. It bothered me so much that I took it upon myself to do something about it.

I crawled from my sleeping bag and told the kid next to me I had to use the restroom. Carefully, I picked my way over a few huddled bodies the way you might step through puddles, aiming for the dry patches. I could see Stevie and his girl on the floor. I navigated strategically, so they wound up in front of me, to my right. As I neared them, I made a show of putting my hands out before me as though I were feeling my way through a place of total darkness. I remember wanting others to support me in what would surely be a discussion with Scott afterwards. "He couldn't see them," they would say. "We could tell by the way he was walking."

When I got close enough, I pretended to stumble. When you navigate obstacles in darkness, such a thing is bound to happen. Kicking Stevie in the head would appear as nothing more than an honest accident brought about by dark, crowded circumstances. When he jumped up with his hand over his face, in the place where my big toe kicked him, he towered over me.

I backed away and put my hands up. I thought he might slug me. I said, "Oh, sorry." Stevie's girl sat up and leaned on her elbow. She looked at me with hard eyes and smirked. Stevie worked the ache from his jaw and looked around the room, maybe for his brother. Then he looked at me with disgust.

"Whatever," he said. If Stevie had seen the mischief in my heart, he might have forced me to the ground and rained all manner of trouble on me. It was clear, though, that he knew better. This wasn't the place for violence. Lust, maybe, but not violence. In that dark corner where Stevie could have done a lot to me, he did very little. He took a step forward, put his hand on my shoulder, and told me I'd better be more careful. He said this with a kind of growl, as though he wanted to make sure I knew he was letting me off easy.

On my way back from the bathroom, I was more careful. I tiptoed to my sleeping bag, where I tucked myself in and struggled to sleep. I missed my mother. She made my world more stable, and on that night, lying among children I only vaguely knew, I felt far away from her. I didn't like trying to fall asleep knowing that I might reveal things to strangers. I was scared, and spent the whole night in a restless predicament.

The next morning, Stevie sat beneath a window with his back to a wall. Redemptive sunlight spilled over him. His girl was on the opposite side of the room brushing through her hair. A tribe of girls clustered around her, their faces glowing.

I was exhausted. My nerves were raw, and my mind ached with fatigue. I was not in a place to think clearly and I remember how heavy I felt, beginning with my eyelids. Everything was slower that morning, every movement and thought, everything but my beating heart, which thrashed inside my chest. I couldn't wait to get home.

Things got worse for me when I reached into my pillowcase and realized my wallet wasn't inside. I inhaled and tried to calm myself, then I unpacked everything I had just put away, turning out my overnight bag to be sure it was empty. I looked inside my toothbrush kit, every zippered pocket of my bag, every pocket of every piece of clothing I had: jeans, sweatshirt, cutoffs. I looked inside my socks. I didn't understand how this could happen. I had my wallet all afternoon; I remembered putting it into my pillowcase that evening. I retraced my steps to places I'd been, the same path I'd taken from my sleeping bag to Stevie's head, then to the bathroom and back, but I knew I wouldn't find it. I knew I had never taken it from my pillowcase. I felt like God was punishing me for kicking Stevie.

I ran back inside. My chest tightened. I went straight to Scott, who sat perched on a stool with a guitar in his lap, strumming something energetic and holy.

"My. Wallet. Is. Missing."

He said the things you'd say to a boy in a panic over something lost. "Are you sure you checked everything? Your pockets? Your sleeping bag?"

"Yes. Yes. Yes."

Scott got everyone's attention. "Clap once if you can hear me," he said. *Clap.*

Then he made an announcement: "Missing wallet, navy blue? Look around the floor, look through your things." Some kids milled about. They shoved aside pillows with their feet, picked up and shook out sweatshirts, patted around lumps of clothing on the floor. But their efforts were half-hearted. Some, like Stevie and his girl, did nothing. Stevie yawned coolly and didn't move from the wall he'd been leaning against. His girl still sat, brushing her hair. They remained where I'd first seen them that morning.

Scott encouraged me to keep looking, especially once everything got packed; the floor would be clearer then, more visible. "It will turn up," he said. "Don't worry." Meanwhile, he busied himself organizing his group into action. "Get your money," he told them. Everyone needed to meet on the lawn downstairs. He told everyone to stay together. It was important they not get too far apart. "And remember your manners," he said. "Remember your pleases and thank-yous."

While Scott said these things, I crawled around the floor among stacked bags, peering into the carpet and around kids' legs as they stepped over me. Scott asked if I'd had any luck.

"No, no luck," I said.

I heard feet paddle down a concrete staircase, voices collect on the lawn below, laughter, and sparring over who stayed up the longest, who kept farting all night, who rolled into someone else. Then, a headcount. "Do we have everybody?" Scott said. "I need to make sure I come back with just as many as when I started."

I kept searching, listening to the voices grow faint before they bled into the sounds of Saturday morning traffic, through the crosswalk, down the street to Winchell's. I listened to them go, Scott and every one of those kids, then I stood among their belongings, knowing that somewhere in that room, something that once belonged to me was there but now gone for good, and I blamed myself for not being more careful.

Then I saw the phone on the wall, an ivory Trimline with a handwritten note taped to the base: "Dial 7 for an outside line."

I dialed 7, then dialed my mother and told her what happened, that I lost the wallet and the two dollars.

She told me the money didn't matter, "not one bit it didn't." She would drive right over, so I should get all my things together and wait for her in the same place she'd dropped me off the day before. I hung up, stuffed my bedroll and pillow and jacket into my duffel and walked out of the church to the curb.

I wasn't waiting more than a few minutes when Mom pulled up in the Corolla. I told her again I was sorry about the money, and she assured me again that it was nothing. But there was this other thing that really burned at her, something that would ensure we wouldn't see Scott or Stevie or Stevie's girl or the woman at our kitchen table or the jelly-jawed preacher ever again.

"They didn't even offer to buy you a donut," she said.

She said this to me as she drove us home in the Corolla. It was a cool fall morning. She found me sitting on my duffel, before anyone else had come back from their morning walk, probably before anyone had even thought to say, "Hey, where's that new kid?"

10

In My Trash Bag, I Met Kathy

"She has been concerned about being unable to raise her 12-year-old son on her own and whether she will be crippled or unable to work in the future."

—R.T.M., MD, Progress Notes,
March 18, 1981

I CHANGED SCHOOLS THE YEAR I STARTED EIGHTH GRADE, just after my thirteenth birthday, and for the first time in my life I had a locker for my books. This felt like a big deal; it felt grown-up to me. I went from one class in one room to a second class in another, and so on and so on, six different periods, six different teachers, six different classrooms. I stopped at my locker between classes, sometimes for no reason other than to roll the tumbler on my shiny combination lock and abide in the satisfaction of it opening. I horsed around with a couple boys, Steve and Billy, whose lockers were next to mine, and we talked reprehensibly about which girls were hot, who had the biggest knockers, and who was so flat-chested as to not be worthy of our scrutiny. Steve and Billy were popular and well-liked. I admired them for their 501s and slip-on, checkered Vans. My mother had been working steadily all year, but trendy jeans and shoes were too rich for our budget.

Before the school year started, Mom got transferred to a junior high in central Fresno. She was part of a pool of clerk typists, a designation given to lower-skilled employees whose school assignments could change from one year to the next based on need. Their jobs were fairly basic: type forms, answer phones, take attendance. At her new school in the fall of 1981, she started out at the front desk, but questions came too fast, things she didn't know how to answer. She asked coworkers, who responded, though impatiently. One woman asked her how it was that she ended up at the front desk to begin with. "If you can't do the work," she said, "then we'll need to find someone who can."

The phone rang nonstop and it hurt to transfer calls because the buttons required a level of strength Mom's fingers couldn't muster. She grew anxious and confused and dizzy, sometimes leaving her post for the bathroom where she sat on a toilet and rested her forehead against the stall door. She swallowed a Cyclizine, which Dr. M. gave her for vertigo, then waited for the spinning to stop. Her coworkers glared at her when she returned. At some point, she snapped at a caller, who hollered at my mother for disconnecting her. Mom was written up for bad phone manners. That was followed by a poor performance review, during which she broke down in tears in her principal's office; she left thinking she'd be fired.

Instead, she was moved away from the front desk to the back office, a place she didn't have to answer calls or interact with people, but she did have to type more than she ever had in her life. She was much slower than the able-fingered clerk, but she persisted for eight hours a day through form after treacherous form, until it was time to leave. She came home every day with swollen, achy hands and was up to ten aspirin a day, plus Tylenol with codeine, plus her prescriptions for inflammation and depression and vertigo. Her pill bottles stood like little soldiers on her nightstand, but there was no combination that made her feel like doing anything but sleep. She was in bed before nine every night, some nights even earlier.

By now, we'd lived in our house on Malsbary Street for two years. Our landlord, Duane, was a kind man who kept our rent at $395.00 a month.

Mom made enough money to cover the rent and buy food, but there was little left for anything else.

We had nice neighbors. The most important of them to me was a chain-smoker named Frank who managed a concrete pipe plant. He showed me how to run a lawnmower and taught me the difference between metric and Imperial. He had a cluttered workbench with glass jars full of nails and screws. Once home from the plant for the day, he changed into frayed cutoffs and flip-flops and unbuttoned shirts and remained in constant possession of a lowball filled with ice and whiskey. His two front teeth were false, and he popped them in and out with his tongue when he puzzled over an engine part. He could do an entire engine rebuild while smoking. He had been a boxer in the Navy, even though he was on the small side.

"Small, but mighty," he once said. "Nobody wanted to fight me because I was tough."

I wanted to be tough like Frank, and I thought there was no better way to do that than to join my school's wrestling team. I told Frank about this, and he thought it was a good idea.

"Wrestlers are tough little bastards," he said, and that was all I needed to hear. I would be a tough little bastard. I was thin and wiry like Frank, and thought my body frame gave me a quickness advantage over bigger boys. The problem was their seasoning; these weren't playground fights where you could just shoot the knees and drive yourself into your opponent's gut. There were actual moves I hadn't learned yet and these other boys had. The worst was the pile driver, which happened every time I lunged at my opponent. He'd clamp his arms around my waist and drop me head-first to the floor, then flip me like a hotcake so my shoulders lay flat and my legs flailed at the gym rafters. There were contests to see who could pin me the fastest.

My coach's solution to my ineptitude was weight loss. He wanted me in the lowest class, where I stood a better chance at not getting squashed. There was also a greater likelihood in that class to win by default. Some schools wrestled with no lightweights, which meant I could get a victory for the team by doing nothing more than showing up. In short, I was being relegated to the place I'd do the least damage. So, every day after school, while the other boys wore singlets in the gym and learned techniques vital to success on the mat, my coach dropped a Hefty bag over my head with a hole cut out and dispatched me to run the fence line alone until I could sweat myself down to one-thirty. On one of these afternoons, as I plodded along the fence line in my trash bag, I met Kathy.

She was thin and pretty and in the seventh grade. She had sparkling brown eyes and straight, shiny hair that curled at her shoulders. She also wore a strawberry-flavored lip gloss I would have licked off her face if she had let me. I was smitten from the moment I saw her waiting at the gate for her father to pick her up. Like me, she found herself alone on the back side of the school every day after practice. The story she told me initially was that her dad wanted to pick her up there, along the busy street by the gate, because he didn't want to trouble with the crowded turnaround where parents normally fetched their kids. I would find out later that Kathy had asked her dad to pick her up there so she could watch me run.

Because Kathy was cute and a cheerleader and looked fantastic in a sweater, she'd drawn a lot of interest from the eighth-grade boys with feathered hair and button flies, but talk around the lockers was that she wanted to be my girlfriend, a development that was as surprising as it was welcome. Kathy's friends made her affections for me obvious, running up to me in a small posse, every one of them chattering simultaneously: *Do you like Kathy do you like Kathy she likes you she likes you so much do you like her, too?*

Kathy made me feel different about myself, and soon, she was lying to her father about what time to pick her up. One day after school, with a nonchalance she'd helped me rehearse, I walked up in street clothes to my wrestling coach and handed over my Hefty bag. At that moment, I went from being the kid on the bottom rung of the wrestling team to the kid *formerly* on the bottom rung of the wrestling team, and Kathy and I began making out every day in an inconspicuous door well of a six-sided learning annex. We French kissed until our jaws ached, which Steve and Billy said was an accomplishment, but not that big a deal. They wanted more from me, and they were disappointed that I couldn't deliver.

I shared very little with them, not because I didn't want to, but because I didn't have a language for it. I coveted their approval as much as my bones ached for Kathy, but I could be crude only to a point, after which the words got so foreign that I clammed up, sweaty-palmed and petrified by my ignorance. My new friends were far more advanced in the vernacular of sex, their language a product of access to older brothers who had experience with such things, along with a fine library of nudie magazines. They lived in an upper middle-class neighborhood near the school, where four tranquil streets of tidy ranch houses converged on a park of green grass and swing sets. Steve and Billy often spent their after-school hours in the company of seventeen-year-old longhairs passing roach clips and listening to AC/DC from one of several Trans Ams parked on the dead end, a place where, right under the noses of respectable nuclear families, deals went down and sometimes soured amid violent cursing and split lips and screeching rubber.

I spent my afternoons with Kathy, our standing after-school date something I looked forward to more than anything else in my life. Each time we walked up to one other, she tucked her hair behind one ear and smiled, looking hopeful and eager. After we'd finish kissing, we'd stand in the door well and hold each other sweetly and look deep into the shimmering pools of one another's eyes, the same God-awful words I probably barfed-up in my lovesick notes penned during Algebra—*holding you sweetly while looking deep into the shimmering pools of your eyes*—every so often peeking around the bricks to see if her dad's Mercedes was on the curb, and if it was, we'd kiss one last time, our tongues in each other's mouths, her fingers wrapped around the back of my head before she'd scamper away, leaving me to ride my bike the nearly three miles home, each crank of the pedals accomplished with little effort since I couldn't get Kathy out of my mind, and since distance, like time, seemed to melt into a suspended, dreamlike haze.

In the days and weeks that followed, Kathy and I spent every minute we could together, most often at lunch where I'd sit on a picnic table and she'd sit on the bench between my legs. I rubbed her shoulders and combed my fingers through her hair. Sometimes we changed things up where she sat on the table and I sat on the bench. At school, kids got to the point where they didn't say one name without the other: "Where are Chuck and Kathy?" but never, "Where's Chuck?" or "Where's Kathy?" We celebrated one month as a couple, then two, but during the time we were together, I never once went to her house nor did she ever come to mine. All of our private tenderness played out in a remote, unseen door well.

At home, we talked on the phone like addicts, our ears sweating from being pressed against the receiver for hours, her whispers meant to hide from her parents the fact that she was awake beyond what was healthy for kids our age; then at times late beyond reason when our conversations had become redundantly affectionate, we'd quibble over who would be the first to hang up.

"You go first."

"No, you."

"At the same time then—"

"One, two, three."

My mother was in bed asleep early every night, aided largely by the pharmaceutical regimen—Clinoril, Ativan, Tylenol with codeine, prednisone—designed to bring her relief in a world that was growing ever more painful. Unlike Kathy, there was no need for me to be so furtive. If Mom was lucky, she made it through the night without waking, but her comfort came in small doses and her sleep was mostly fitful. She wasn't eating well, telling Dr. M. that her diet for the most part was cheese and crackers. She cried out during flare-ups, howling into the unsettled darkness about feeling tender all over, about shooting pains in her arms and legs, about the bed of nails beneath her.

On one of those nights I was on the phone with Kathy, my mother called out to me. "Water," she cried. "Chuck? Water!" At first, I ignored her. I knew she wasn't going anywhere, but I couldn't say the same for Kathy, who was rumored to be hanging out with a kid named Keith, a guy with real Vuarnets, not cheap knock-offs. Keith's family could afford

Vuarnets and ski weekends. Keith collected lift tickets on his parka and his face was always tan, except around his eyes. *Keith, Keith, Keith.*

On the phone, Kathy asked if I was going to play baseball in the spring. I said I didn't know.

"Keith is going to play baseball," she said.

She asked if I was going to Tina's Halloween party, and I said I didn't know that, either.

"Keith is going as a vampire," she said.

Keith, Keith, Goddamned Keith.

From her bedroom, my mother called: "Can you bring me water?"

It was a bad night for my mother, one of many bad nights, but one that seemed worse than others, somehow. Normally, if I didn't come right away, she managed on her own. The idea of total dependence was humiliating to her. Mostly, she willed things to happen. But there were times total dependence was all she had. She wanted freedom from my help as much as I wanted freedom from her need, but neither option ever offered itself unequivocally. Rather, we orbited about one another in a murky, uncertain anti-pattern, dictated by her brain's chemical imbalance and her body's intermittent pain.

"Chuck? Water!" A third call, one I could not ignore.

"Keith's gonna get a Porsche when he turns sixteen," Kathy said.

I told Kathy to hold on. I told her there was something I had to do. I put the receiver down and went to my mother. She was sitting up in bed. "There you are," she said. "I was worried."

"I'm here," I said, but I was bratty about it. I was thirteen and had a chemical imbalance of my own to work out, one that for months had made me irascible and selfish and prurient. I was on the front end of discovering things about myself that confused and terrified me. I was always irritated, especially with my mother, because I felt I deserved things like ski weekends and Vuarnets, and her inability to provide those luxuries was spoiling my relationship with Kathy.

In the dim light of my mother's bedroom, I gave her water. I lifted the glass to her lips and let her drink. She then asked for pills, which I took from a bottle and dropped on her beefy tongue. She swallowed the pills and took some more water, then she asked if I would help her lie back down. "Be gentle," she said, and I knew why; when she got like this, the tips of my fingers against her skin were too much for her to bear. They shot through her with exquisite pain. She lowered her chin then raised it, which she did to force the pills down her throat. Then, with my hand on her back, she eased herself to bed. With her eyes closed, she whispered "thank you."

I said "you're welcome." I covered her with the bedsheet and turned out the lamp on the nightstand.

In my bedroom, the phone was as I'd left it, receiver-side down on the carpet, and I picked it up from the floor. I pressed it to my ear and said, "Kathy? I'm back." I said, "I'm here now, sorry," but Kathy was not there.

I guess I had been gone too long. I guess she just figured we'd see each other at school, and we did, the next day, between classes, me standing near my locker, she standing near hers alongside Keith—*Keith, Keith, Keith*—who was wearing his Vuarnets and talking about Tina's Halloween party, and who was going, and what he was going to be. When I saw Kathy tuck her hair behind her ear, I knew Keith had drawn her away from me. For that, I hated him. But really, how much could I hate a guy who knew who he was and wanted to be? In truth, I envied him, and while I wished he would move on to some other girl and leave Kathy alone, I knew even then there was nothing I could do about it until I became a different kind of person: tougher, more grown-up, and radically uncoupled from my center of gravity.

11

We Kicked Over a Few Tricycles Along the Way

"She continues to complain of her episodes that sound like vertigo. She is quite tearful and upset today and is concerned that these problems may result in the loss of her job."

—R.T.M., MD, Progress Notes,
December 21, 1981

W E WERE AT STEVE'S PLACE ON NEW YEAR'S EVE. THE houses on his street were brick and wood-sided with shutters on the windows and naked tree limbs bending over shake-shingled rooftops. Picture windows featured lit Christmas trees, and lights hung from every eave. The hedges were clipped into long boxes and the fescue lawns were broad and groomed and deep green, unlike the houses in Stuccoville, where the Bermuda that time of year was dormant and drab. There were flowers in neat, colorful rows beside walkways, and mailboxes set in brick or stone took their sturdy places on the curb. I had ridden my bike over there earlier that day, and we'd spent the afternoon throwing a football in the park with Billy. It was cold but sunny, and when we got tired of throwing the ball, we sat on the swings and let our sneakers drag through the sand and talked at length about the nearby girls with morally casual attitudes and permissive, disinterested parents.

How it came to be that three, thirteen-year-old boys had a sprawling, well-lit house to themselves on New Year's Eve, 1981, is anyone's guess. I do know that Steve's parents went to a party. I watched them leave. Steve's dad wore a suit with polished shoes and Steve's mom wore something that glittered. I cannot imagine me calling my mother and telling her that Steve's folks were gone, and it would just be the three of us boys home alone that night, and was that okay with her? I wonder if I had to lie; I wonder if I called her late that afternoon and asked her if I could stay, maybe thinking she'd give in easily because she was in pain, had no energy, had no will to argue. Maybe she said, "Let me talk with Steve's mom for a sec," and Steve, who saw this coming, had his older sister Jill take the phone from the side of my face. And maybe Jill, who had possibly pulled these kinds of stunts before, was flawless in her mimicry and completely convincing in her role as Steve's attentive mother. There would be board games and pizza, Jill might have said, and Atari for when the boys wanted to play Defender. *You know these boys and their video games, ha ha,* and *I'll be sure they hit the hay right after the ball drops.* Is it possible that Jill then handed the phone back to me and stuck her long finger and sharp chin right up to her little brother's face and whispered, "You owe me," before capping her lipstick and grabbing her car keys off the counter as she whisked out the door?

That's all speculation, because I honestly don't know how the three of us were there, by ourselves, with an Atari, a large pizza, my mother's trust, and a wide-open liquor cabinet.

We first walked the neighborhoods near the park and the junior high looking for girls, preferably in a group of three but certainly open to the idea of four or five, any young ladies who may have shared our burning inclinations toward freedom and adult living. We drifted toward lit bedroom windows, on the other sides of which were presumably girls our age, some from our school, but others—the girls we *really* wanted, Steve said—from St. Anthony's, the Catholic school chicks aching to bust free for a few hours and break some rules with three irresistible, prowling hoodlums who epitomized cool. Steve and Billy were confident that our mere presence in their manicured flower beds would emit pheromones powerful enough to coax these girls from their cozy homes and join our rebel march to Steve's place, where our charm, some wine coolers, and Cyndi Lauper's "Girls Just Wanna Have Fun" would lay the groundwork for some serious French-kissing. We kicked over a few tricycles along the way and moved newspapers left on driveways to places we felt more appropriate, like rooftops and birdbaths. We rang doorbells and ran, threw rocks at cats, and opened car doors left unlocked. Our path of lawlessness took us to a 7-Eleven, where Billy and I palmed M&Ms while Steve sparred with the clerk over a *Penthouse* magazine he swore his father had sent him to buy. In the end we cobbled enough pocket change for one Super Big Gulp and headed back to Steve's house with waning spirits, no *Penthouse*, and pilfered candy stuffed into our jeans.

The house was just as we'd left it; every light was on and MTV was blaring. The kitchen still carried the heavy aroma of pizza even though the open box revealed just one curled slice, the cheese having long ago congealed into something rubbery and unappealing. Billy scarfed it anyway, then drank straight from the two-liter Coke bottle left open on the counter.

"Dude," Steve said. "We need that."

"Relax, dude," Billy said. "There's a ton more at my house." Billy lived just across the park from Steve. He could be there and back within minutes with anything we needed, he said. "So, relax, dude."

"We don't need that much, anyways," Steve said. "Mine's gonna be mostly rum." I sat at the kitchen table. The liquor cabinet stood next to me. It was white, and there were brass knobs on the doors. You could see into the cabinet through small glass panes, and on the other side of that glass, rows of bottles, some filled with colorless liquids, some more amber-looking, all with distinguished labels intended to convey the same general message of abundance and good fortune. Steve asked me to grab the rum. I pulled open the cabinet door and read the labels; there were several bottles with the word "rum" on them. I grabbed the one in front; its label had a red-orange sun behind a palm tree. Apparently, that's the way it worked with liquor; it made you believe you were in perpetual sunset.

Steve put ice in a glass and poured it half full with rum, the other half with Coke. He stirred it with a spoon, then handed it to me. I took it like it was no big deal, like this was all part of the life I was meant to slip into, one of ease and high living. Steve said "cheers" and I said "cheers" right back. There we were, just a couple of grown men enjoying a cocktail on New Year's Eve, just like Steve's dad was doing right next to his glittering wife, and maybe Billy's dad, too, probably in the same place, in the lap of good cheer and enormous possibility.

I drank. One gulp, and it felt like I had dropped a burning match down my throat. Right away it came back up, out of my mouth and through my nose. I wondered how people could do this, how they could swallow fire and then, *willingly*, do it again. Steve and Billy didn't flinch.

"Come on," Billy said. "Get the first one down and you won't taste it after that." I tried again, and again, the fire raging in my throat. But this time I kept it down. I squinched up my face and rattled my head around and the sensation of the rum going down was soothing. It was a warmth that traveled the length of my esophagus and into my stomach, where it mixed with undigested pizza in a kind of pleasant fermentation, one that broadcast itself within seconds to the nerves in my extremities, all the way to the tips of my fingers and toes. I was warm all over.

"That's the stuff," Billy said. "The next one will be easier."

I drank again, and he was right. No fire this time; my insides had been primed. There was only warmth now. I threw back another gulp, and then one more. The rum became a great comfort. And soon, the glass was empty save a few ice cubes with soft, rounded edges. Steve, of course, filled my glass once more, same recipe, half rum, half Coke, and the three of us retired to the family room and sat in front of the Atari. My head was swimmy and my body light, like a helium balloon I fought to keep anchored. The room was frowzy and off its axis and I worked to maintain my balance, though I wasn't moving. Billy passed me a joystick and I toggled it dumbly through games lasting less than a minute as my lives were siphoned away quickly at the hands of faster, more agile aliens and enemy rockets. Green lasers blew my spaceship into electronic flares on the screen, but then a new ship appeared, a new life, which I maneuvered against the spacey backdrop until another, faster-moving green hyphen ripped through my hull and blew me to smithereens.

It was all going down so smoothly now. Billy said, "I bet you can't even taste it."

"Smooth," Steve said.

I tasted nothing but caramel and butter. It was like drinking cold pancake syrup. Naturally, when Steve brought me another, I couldn't fight it. By the time drink number three was inside me, the room was spinning, a condition I struggled against by slamming my eyes closed, squeezing them together as if somehow that would generate enough force to bring the tailspin to a halt.

I had to puke. I pulled myself up on all fours and crawled toward a narrowing hallway, one with kids' school pictures in frames hanging on the walls. There was Steve, with ginger hair and freckles, and Jill, her hair straight and blonde, both poised and smiling, Steve with a mouth full of braces, Jill's teeth like tiny piano keys, straight and white. Their faces wouldn't hold still. Even when I closed my eyes, they spun through my brain, and it was at that point I felt myself being dragged along the carpet, Billy holding one wrist, Steve the other, the two of them tugging me, taking a corner too tight and bending my body around a wall and into a bathroom with a pink rug, Jill's bathroom, which was too bright. There was a damp towel in a bundle on the floor next to my face.

Steve and Billy dropped my arms. "Dude," Steve said. "You're wasted."

If wasted meant disconnected and out-of-control and completely freaked out, then yes, I was wasted. Billy left, then came back and sat on the edge of the tub. He flipped through the pages of a nudie magazine he'd stolen from his older brother, and ordered me to look at a picture. But it was no use. There was no focus, only spinning, and I dug my fingers into the pink rug to slow it all down. Steve stood over me and sang something by J. Geils, then Billy picked up the riff, and the two of them carried on in song about the angel in the centerfold. I opened my eyes once more and saw her there, unfurled next to Billy's face, multiple versions of them both. It was like a hospital drama where the patient, his head wrapped in gauze, opens his eyes and sees four revolving faces of the same person staring back at him. I tried closing one eye, but it was still a kaleidoscope, and the dizzying rush of images grew unbearable. I felt my head slam into a cabinet as I pulled myself to the edge of the toilet and hurled. My rummy guts overshot the bowl and splashed against Jill's white bathrobe, which she had draped over a shower curtain rod. This happened two or three times.

"Duuuude," Steve said.

Billy tried to spin out of the way, but he was too slow. "You got some on me," he said. He dropped the nudie magazine in the bathtub. I turned to look at him, feeling guilty. He wiped vomit from his arm with the shower curtain.

I pressed my cheek against the cool toilet seat, and when the next round came, Steve grabbed my hair and held my head over the bowl. He pushed my face toward the water so that puke splashed back into my eyes. There were long, painful heaves during which vomit streamed from my mouth and nose and I was forced to taste my own stomach acid on its way out.

Steve shook me awake in the morning. I was on his bedroom floor. There were pans banging around in the kitchen.

"What happened?" I asked. My eyes were open, but just barely. I was sweating. A wave of nausea passed through me, and my mouth felt like it was stuffed with a dirty sock.

"You got hammered, dude," Steve said. "Come on, we have to go."

He had been out of bed for a while, enough time to get dressed and take the lay of the land. Billy was gone, left early that morning, and Steve's mom was in the kitchen making bacon and eggs. Jill was in her bathroom. She was apparently more than just a little upset with me for the way I'd treated her robe.

I didn't feel like moving, but Steve prodded me with his toe. "Come on," he said again. "Before my sister gets out of the shower." There were those words I'd longed to say, *my sister*, words that tumbled so easily from

Steve's mouth, words he took for granted. He was being protective of me, not wanting me to be subject to Jill's wrath. It might cause a ruckus, get his parents involved, and we didn't need that. As it was, we'd be able to escape on our bikes through the garage and Jill would probably forget about the whole thing by the end of the day, once her robe had gone through the wash.

For the most part, I stayed away from mischief after that night, which I believe—though she never brought it up—my mother knew about in that cryptic, intuitive way mothers know when things aren't right with their children.

There was one notable lapse in the spring of 1982 when Billy and I went on a stealing spree, riding our bikes from one grocery store to another, idly roaming the candy aisles and waiting for just the right moment to slip a Snickers into our pants. It was easy and thrilling, the adrenaline of petty theft clever fuel that made us feel bulletproof. And then came the fifth store of the day, a Food Land, our final stop before we rode off into the sunset of our glorious achievements.

With our stolen goods, we strolled out side-by-side, getting just a few feet before the undercover security man clamped onto the backs of our necks with his strong fingers. He bent low so his mouth was right between our ears. "Let's talk about that candy in your pants," he said. He turned our bodies hard to the left, toward the entrance, and Billy and I caught each other's eyes, probably with the same thought: *We can outrun him.* That was probably true. He was a big man who didn't stand a chance had we gotten loose. But in truth, we were the ones who didn't stand a chance, because when power grabs the early advantage, power usually wins. As we tried to wriggle free, his grip tightened, and I swear his thumb and middle finger met at my Adam's apple, so complete was his hold on me. He marched us right back into the store, past a grinning checkout lady, up a staircase near the produce section, and into a covert office behind smoked glass windows.

All the while, from the side of his mouth, he whispered the same petrifying refrain, which I have never forgotten: "You're fucking going to jail. You're fucking going to jail." I believed him. I had no doubt as to the truth of it, and I imagined myself behind bars alongside real criminals who would waste no time in hurting me, all because I got a thrill from stealing candy.

We did not go to jail. Instead, we had to sit in that dark office while the security guy called our mothers, both of whom were home and both of whom were forced to pick us up from the Food Land. Mom and I twisted and folded my bike into the Corolla. When I got in the car, I folded my arms over my chest and in my most authoritative, adult-sounding voice, I made the following pronouncement: "I don't want to talk about it."

She would have none of this. Her impatience with me was at its peak. This was the only time I ever remember her touching me in a way meant to pose a threat or send a message of harm. She grabbed my cheeks between her sickly fingers, something that must have brought her great physical pain, and turned my face so her eyes bored into mine. She spoke through her teeth: "You're gonna talk about it, pal." And if I wasn't willing to talk about it, she had another idea. "It might be time for you to live with your father."

She let go of my face. Her own flushed with fear and regret. The words had escaped her, and they couldn't be taken back.

While the idea of having a dad was appealing, I didn't want *my* dad, the man who'd made it pretty clear he didn't want me, either. My mother knew this, though it was a pretty big bluff to call at the time. But why wouldn't she want to be free of me? I lied, I stole, I broke other people's things, I ran away from her, and the absolute worst of it was that no matter how hard she tried, I was never content. I let her know in most everything I did that our lives were insufficient. Back then, I'd have given just about anything to be someone other than who I was.

I remember how I felt the morning after I got drunk on rum at Steve's house, the first day of 1982. I remember the nausea and the regret, mostly. But I also remember how Steve and I escaped his sister and met Billy, and the three of us rode our bikes through the same neighborhoods we'd walked the night before. Like proud conquerors, we took in our handiwork: the rooftop newspapers, the upturned trikes, even one driver's side door still open. The air was crisp on my face and provided fleeting moments of relief from the pounding in my head.

Steve and Billy carried on about me, about things I said and did, stuff I'd blathered about Kathy and how much I'd missed her, the love of my life who was now with Keith, and how I was going to kick his ass for stealing my girl, the brave drunk in me talking as though such a thing were actually possible.

"You should have seen yourself," Steve said. "You should have seen how you acted!" He said I wasn't like the Chuck he knew at all. He said I was crazy and bulletproof and brave. He said I was this totally different person, which made me feel accomplished and cool because, after all, wasn't that my goal?

12
Our Cupboards Were Full of Her Profits

"She continues to complain of pain in her joints, primarily in the morning with some swelling in her hands [. . .] I have offered to support a disability status for this to allow her to pursue a full time Tupperware career."

—R.T.M., MD, Progress Notes,
August 27, 1982

OUR RENTAL ON MALSBARY STREET WAS ONE HOUSE south of Bullard Avenue, which turned into a narrow country road not far past Stuccoville. It ran west all the way to the railroad tracks, after which it became nothing more than a strip of old tar that looked to have been laid down a half-century ago by a farmhand with a flat shovel. It was pockmarked and crumbled along the edges. On the hottest of days, its surface was like candle wax. As a boy, I rode my bike on that section of road during the summer, leaving tire tracks like fossils in the soft tar. Years later, my high school cross country coach—a thin, bearded man named Dennis—ran our team along Bullard as far as it would take us. Beyond the railroad tracks, passing beneath my pounding feet, were the impressions my tires had left nearly a decade before.

Back then, if you drove west on Bullard from the center of town, you passed St. Anthony's Catholic church, across the street from Monterey

Pines; a bit further, and you saw on your left the Food Land where Billy and I got caught stealing; you passed Tenaya Middle School on your right, and from the passenger window, you saw the door well of the learning annex where Kathy and I French-kissed. You crossed Van Ness Boulevard, a street that north and south featured sprawling yards and colonial mansions, homes to the wealthiest people in town, the surgeons and bankers and cotton farmers and homebuilders, truly jaw-dropping properties that made you wonder how so many rich people wound up in Fresno and where all that money came from.

Sometimes, Mom and I hopped in the Corolla and drove up and down Van Ness just to imagine what life was like on the other sides of those tall oak doors. These places had verandas and flying buttresses and porte cocheres, words my mother acquired during her stint as a real estate agent in Simi Valley—after Paramount, before Oregon—a venture gone sour. One of these Van Ness estates had a backyard aviary full of peacocks with grand, iridescent plumage that we could see over the fence as we drove by. So much extraordinary wealth, so close.

If you drove past Van Ness, about a mile west to Marks Avenue, you were in neighborhoods full of custom ranch homes with indoor water features and long tables for twelve, china hutches and front rooms that didn't get used. More doctors there, and lawyers, and financial planners, and people who generally made solid investment choices at a young age and were now in positions to take Hawaiian vacations every year and weekend jaunts to Carmel to shop garden boutiques.

Further west, a strip mall: another Food Land, a Thrifty Drug, an Armenian deli, a Guarantee Savings and Loan. Then more ranch houses, smaller as you drove west: schoolteachers, store managers, pharmacy clerks, double incomes, manageable debt, and trips to Disneyland every few years.

Then, on your left, Stuccoville, the bottom of the funnel, the hillbillies, pot-smokers, plate-smashers, and door-slammers; the sullen teens, spurned spouses, delivery drivers; the grocery clerks, the prison guards, the factory men, the substitute teachers, the barbers, the bank tellers, and, sometimes, on Saturday afternoons, the Tupperware ladies.

The women arrived wearing autumn scarves and earrings. They handed me their coats as they walked in, which I piled in a mound on Mom's bed. They smelled of perfume and cigarette smoke, the coats and the ladies.

This wasn't the first time Mom had tried to make it in direct marketing. At Monterey Pines, she sold Mary Kay, the pink Cadillac her goal from the get-go. I remember conversations she had with my father about what it would take to get her behind the wheel of a pink Caddy, and if she did really well with the company, it could take them places, maybe Florida.

"Wouldn't that be something, to drive around Florida in a pink Cadillac?" she said.

My father, who had dreams of his own, spoiled her fantasy. "You'll have a few parties," he said, "then we'll wind up with all this Mary Kay stuff we don't need."

After he left us alone in the yellow Stuccoville house, Mom gave it another shot, this time with the world's leader in fragrant bric-a-brac, Avon. Her bureau and bathroom countertops were overrun by decorative perfume bottles with cork stoppers, and I wondered which of them held the genie I would summon to grant our wishes. There were other scents in statuettes, little garden girls in yellow dresses holding bouquets and jumping rope. My bubble bath was inside an enchanted frog. Mom had perfumes and colognes in a brown glass Basset Hound, a big game rhino, and the Liberty Bell. She even gave me three fragrance decanters for my bedroom—bronze busts of Washington and Lincoln, along with a 1927 Bugatti—all full of a scent called "Deep Woods Aftershave." I remember slapping it over my cheeks mornings before school, feeling very much like a lumberjack, even though I wouldn't shave for years. And the cameos! My mother had them on rings and brooches and compacts and pendants. They were tiny works of art to her, things that made her feel refined and regal.

So, when she hosted a Tupperware party in 1982, it must have felt old hat to her. She had me help with the display before her guests arrived. I stacked pastel bowls in tiers, biggest on the bottom, narrowing to the top. She stood a few yards away providing directions. "Put the tumblers on the right, next to the coasters," she said. "And the salt and pepper shakers alongside the picnic pack." She tapped a painted fingernail against her tooth and clicked her tongue, an artist at work, getting things just right. She wore pantyhose and a skirt with pleats.

There was an air of optimism about my mother, as though this was, at long last, our Big Break. Tupperware spoke to her dreams for a better life and she could hear its message clearly. I heard it, too, and it sounded like coins pouring from a slot machine. Maybe Mom wouldn't be the next Tupperware Queen Brownie Wise, but she believed she could do enough parties to move quickly up the ranks from dealer to manager and then, who knows? Women like Brownie Wise had been making a fortune in Tupperware for years, so why not her, why not now?

We set out lunch boxes and sunburst canisters with fan lids you could seal by pressing down in the middle. There was a cake carrier, a contraption that made freezer pops, and nesting measuring cups. As the ladies gathered, once I'd dispatched their coats, I served them tea in Tupperware mugs and cookies on square Tupperware plates with rounded corners. We didn't have enough places to sit, so some of the women perched on the arms of the sofa and our vinyl recliner. We put our four dinette chairs in a small half circle. There had never been so many people in our Malsbary rental at one time.

I was my mother's trusty assistant. I hammed it up as a butler, asking the women if they wanted more of anything or if I could clear their dishes. I directed them to the powder room, which is what Mom told me to call it, "down the hall, first door on your left." We had an Avon fragrance candle burning there and monogrammed hand towels Mom only put out for guests, so they hadn't gotten much use. When it came time to show off the *product*—Mom kept saying we had to *move product*—she relied on my stronger fingers to demonstrate the signature burp and seal. "So simple a teenage boy can do it," she said, stepping aside and waving her arm in a flourish, like a ringmaster, making me the star of the show. I burped and sealed over and over, a showman's grin on my face.

"Just think of all the money you'll save by keeping your leftovers fresh!" Mom said. "We haven't had a head of lettuce turn brown in six months, have we?"

"No ma'am," I said, in a kind of over-the-top, comedic way, like Jerry Lewis. "Our month-old lettuce is as green as the day we brought it home from the store, ha ha," and the ladies loved me. I had them bent over laughing. I saw the potential for our success as a duo right away. Mom just needed to provide the business savvy and I could do all the demos and offer comic relief.

The party guests filled out their forms and placed their orders, and as I collected them, I glanced at the dollar amounts and thought all that money was coming straight to us. I felt buoyed by the sense we'd finally hit it big.

As the women left our "lovely home," I was gentlemanly as I fetched their coats. They all said I was a real charmer and handsome to boot. Did I have a young lady in my life? "Oh, my, I bet you must have to beat them off with a stick," one of them said. "He's gonna be a real heart-breaker, Barb."

My mother glowed. She was pleased with me. And for a short while, when I felt like we were making it, I was less of a pain to her.

We put on a good show, Mom and me. I thought we would take our act on the road, three parties a day, five days a week, and that riches weren't far off for us. By my estimation, we could bring in close to six grand a month with that schedule. I could quit school and get private tutoring when my busy schedule allowed it. For a while after that party, I badgered my mother about doing more. And there were a few, on Saturdays, but she left me home, saying she wasn't the hostess so she didn't get to decide how exactly the show would go. She was just pulling in recruits, she said, not "moving product." She told me we'd be fine, that Tupperware was no great shakes, really, and that money didn't pour in the way I thought it did. It wasn't, in fact, that easy.

In the end, Mom couldn't devote the time to it she would have liked. She was still working eight hours a day for the school district, and that was income she could count on. There was also the matter of her health.

Her bursts of energy and optimism were followed by long bouts of withdrawal and fatigue. As a result, our cupboards were full of her profits: cups and bowls and food storage containers with airtight, spill-proof seals my mother needed me to open and close.

I developed a fever for money. It came upon me after the Tupperware party, but got worse one Saturday after Mom came home having earned $292 for recruiting new Tupperware dealers. She had a pink ticket in her hand that she waved over her head like a flag. It read "Lucky! Lucky! Lucky!" There was a black ink stamp of a treasure chest within a halo of dollar signs. This was as bright as I'd ever seen her. Having money made her feel lighter, and I wanted that same feeling.

As good fortune would have it, about this time Stuccoville was in need of a new paperboy. Our neighborhood route opened up because the kid who had it kept oversleeping and papers weren't getting delivered. Residents were indignant. In the mornings as I'd walk to my bus, I'd see them collect on their driveways in bathrobes and house-slippers, coffee in one hand, no newspaper in the other. In a neighborhood where pennies counted, these folks didn't cotton to getting ripped-off. They called in complaints to the paper, besmirching the name of the good-for-nothing slacker currently assigned to the route and calling for his dismissal. Reparations were made in the form of subscription discounts and vouchers to all-you-can-eat buffets.

Then one afternoon, there came a knock at my door. Mom was at work. I was watching sitcoms, most likely reruns of *Gilligan's Island* and *I Dream of Jeannie,* the sum total of my after-school existence back then. I didn't entirely mind this because of my acute and mostly inappropriate longings for Tina Louise and Barbara Eden, who—thanks to a mouth full of subsidized braces and my own colossal insecurities—were the closest things to love interests I could hope for. They were as important to me as Kathy had been, only without the heartbeat and whispered declarations of love. It was a difficult time for me hormonally, and my mother was ill-equipped to give me The Talk. The previous summer, on our way to a golf course in Oregon, Grandpa Leo tried.

"Charlie, my boy," he said, "The summer—no sweeter was ever; The sunshiny hills all athrill; The grayling aleap in the river . . ."

For the second time in my life, I was sitting shotgun in a Buick next to a man whose prelude to a difficult subject was "The Spell of the Yukon."

Grandpa Leo finished the stanza, then I saw his hand move into my peripheral vision. It hung in the space between us and his fingers curled as though holding a beer can. He said the words "urges" and "blood pumping," which I absorbed with some discomfort, but once he got to "Your penis gets hard" with his curled hand still floating before me, I stopped listening and turned my eyes to the passing trees. As a result, I played a lousy round of golf that day.

The knock at my door turned out to be a man named Jim. He was large and jolly, with a bright pink face and a fleshy wattle beneath his chin. Later, he would begin referring to himself as "Big Jim." On the street behind him, with the engine still running, was a metal-sided cargo truck with sliding doors. In blue letters on its side were the words *Fresno Bee,* and next to that, a happy little cartoon bee holding a newspaper.

"Hello, young man," Jim said. I shook his hand when he offered it. My mother would have appreciated this. I thought Jim was there to sell me a subscription, and I was prepared to tell him that he'd have to ask my mom, but she was at work, and anyway, he didn't need to bother coming back; she'd probably say no because we were so broke, we couldn't pay attention. That was what Mom always told the solicitors who came up the sidewalk of our rental bearing cases of cleaning supplies. She thought it best to be honest with them, to let them know right from the start they stood no chance with her. "You can't suck blood out of a turnip," she'd say, which I came to know meant that you couldn't get money from someone who had none.

But Big Jim wasn't peddling newspaper subscriptions. He was there to offer me my first real job. "Some of your neighbors said you were the right young man for this," he said. He paused to consider me. "I need someone to start right away." He was looking for a real hustler, he said, someone who didn't mind being in business for himself. There'd be some training, some time spent learning the ropes, but it was a big route, and there was some good money to be made. The kind of money a handsome young man like me could certainly use, what with all the pretty girls I must have coming around. "Whaddya' say," he said. "You interested?"

Was I ever. I took it on the spot, without even asking my mother.

"That's what I thought about you," he said. "I could see you're a real go-getter." Before he left, he gave me a canvas bag, the kind you throw over your shoulders or on the back of a bike. He gave me a box of red rubber bands and a receipt pad where I'd have to write the names of my subscribers and their addresses and what they owed. Then he gave me a list of my customers. Ride around the neighborhood, he said, and get to know your route. Do a few dry runs to figure out the fastest way.

Our neighbor Frank helped me fix up an old red beach cruiser he had lying around. Truth be told, he stood and gave me instructions with a cigarette dangling from his lips. He tinkered on all kinds of engines and bicycles with a cigarette in his mouth and a glass of whiskey nearby. He said I needed to start with my own skin in the game. This turned out to be literal after I tore up my knuckles on concrete when a wrench slipped free of a stuck nut. The blood came up straight away as I flexed my fingers and shook away the pain. "Work through it," Frank said. He left and came back with a clean white roll of gauze and a can of Bactine. He sprayed my wound and wrapped my hand. I freed the troublesome nut as the bandage soaked up my blood, turning the gauzy white, crimson. I felt like a prize fighter, as manly as I had ever felt in my life.

I replaced the tubes in the tires and filled them with air. I oiled the chain and the sprockets. I polished the chrome and wiped away cobwebs and shined up the spokes and rims with a tuft of fine steel wool. And the best part, I attached plywood side panels to a rack behind the seat so my canvas bag wouldn't get caught in the spokes. For this, I used a drill and four bolts with nuts and lock washers. This took a good part of the day, but in the end, I had a work bike I was proud of.

Frank said we had to christen her. He handed me his rocks glass and told me to pour whiskey over the frame. I did this. I then ran my finger over the frame and brought that same finger to my lips, which went numb and tingly. Frank said I had to name her, that normally when you did things like this you chose the name of a girl who was real important to you, like a wife or a daughter or an old love you wanted to remember forever, and it took about three seconds for me to tell Frank my new cruiser would be called *Kathy*. He raised his whiskey to his lips. "To Kathy," he said.

"To Kathy."

That evening, I rode around Stuccoville and learned my route. *Kathy* and I did this after dinner, and I waved to my neighbors sitting in lawn chairs with their faces turned toward the setting sun. Men hoisted their beer cans in my direction. One guy named Floyd hollered "Here's to the new paperboy!" and his wife Sandy called out, "Hear, hear!"

Before I even started, I was appreciated.

I memorized addresses and matched them to house colors. One of them was easy: 3444 went with the yellow house on Oswego, our first home in Stuccoville, the place my parents bought and my mother sold. I stopped and looked at it through new eyes. It seemed smaller, and still durable, but I felt unsettled by it; the memory of it was too close, the house too familiar, as though I could still walk through its front door and see my mother in her housecoat at the kitchen table, her legs crossed at the ankles, cigarette smoke slipping from her nose. I thought if I watched the front door long enough, it might open and my young self would tumble out.

I pedaled the neighborhood and created a route in my head: from the Malsbary rental, stay on the right side, into and out of two cul-de-sacs; then turn right and serpentine along three streets, up one side, down the other, until I had wrapped myself all the way around to the back side of Malsbary. Next up, a street called Valentine, which sprouted cul-de-sacs of its own to the east, and on its western edge featured a block-long, single-story apartment complex, a place designed with order and integrity and ease, where I could ride close enough to front doors to land papers on welcome mats by simply dropping them from my hand.

I learned as well about the business, what Big Jim called "overhead." The first box of rubber bands was on him, he said, to help get me started, but once I ran out, I would have to order more and that would come out of my earnings. I had to make sure I had a ready supply of them, in addition to plastic sacks for rainy days, which I also had to buy. And if I wanted another canvas newspaper bag, maybe one for my shoulders so I could tote all the papers in one trip, then that was on me. Big Jim called it "the cost of doing business" and these were things to consider as my enterprise grew.

After a couple of days, he turned me loose. I heard his big truck in front of my house every morning when it was still dark outside. He dropped bundles of newspapers on my driveway, and after he motored off, about four-thirty every morning, I got out of bed to fold them in the predawn chill of my garage. I delivered to a hundred and twenty subscribers in Stuccoville, then after school on most days, I knocked on doors with my receipt pad and said, "Collecting for the *Bee*." I got really good at my job, really fast. I always had the paper on the doorsteps before six-thirty and my neighbors gave me tips on top of their six-dollar and fifty-cent monthly subscription payments. Usually, they just rounded up to seven and told me to keep the change, but there were some real generous folks who occasionally slipped me a five-spot like it was meant to be a secret. *We appreciate you,* they seemed to say. *Keep doing what you're doing.* I collected close to eight-hundred-dollars in cash and personal checks every month and gave Big Jim ninety percent. The other ten percent and my tips went straight to me. I got Sunday's ads and comic section on Saturday, and my mother enjoyed reading the *Parade* magazine before everyone else.

This experience changed me. Now that I was collecting money in stacks, I wanted more. It didn't matter that I was turning most of it over to Big Jim. What I managed to keep still felt like a lot. With every tip, no matter how small, I walked away feeling as though I had just found the golden ticket, that I could wave it over my head like a flag stamped with the words "Lucky! Lucky! Lucky!" But it was more than that. Money was like praise, something I also longed for. When I collected and my neighbors told me I was good, *the best in the business,* I felt buoyed and light. I was much stronger and more capable than the loathsome and awkward boy who dwelled inside me. I suppose you could lay me on a sofa and open my soul with the right questions and some soothing nature sounds and figure out pretty quickly that this had everything to do with my father leaving. That theory is self-evident. For me, praise from others became vital, like water and air. Without it, I was detestable to myself. The problem with self-loathing, of course, is the proximity of your attacker, and that's the way it was with me. I couldn't escape myself. In the absence of outside affirmation, I assumed the worst about my insides; my heart was rotten and full of nothing but lust and greed. I spent long hours trying to purify my soul, which was exhausting, especially since I was trying to do other things at the same time. I continued to seek perfection in everything, answering to the bothersome voice in my head, which most of the time carried just one message: "You can do better than that." I felt the enormous weight of responsibility, and I couldn't bear the thought of letting people down.

I wanted everyone, even people I didn't know, to be happy with me. That's why every newspaper, every day, was on the porch and on time.

When I was a freshman in high school, after finishing my paper route, I caught the bus for Edison High School on the poor west side of town. It was a kind of social experiment put in place by the school district to integrate the student body and make strides toward civic unity. The flaw was that the big yellow buses only went one way. All roads pointed west to Edison, and no buses carried poor black freshmen north to the more gentrified Bullard High School, from where I'd eventually graduate. As a result, Bullard hadn't had a freshman class since the mid-1970s. I suppose the district felt it was more important for the wealthy kids to be exposed to lives of struggle than it was for poor kids to be integrated with lives of prosperity.

On the first day of my freshman year, I watched a cage fight, a brawl inside an island of lockers enclosed by a chain link fence. These happened weekly, at least. Students scaled the sides of the cage like bugs, all screaming and cheering, all scrambling for the best view until someone, usually the football coach, charged inside to break things up. Kids always emerged with bloody lips and ripped T-shirts.

An older kid in Stuccoville who'd gone to Edison gave me some advice: Guard my lunch tickets, avoid going into bathrooms alone, and learn what a switchblade sounded like. In Mr. Good's freshman English, where I read *Lord of the Flies,* one such knife was on display over the door, driven through a sneaker into the wall. It was a symbol of what would happen if I tried to run. That's what this older kid told me, and it was good advice. Once, when I was in the bathroom alone, I was startled at the urinal by the click of a switchblade and was forced to surrender my lunch tickets. I remained still and didn't run and later that day, I bought four lunch tickets for a dollar from a scalper so I could eat. They could have been my own lunch tickets.

I was also told that at random points during the day, depending on the shifting wind, I could be sickened by the nearby rendering plant, Darling Ingredients, the place where they turned slaughterhouse leftovers into animal feed. Our freshman baseball team practiced and played its games close enough to the plant to hear its machinery grind horse parts into dog food. I never got used to the odor, which seemed to attach itself to me. There were nights in Stuccoville where I might catch a whiff of decayed meat caught up in my hair or in the sweat trapped in my ballcap.

Our only way out was for our parents to enroll us for one year in the Catholic high school and pay tuition. Many did. The rest of us went to Edison, home of the Tigers and a student body that was more than ninety-five percent African-American and, it seemed to me, one-hundred percent poor.

I knew this because on the privileged north side, I was living poor; poor had a countenance I recognized.

Most of those early mornings before school, Mom got up when I did. She sat in a lawn chair in her bathrobe and handed me rubber bands one at a time from a Tupperware bowl as I worked my way through the stack. In the winter months, she made me hot chocolate and I dipped powdered donuts in it. I ate and drank and folded, alternating from one to another to the next and back through the cycle, over and over. Mom smoked a cigarette with her instant coffee. We didn't say much to each other. I operated with fervor and focus. I double-folded my papers and wedged them into my canvas bag. Double-folds were more aerodynamic than a simple fold-over, and when I flung them just right with some loft, they left my hand like pigeons and landed softly on doorsteps. Each successful toss was a small victory, each failure a study in what I'd done wrong. *Bad arch. Poor timing. Too firm a grip.* For those times I was off-target, I took care to stop and fix my mistakes, which sometimes made for more time on my route, but that didn't matter. I'd climb off *Kathy* and retrieve papers hung up in bushes or within flowers. I replaced muddied papers with clean ones and left them in places easy to reach.

After my route one day, I parked *Kathy* in the garage and went into our house for a shower. It was springtime, late in May. My mother was standing at the sink rinsing a dish. She heard me come into the kitchen and asked if I had a minute. "I have something to tell you," she said. I really didn't have that minute. My bus to school would be on the corner within the half-hour. I hadn't showered. But something was off. She was dressed for work as usual, but there were lines in her face that told me I had better do as she said. I made myself a glass of Instant Breakfast and sat down at the kitchenette.

"I'm here," I said. I remember making a production of being inconvenienced. I would become an expert in doing this.

She sat down next to me and wrung her bony fingers. "Today's my last day with the district," she said. "As of tomorrow, I won't have a job there anymore."

At first, I took this as fine news. She must have gotten something better. "Where are you gonna work?"

"Nowhere," Mom said. "I'm not going to work anywhere."

"What?"

"This probably isn't the best time," Mom said. "But I thought you needed to know that I'm going on disability."

I asked her what that meant, and she said it had to do with the government supporting people who could no longer work because their bodies were too "broken down."

"That's me," she said. "I'm just too broken down. These fingers," she said. "How am I supposed to type with these fingers?"

She slid her hands across the table so I could get a better look, but I had been seeing them for years now. They were gnarled and tar stained. Still, she made me look upon them, two hands, eight knuckles in little peaks over bowed fingers. Her thumbs curled outwards in the shape of fishhooks. "I'm a typist!" she said. Her cheeks reddened and tears formed in the wells of her eyes. Then, to herself, she said, "How can I be a typist with these fingers?" She slid her hands off the table into her lap. She kept her head down, as though continuing to examine them.

We wouldn't have to move, she told me. We could stay where we were. It would work out. "Just do what you've been doing, and we'll be fine," she said. "Just don't worry." But I did worry. I worried a lot. I didn't believe her. I didn't see how we were going to be fine with her not working. I didn't see how we could stay where we were.

But there was another thought that terrified me even more. I didn't see how she was going to stay alive much longer, and if she died, what would become of me? Where would I go?

I had seen all of the pills. Jesus, I had fed her most of them. No one should be able to take that many pills in one day and not die. At that point, she was taking ten aspirin every twelve hours, plus all of the prescription stuff, long words I couldn't pronounce for the treatment of ailments I couldn't fathom. She probably swallowed twenty-five pills a day. She was forty-four, and had been smoking since she was twenty-one, close to a carton of Virginia Slim menthols every week. She subsisted on cheese and saltines and nicotine and Maxwell House.

I knew that my father was living in a studio apartment in Bellflower, selling advertising in the *Long Beach Press Telegram,* living a miserable bachelor's life. I knew this because on the fourth of July, 1982, he wrote me a letter: "I'm doing all right down here, I guess. I think about you and your mother every day." If Mom died, I worried that he would come for me. I worried that he would pull up to our Malsbary rental in his El Camino and offer to help me pack my things. He would say there were good schools in Orange County and he could rent us a two-bedroom place, not far from the ocean. "Imagine," he would say. "A couple of bachelors on the beach. You could learn to surf. You could hear the waves from your bedroom window. And the girls! With your blond hair, you would fit right in. I'm sorry about your mother, pal. I know you two were close."

I wouldn't tell him. I would live in the Malsbary rental by myself. I would get a night job to pay for things, and if my father did find out, I would jump on the Santa Fe and go wherever it took me. It would be easy. Empty boxcars passed through Stuccoville all the time, moving real slow. I knew this. I knew this because I had been hearing them and watching them pass by my neighborhood for years. I knew I could walk out the door with Mom's ashes in a Tupperware bowl and keep walking west on Bullard until I got to the tracks. Climbing aboard would be as easy as getting on an escalator. I would escape my father in darkness. And then, once on the train, I would rumble through the fig orchard, where the kids from my high school drank beer and smoked pot and felt each other up beneath a canopy of gnarled tree branches. I would light a cigarette in honor of my mother, and as the train picked up speed, as it put some distance between me and my dad, I would open that Tupperware urn with my able fingers and release my mother's ashes to the night wind.

"Honey," she told me again. "Just don't worry." She reached across the table then and touched my hand. "Look at me," she said. I did. I looked right at her, not at her hands but at her face, right into her hazel eyes.

"We will be fine," she said. "We will be just fine."

13

There Hung in the Air a Sense of Unease

Counsel: Okay. How do you spend your time now?

Witness: I do things for my son. I pick him up from school. I usually don't get up until late in the day.

Counsel: So, he gets himself off to school and fixes his breakfast and lunch or whatever?

Witness: He does everything, yes.

Counsel: And you pick him up after school. Who does the housework? Does he do it, or do you do it, or what?

Witness: We both do it.

Counsel: I gather he's been helping with that for a number of years now. Is that a correct assumption on my part?

Witness: Yes.

—Workers' Compensation Appeals Board,
December 12, 1983

IT WASN'T OUR FIRST TIME ON WELFARE. WE HAD BEEN ON it about six years earlier, just after Dad left. For four months in 1976, before Mom finally got a job at the end of the year, we had bricks of government butter and cheese in our fridge. Mom shopped with food coupons she discreetly handed to clerks at Alpha Beta. "Just until we get back on our feet," she'd whisper.

And now, the summer before I turned fifteen, we were on it again.

It wouldn't last long, Mom told me. Things were going to be tight for a while, at least until the Medi-Cal got approved. Then we'd be set. "We'll actually be better off," she said.

Someone from a government agency came to our Malsbary rental. She wore a dark blue pantsuit and walked around with a clipboard. She opened our cupboards and refrigerator. She looked with a penlight in the narrow spaces between cabinets and under walls, inside and behind our kitchen trash can. Her name was on a badge pinned to her lapel, along with an official-sounding title, *Examiner* or *Agent* or *Investigator,* or something. I remember her height and stiff blonde hairdo worn like a helmet. Her cheekbones were sharp and touched with rouge. She was thick and unfeminine and built for power. Still, she struck me as kind in the easy way she moved about and smiled. She chatted as she worked, as though the act of speaking were more important than anything she might uncover, anything that might betray my mother as incompetent or care-less: mold, weevils, mouse droppings, exhausted beer cans. She checked boxes on her clipboard with great efficiency. "Just routine," she said. Then we all sat at the dinette and she asked us questions, starting with me. Was I active? *Yes.* Did I get good grades? *Sure, I guess.* What kinds of things did I like? *Baseball.* For a few minutes, I was the subject of her scrutiny. She gave me a once-over, checking for obvious flaws—scratches, bruises, rotten teeth—then she said I looked like a healthy and helpful young man.

"Very helpful," Mom said. She placed her hand over mine and worked her fingers into my grasp. I held her fragile bones there for a moment, then let go. The woman asked if there was other family, anyone else close enough to help.

"My mother and brother are moving to Fresno in a few weeks," Mom said. "More for moral support, than anything. They aren't in a position to help *financially.*" Mom needed to make that last point clear. I saw then that proven and legitimate penury was the only way to government relief.

Assets of any kind were a path to denial. You had to be picked clean, like a carcass in the desert, before restoration could begin. At the same time, you couldn't look like a carcass in the desert. You had to prove there were still things you could offer, that you were doing the best you could with what you had, even when what you had wasn't much.

The woman wrote things down, things that didn't seem relevant. She inquired after Jack's and Marzelle's ages and health. Mom told her that Jack was forty-seven and Marzelle was seventy. Health-wise, a five or six out of ten. What of Marzelle's husband, my mom's father? "He died of cirrhosis in 1970," Mom said. The woman checked a box and shook her head. "I don't drink," my mother said. "Not one drop, ever."

"Oh, I didn't mean anything by that," the woman said. "Just too bad, is all."

Mom said she had seen what drinking could do to a person. The woman nodded, as if she knew, too. There was something shared, but not stated. Mom said she wished she could say the same for the cigarettes, though. Unfortunately, those had a hold on her. "They help keep my weight down," she said, which she had been saying for years. The woman nodded again. She said that cigarettes didn't disqualify anybody. "So, don't you worry, honey." I remember that. This woman we had just met, this woman who looked so harsh, called my mother *honey*.

My mother continued to answer questions: Marzelle had emphysema and osteoporosis, the kinds of things you'd expect of a woman in her seventies. She and Jack were both smokers and *occasional* drinkers. Because I was good enough with words, I recognized this as an outright lie. My mother may have called it a "white lie." She may have said she "fudged the truth." Whatever she might have named it, her transgression came as a surprise to me. Still, I understood the purpose behind it, even then. She needed to present as unblemished a family portrait as possible, because she feared our real life would be found too defective for relief. And we needed relief.

My uncle, Mom said, was a very capable driver. He would help with things like doctor visits and filling out forms, when those needs arose.

"He used to be a driving instructor," I said.

The woman said that was good news. She said that would serve us well.

She checked a few more boxes on her form, then I watched her signature flow from her pen in a few indecipherable loops. She tugged the yellow copy free from the carbon and handed it to Mom. There was a checkmark in a box at the bottom next to the words *Recommended for Approval.* "Stick that to your fridge," the woman said. Mom did. It remained stuck there for a good long while. I remember the thin yellow paper, held in place by an apple magnet, eye-level, so that each time I went to the fridge, I looked right into the word "Approval," a word that meant more than anything else in the world to me.

They thanked each other, my mother and this woman, and we all stood and walked to the front door. She said Mom had a lovely home. I could see that my mother took pride in this. She squared her shoulders at the compliment and thanked this stranger who had just given us new life. My mother corrected her, just slightly: "*We* have a lovely home," she said. "This boy and me." She stroked the back of my head, and the whole bit brought a satisfied grin to the woman's face. An official letter would be coming in the mail within the week, she said, along with Mom's first allocation that would keep us afloat until something more stable kicked in. She took my mother's hand, gently.

"And you, young man," she said. "You keep being helpful."

I said I would.

I didn't tell her about my paper route. I didn't tell her because she didn't ask.

Weeks later, just as Mom had reported, Marzelle and Jack relocated to Fresno. They moved into an apartment six miles east of our house, and for the first few months, they were over a lot to visit, often bringing groceries. Marzelle put whatever she could on the table for us: hot dogs, chips, Jell-o cups, 7-Up, fruit cocktail in heavy syrup. Most meals were like picnics. Marzelle sometimes got creative. She spooned out a pile of cottage cheese and topped it with a canned peach half so it looked like an egg, sunny-side up. She made ambrosia with marshmallows and coconut and mandarins, which sat on our table in a translucent green Tupperware bowl.

We also went out to eat once a week. Nothing fancy, just places Marzelle called "greasy spoons." We always sat in the smoking section, Jack and Marzelle on one side of the vinyl booth, Mom and I on the other. This was strange for me, having them in the same town. Mom said it was fun to have family around to do things with. I didn't think so.

Those nights at dinner, Mom tried to get me to talk about my life. "I'll bet you have some interesting stories about your paper route," or "Tell us about the football player you're helping in algebra." And then she'd offer an addendum to make my answer sound more compelling.

"They've struck up quite a friendship, those two," and Marzelle would take a healthy drag from her Lucky Strike and try to look intrigued while Jack blew cigarette smoke out his nostrils. His attention was always elsewhere, usually on the broad-bottomed waitresses in brown skirts and tan hose. Marzelle might start off listening, but I would lose her quickly to an unruly sugar packet or a dirty teaspoon.

If I had shared more than just shrugs and short answers, I might have told them I was on the baseball team at school but played very little. That my job with the *Bee* had allowed me to start a fine collection of department store lingerie ads. That I had saved over $400 from my paper route, money I'd hoped to put toward a car, and that the only smudge on my otherwise perfect report card was the *C* I'd earned in Basic Typing.

One night, though, I tried to talk with Jack. I told him I thought it might be time for me to start shaving. There were the beginnings of blond whiskers on my upper lip and chin, soft fuzz on my cheeks.

"What did you think?" I said.

"No way," he said. He shook his head and mashed out his third Camel in the ashtray between us. "Nope."

"Why not? I have whiskers, see?"

I pushed my face across the table so that he might get a better look. Once he saw how bristly I'd become, he'd have to agree that shaving wasn't such a bad idea after all.

He examined my lip and held my chin between his thumb and forefinger; he moved my face from one side to the other, considering each cheek. Even though he'd already finished his cigarette, wisps of smoke still trickled from his nostrils.

"No," he said. "You're too young." He told me to hold off on shaving for as long as I could because once I started, I could never stop. "You take the boy away and become a man," he said. I thought, *That's exactly what I want to do!* I wanted to nick myself with a blade and soak up blood with toilet paper. I wanted to feel razor burn. I wanted to slap aftershave on my cheeks after actually shaving.

"So, when will I know I'm ready?"

"You'll just know," he said. He shook another Camel from the pack and dropped it on his lower lip, then left the table clutching the dinner ticket and his sour disposition, making it clear that he had given all he had to offer on the matter.

In June of 1984, we were in the backyard of the Malsbary rental, celebrating Mom's birthday. Jack and Marzelle came over, along with Frank and his wife Nancy. They sat in lawn chairs around a table, at the center of which was a single-layer birthday cake with white frosting. I have a photograph of this. Frank, Nancy, Mom, and Marzelle were there, but the chair next to Marzelle was empty; it was the chair where Jack had been sitting. It was dusk and the sunlight glowed amber on our fence pickets. I must have taken the picture because I am not in the scene, and I am sure it was at that exact moment, after I snapped the photo, that Mom said, "Why don't you go check on Jack?" I was already standing, and along with cigarette smoke, there hung in the air a sense of unease; Jack had been gone a long time.

It didn't take long to find him. I went inside and followed the sounds of his retching to our bathroom, where I discovered him on his knees over the toilet, resting the side of his face against the seat. His neck and ears had gone blue and he had a finger in his mouth. When he saw me, his eyes filled with terror, like maybe I was Death coming for him. He backed away from me, his long legs scuttling over the tile, one foot pulling free of his shoe. I could see from his wide eyes and taut neck that there was something hung up inside him, something he was working to get out. The water in the toilet bowl was beer-colored, foamy and tinged pink.

I hollered for Frank. I called out his name again and again: "Frank, Frank, Frank, Frank, Frank." I did not call out for my mother. Perhaps I thought Frank the most capable, this man I'd watched repair broken things.

Frank came, and so did the others: Mom, Marzelle, Nancy, and all four of them crowded the bathroom as Jack struggled to find air. His eyeballs darted from one face to the next; he lurched in the direction of the toilet bowl, his hand in his mouth up to his wrist, it seemed. His back became a hump that rose and fell, rose and fell, and then out of him came a deep, guttural, repeated gagging. Mom steadied Marzelle. Frank stepped in front of me and dropped to a knee behind my uncle, a cigarette in his lips. Nancy was in the kitchen calling out our address into the telephone.

The paramedics responded quickly. They intubated my uncle, then took him to St. Agnes Hospital, where he was cared for by a nurse named Gayle, who had curly red hair and green eyes. She dressed like my mother, in light, patterned blouses and culottes that flaunted chubby ankles.

Months later, without warning anyone, Jack and Gayle got married.

At first, Jack was buoyant and affectionate, as if he realized how lucky he was to have this ship come in. He acted lovesick for Gayle. He jumped from the table at meals to fetch things from the kitchen, he warmed her coffee, he massaged her shoulders and feet after she worked long shifts at the hospital, and he generally displayed the kinds of behaviors that might win him favor in a house where everyone, including his new wife, saw that his tenderness was a sideshow. He colored himself as big-hearted and sacrificial. He asked me about shaving, said I was look-ing like a real man, and gave the impression that for years he had been doing all he could to ensure I would want for nothing in the absence of a father. I had seen this before, from my mother, this false rendering of family, this spackling-over of truth.

One Saturday when we were all together at the house he now shared with Gayle and her two sons, Jack asked if I remembered the time he took me to Dodger Stadium for my first game. This was true; Jack had done this. He bought two tickets in the upper deck for a game against the Cincinnati Reds in August of 1976, just a week after my dad left. Mom drove us to LA so she could piece things together with some help from Marzelle. "Yes," I said. "I remember the game." I remembered the palm trees beyond the outfield wall. I remembered green grass and blue hats and red hats. I remembered the crack of the bat and that runners were a full two steps out of the box before that sound reached my ears. I remembered thinking it was a long, long way down from the upper deck, and my knees were weak as we ascended the concrete steps to our seats. I remembered how far away it seemed.

I remembered all of that, but I didn't say so. All I said was that I remembered. Jack wouldn't let my response end at that, though. He had to drag more out of me: "It was a fun time, wasn't it? And who was your favorite Dodger? Do you remember who you just couldn't stop talking about?" And I had to say Steve Garvey, because this was true, too. I had made a production of my adulation for the Dodger first baseman when I was a boy; for years, I mimicked Garvey's rigid batting stance on every one of my Little League teams.

"Steve Garvey. That's right," Jack said, as if it had just come back to him all over again, reconstructing itself piecemeal in his memory. But this was part of the pretense; he knew Steve Garvey would be my answer. Jack was mugging for his new family. "You know," he said, "when I lived in LA, people used to mistake me for Steve Garvey."

Gayle said, "Oh Jack, stop. Where'd you come up with that idea?" She waved her hand at him as if to dismiss such a wild notion, as if they were an old couple married for years and not months.

"It's true," Jack said. "You don't see it?" He said that not so long ago, the resemblance was striking. He looked to my mother and then his mother, but neither of them said anything.

"You don't remember that, Barb?"

She said no, she did not remember it the way he did. She had not remembered anyone mistaking my uncle for Steve Garvey.

Then he turned to me. "You probably don't remember, either," he said. "You were too young," which was true, but I did know all about Steve Garvey and his dark hair combed in neat rows, his neck muscles, his Popeye forearms, his prominent chin. I knew about this man I idolized, and my uncle was not him.

At that point, one of Jack's new stepsons asked, "Who's Steve Garvey?" and I of course thought he was a blockhead because everyone knew Steve Garvey, even people who didn't know baseball. I started to say something caustic, something like "How could you not know Steve Garvey?" But before I could get the words from my mouth, Gayle interrupted me. Her hand waved like she was shooing a fly. Without looking at her son, without even considering that someone else might have an answer, she said, "No one, dear. Steve Garvey is no one."

14

If I Were, If I Were, If I Were

"Margaret got me a lot of nice clothes for school. I got a
new fall jacket, a new pair of shoes, lots of new socks, three
shirts, and I'll get a pair of pants later."

—Letter to my mother, August, 1984

IN THE 1980S, BULLARD HIGH SCHOOL—HOME OF THE
Knights—was Fresno Unified's repository for the wealthy. Because
Bullard was one of only six high schools open at the time in a city of a
quarter million, it enrolled students from all over the mostly wealthy
north side, a geographic area that seemed roughly the size of Rhode
Island. That there were so many rich kids concentrated in one region
of the city was a wonder to me, but no more wondrous than the fact I
was among them in the first place, the beneficiary of a quirky yet generous southwest boundary line that stretched like Italy's boot to include
our Malsbary rental, though just barely. Move northeast in a spray pattern and the neighborhoods grew progressively more affluent. Push our
house a half-mile west, to the other side of the Santa Fe, and I would
have been in the rural district where migrant farmworkers' kids picked
vegetables before sunrise instead of throwing newspapers.

Thanks to my paper route, I fit in well enough at Bullard. My earnings
allowed me to buy decent clothes. With my own money, I bought two
Ralph Lauren polos and some Levi's 501s, then I sprung for some Stan

Smith Adidas, shoes that falsely identified me as a dues-paying member of the Sierra Sport and Racquet Club, where I was able to hang out as an after-school guest with some guys who were doctors' kids. The Stan Smiths, in fact, were a requirement; only white soles were allowed on the court, but all I had at the time were shoes with black rubber bottoms, which left skid marks the rich folks wouldn't tolerate. I held my own on the court, however, thanks to hours of banging a tennis ball off the dog-eared fence across the street from our rental with a wooden racket borrowed from Frank's garage.

The parking lots at Bullard were filled with fine German cars and elevated trucks with knobby, oversized tires. Upon hearing of my new school and its dignified mascot, my father contrived a majestic vision for me as I neared driving age. His 1975 Chevy El Camino would be all mine, a birthday present for my "Big One-Six," he said. There would be some body work, but not much, then he would take it to his local Earl Scheib and have it painted a deep cobalt with light blue rally racing stripes to match my school colors. But that wasn't the best part. It was the tailgate he was most excited about. "Like a mural," he told me. A partial moon and twinkling stars would make the backdrop for the words—in white Gothic script—*Mid-Knight Blue.* He wanted to be sure when he explained this to me over the phone that I understood his clever pun. "Mid-Knight, with a *K,* because you're a Bullard Knight," he said.

The tailgate's centerpiece would be a knight's armored bust in profile. My father sketched the design for it on a piece of *Press Telegram* stationery and sent it to me, asking forgiveness for his rendering of a medieval mask, which looked more like a steam iron with a feathery plume than something that might protect a nobleman from the business end of a steel-tipped lance.

"You get the idea," he wrote.

He would have the car ready for me in a few months, then he'd drive it up himself and deliver it personally. From what I came to know of my father, he had a cinematic vision for its presentation: the sparkling car parked at a showcase angle in front of the DMV as I walked out with my license and took the keys from him. There would be a long embrace as we reunited after years of separation; there would be tears shed and hatchets buried. There would be forgiveness for his infidelity, his poetic leaving, and nothing now but forward-thinking, of letting the past stay there. I knew it would never happen, not one bit of it. My father had conditioned me to expect nothing, and that's what he delivered. The El Camino was never painted. My father didn't visit on my birthday, and he never wept tears of regret as he held me to him, at least not then. It was all for the better. His intentions may have been good, but they were conspicuously hollow, and he was behind-the-times when it came to grand gestures. Airbrushed car art was an artifact of the seventies, something that would have led to public ridicule in my high school. By the mid-1980s, kids were more sophisticated in their style, with their fog lights and rear window louvers, with their aerodynamic whale tails.

About this time, I had gotten word that Wienerschnitzel was hiring. I was fifteen. My best friend was Steve M., who everyone at Bullard called "The Monk," which was appropriate for a guy most admired for his reserve and unflappable nature in the face of normal teen dread. The Monk was always in control. He was sixteen and had a stable home life, one I perceived as free of confrontation. This is why I felt calmer around him than I did anyone else. I trusted his constancy, a quality I recognized in so few others around me, certainly in no one my age. He drove me to Wienerschnitzel one afternoon, and he sat in the car while I ran in to pick up an application.

The place was empty inside, nothing but a field of mustard yellow tabletops and red swivel chairs. The air smelled like a county fair, like fried batter and cooked meat and lard. A clean-shaven man with brown hair stood behind a cash register. He looked wholesome and tan, like the men in the black and white glossies in Mom's hope chest. He wore a white collared shirt with short sleeves and a brown tie. Pinned over his heart was a badge with the word "MANAGER" on a label in raised white letters, and below that, his name—"JIM"—same as my distribution manager for *The Fresno Bee*. But unlike Big Jim, Wienerschnitzel Jim was fit and broad-chested. I would find out later he was a cyclist and fitness junkie who brought his own lunches to work. As I scanned the place, Jim seemed to read my thoughts. "We're slow now," he said, "but we'll pick up once it gets closer to dinner."

He asked what he could do for me, if maybe I was interested in two corn dogs for a dollar, but I told him no, that I was there to pick up a job application. That was the gist of it, so Jim reached below the register and pulled a stack of applications from a drawer, then walked out from behind the counter to hand me one.

"Would you like to sit down?"

His smile was flawless and white, his voice comforting. We sat in a booth by the window, which offered a view of The Monk sitting in his orange Celica. Jim asked if I wanted a Coke while we talked, and I told him sure, because what fifteen-year-old kid doesn't want a free Coke on a hot day? As he walked to the drink machine, I looked out the window to The Monk, who had a wide smile running over his face. I slid into the booth and Jim set my Coke on the table before sitting down across from me.

Jim asked some questions and we made small talk on the subjects of high school and baseball and the *The Fresno Bee*. He talked about how admirable it was for a young man like me to wake up every day so early and get my papers out, all the while maintaining my excellent grades. It was an outstanding quality, he told me, the discipline to balance work with school with sports. You either had it or you didn't.

"I have to drag my son out of bed," he said. He told me his son was my age and went to Bullard and maybe I knew him, a boy named Ricky. "Tall skinny kid," Jim said, "long horse face, like mine." As he said this, he pushed his neat hair off his forehead with one hand and stretched his cheeks down with the other, so he looked like Stan Laurel. "Recognize him now?" he said. I chuckled. Ricky worked at Wienerschnitzel, too, Jim said.

At the table with Jim, a man I had known for ten minutes, I could already see he was the type of man I would want for a dad, so when he offered me a job, I took it because there was no other choice. Declining would mean losing him, this kind surrogate who had dropped in on me in the unlikeliest of places.

There was no man in my life who was truly, unconditionally, mine. There were, instead, pieces of men. Men who weren't my father filled in blanks here and there: Uncle Ed bailed me out of my first crime; Grandpa Leo taught me to play golf and tried to teach me about sex; Big Jim gave me my first job; and Frank put a wrench in my hand. And there were more, so many who had no idea they were spackling a hole that needed filling, men like my AP English teacher, Mr. Donahue, a bald, quirky goat who taught me about modal verbs, that *could* implied both ability and possibility, while *can* showed ability only. Something that *may* happen is more likely than something that *might* happen, but both are far less certain than something that *will* happen.

I loved English. I loved its nuance and power. And I loved words. I loved how they could be pieced together to make things that moved people. I loved reading. I loved coming-of-age novels and just saying the word *bildungsroman.* I loved J. D. Salinger and S. E. Hinton and John Knowles and Harper Lee and their stories of courage and identity-finding despite alienation and disorder. And I generally loved poetry, but only if it rhymed.

Mr. Donahue taught me about plot and theme and tone and figurative language. He taught me how to read for meaning and introduced me to Chaim Potok's *The Chosen* and Reb Saunders, a man who withheld speaking to his son, not out of cruelty, but as a way to help him turn inward and cultivate his other senses. Reb believed that silence was the path to the enlightened soul. Could this be what my father had in mind? All those years he did not speak to me, was he teaching me through silence?

He was, of course, though without intention.

And Mr. Donahue's most impactful lesson was on the subjunctive mood and its multiple iterations, but what stuck with me was the one that whispered possibility, the one that conveyed a wish: *If I were, If I were, If I were.*

Minutes later, after I'd shaken Jim's hand and walked out, I got into The Monk's car and told him that I honestly didn't know what happened. The nice man hired me on the spot. It was easy. It was so easy, in fact, that

The Monk thought he'd give it a try himself, and within twenty minutes, we were both hired as food prep guys at the World's Largest Hot Dog Chain.

The Monk climbed the ladder quickly—from buns to grill to register to drive-through, then unofficial night manager—but I never made it beyond bun guy. I could never quite avoid the hot steam as it escaped the drawer, and for months my forearms and the tops of my fingers were hairless and blister smooth. I lacked a certain aptitude for fast food, I suppose, that aptitude being *fast*. In less than a year, I left Wienerschnitzel for a job scooping gelato in a North Fresno strip mall. The Monk stayed, though, because staying was all he'd ever known.

One dark morning, over a year later, I was sitting alone in my garage with a stack of newspapers to fold. I saw a headline about a beloved Fresno restaurant manager killed in a single car crash on Friant Road in the foothills. I stopped cold when I saw the dead man was Jim.

I read the article and learned that he had been driving around a curve, maybe too fast, and his Volvo went up an embankment and flipped. His sunroof was open and there was speculation that he wasn't wearing a seatbelt, given how he was thrown from his car. I sat there before the sun rose and cried hard over this. I cried all the way through my route, mostly for Ricky, whom I had come to know at Wienerschnitzel, whom I had come to envy for his father, for the fun ways they needled each other on the job. He seemed to hold his father in such high regard, like there were no others before him. His father was complete. I wondered where such reverence came from and how it was possible.

I would see Ricky over the weeks and months we remained together at Bullard, and every time I did, I felt an unbearable sadness for him. I thought about suffering and different kinds of losses, about how some are worse than others. I imagined Ricky losing his father was worse than me losing mine, because Ricky's dad was part of his present tense, whereas mine existed only in the subjunctive: a hope, a desire, a *what if*?

But my *what if* was Ricky's *no more,* which could explain why, every time I saw him—at school, in the fig orchard, wherever—he seemed rudderless and wanting, his boy's eyes looking forward, looking back, looking everywhere for another possibility in which his father were still around.

That same morning after my route, I sat at our kitchen table with a pen and a piece of binder paper. With the sun just rising in the window behind me, I wrote my first poem, an elegy for Jim, the words of which now totally escape me, but not the idea: that Death had hastened away a great man and there was nothing that could fill the hole except the hope we might see him again. When I finished, I drove to Wienerschnitzel. It was still early in the morning, long before The Monk or any of the other workers would open the restaurant. It must have been a Saturday because I remember knowing I had a whole blank day before me.

I pulled into the same parking spot The Monk had waited for me in months before and stared through my windshield at the restaurant's glass doors. There were bouquets on the ground and wedged in the door handles. I got out of the car and walked to the doors and peered through the glass: a field of mustard yellow tabletops and red swivel chairs. Nothing had changed, but then again, everything had. I would leave for college soon, for UCLA, where, thanks to a derelict father and a disabled mother and demonstrated proof of this indigence, the federal government would finance a four-year bachelor's degree in English, a language I was already pretty good with. The proof of my giftedness was right there in my fingers, still gray with newspaper ink.

I slipped my poem between the glass doors and pushed it like a letter through a mail slot. I watched it flutter for a moment then lilt to the floor before landing face up on the brown tiles I once used to mop, right there in front, in a spot no one could miss it.

It seemed to whisper possibility as it fell.

If I were.

If I were.

If I were.

15

You Will Be With Me in Paradise

"I haven't heard from Dad lately so obviously I have yet to be invited to the wedding."

—Letter to my mother, January 19, 1987

MY FATHER MET HIS SECOND WIFE IN AN ELK'S LODGE bar. Her name was Lucille. She was a chain-smoking Filipina with a weakness for Chablis. Her tiny head darted about chicken-like, which made everyone around her jumpy. She had peculiar, gaudy taste, and she filled their Long Beach house—and later, their Palm Springs triple-wide—with Polynesian baubles, things like battery-operated hula girls, paper cocktail umbrellas, and coconut monkey statues. She hung velvet tapestries of skulking panthers in her smoking porch (not that she needed a designated space to smoke), and atop their console television, she situated a giant porcelain seagull flying from a wave-battered rock. She and my father picked it up for a hundred bucks in a Fontana consignment store, but before that, it had allegedly resided in a vacation home belonging to Connie Francis, a dubious factoid Lucille shared with every guest.

Just for fun, and because it seemed to fit, I referred to her in conversations with my mother as "Loose-Wheel," and Mom, because she was a better person than me, would say, "Now, Chuck, stop." But she was no doubt pleased that my father's new wife was not leggy and attractive, that she was, instead, a drunk and a hoarder and batshit crazy.

She also owned two Pomeranians, both of which yapped and wheezed incessantly at the aluminum screen door, behavior Lucille thought was endearing. She once told me that whenever I wanted, my father would drive up to UCLA and get me, and I could stay with them in Long Beach for the weekend. I could do my laundry and play with her dogs. We could go to the Queen Mary and drink mimosas. We could eat prime rib at a place that had karaoke and still let you smoke inside, and I could watch my father sing Neil Diamond songs. I could think of nothing I wanted to do less.

I was a freshman in college when Dad and Lucille got married. I was eighteen years old and had a neighbor in Hedrick Hall, a girl named Pam who once asked *why* I was an English major, as though my choice was impractical and destined me for a life of poverty. At the time, I told her English offered me a path to avoid failure. But there was more to it than that. I felt called to language, and literature helped me understand my own complicated alchemy. Characters on the page were more flawed than I was, and this made me feel less alone. Reading was a hedge against self-loathing.

I took two English classes in the spring quarter of my freshman year. One of them was Detective Fiction in which I read *The Maltese Falcon* and *The Big Sleep* and *The Postman Always Rings Twice* on a chaise longue at the Sunset Rec Center. Even though it was formulaic, noir fiction brought me comfort because the protagonists reminded me of Perry Mason, with their stiff-necked confidence and cool self-possession.

That same quarter, I also took Celtic Lit, but it wasn't as calming. I could make no sense of Dafydd ap Gwilym, whose poems were unutterable: *Rho Duw gal, rhaid yw gwyliaw,* which when translated means "By God penis, you must be guarded." I suppose the lesson there for a college-aged boy cannot be missed, but since I was neither able nor inclined to address my penis in erotic Welsh, it was a lesson deferred.

The rest of my reading didn't give me the same trouble. When I wasn't by the pool, I was in my dorm with my face in one of several anthologies, books I have kept for over thirty years. I can still read my annotations and see how I was interpreting things at the time. Next to a canto in Spenser's "Faerie Queen," I scribbled "Alexandrine rhyme provides firm closure," and in the margins of Eliot's "The Waste Land," I find this: "the body decomposes in a concatenation of parts. The city decomposes in the same way." I had drawn arrows to the words, *knees, heart,* and *feet.* Shelley's tempestuous wind, I wrote, "kills in autumn to rejuvenate in the spring," and God in J. S. Mill's *On Liberty* "takes joy in human experience." These notes go on and on and on, through hundreds of pages of text, through Milton and Dryden and Swift and Pope, through Wordsworth and Keats and Tennyson. The latter's "Ulysses" was my favorite among them all. "Come, my friends / 'Tis not too late to seek a newer world" [...]

> and though
> We are not now that strength which in old days
> Moved earth and heaven; that which we are, we are;
> One equal temper of heroic hearts,
> Made weak by time and fate but strong in will
> To strive, to seek, to find, and not to yield.

In that one, "strong in will" is double-underlined. I must have felt this was of particular importance. This must have been a quality I admired, and judging by my emphasis, I must have admired it twice as much as other qualities. It must have been something I was aiming for, even as I cowered, even as I felt detached and discouraged and irredeemable.

During the spring quarter of my freshman year, I joined a fraternity, and one of the guys in my house helped me get a job waiting tables at a popular West LA restaurant, a place called Islands, on the corner of Veteran and Pico. We wore Hawaiian print shirts and Bermuda shorts. Thatched grass hung over the bar and surfing videos looped endlessly on the televisions. Our specialty burgers and chicken sandwiches had names like Big

Wave and Sunset and Luau and Pelican. All of this thrilled Loose-Wheel, who once visited with my father and got giddy on mai-tais and prattled on about how being there made her feel like she was on a Hawaiian vacation, that the place could use a few tiki torches and a pig on a spit and you would never know you were a mile from Century City.

I worked five nights a week, Friday through Tuesday, and I found myself with more money than I ever had in my life. I had regular customers who had money to burn. People like Magic Johnson who always ordered the Moa Kai tuna sandwich and fruit punch. People like Jimmy Smits and Susan Dey and the cast of *L.A. Law*, who broke from the set for late lunches and said they didn't have time to wait for change, that I should keep whatever was left of Jimmy's hundred-dollar bill, which was more than the tab itself. Jimmy always gave me a wink on his way out, and I wanted to be just like him: wealthy and famous and charitable. I accomplished this last thing by sending money home to Mom, which I only know because she kept every letter I sent: "If you are struggling bad or feel you can't buy groceries or need money to pay a bill, don't hesitate to ask me for help." At the end of most of them I wrote, "Here's 20 bucks to help you out." Sending my mother money was perhaps my one virtuous act during a time I remember mostly for its moral limbo.

I needed a way to get to and from my job, so I bought a used motorcycle I saw advertised in the *Daily Bruin*. It was a Kawasaki Nighthawk 450, burgundy and chrome, a shiny little workhorse I rode north on the PCH to Malibu on Saturday mornings, to a surfside restaurant called Gladstones. I sat on the deck with my fraternity brothers who rode motorcycles, too. We ate chowder and sourdough and drank Bloody Marys with cracked pepper and celery stalks.

"The hair of the dog," we'd say, because there was no better way to banish the pain from the night before than to indulge in what brought on that pain in the first place. This is how I lived, in a constant state of drunkenness and self-repair, my heart clutching at any girl who took an interest in me, even if it was only for a few hours. Nothing made much sense, but this didn't seem important then. I was young. I was reading great works of literature. And on Saturdays, in a time when helmets were optional, I was riding my motorcycle up and down the Pacific coast with the wind in my hair.

This was the best I'd ever felt in my life, but only if you took away the guilt burden I bore for my mother. It didn't matter if I was hobnobbing with TV stars or reading Shakespeare or boat-racing warm beer in a Westwood pizza joint. None of that ever let me forget who I was and where I came from—*that which I was, I was*—and none of it shook loose the anxiety I felt over my mother being alone. By this time, she lived in a musty mobile home west of Highway 99, near a truck stop. It was a place that in some pocket of her failing brain fulfilled a dream, one that also included a lap dog, a cockapoo she named Reggie because she was fond of Mr. October and the dog—like Mr. Jackson himself—was black. I worried that I'd get a phone call from a well-meaning hospital employee or social worker informing me that my mother had died in that trailer—that she'd been dead for several days, in fact—before her neighbor Carolyn Twitty, whose name I always loved, finally heard Reggie's yapping and peered through the kitchen window, through the white, lacy curtain over the sink, to see my mother's body crumpled on the kitchen floor in a pool of blood. "We're terribly sorry for your loss," that social worker would say. "But we'll need to have you come home and take care of final arrangements."

In 1988, I stayed in Westwood for the Thanksgiving break. I was dating a girl named Laura who looked just like Snow White. She had black hair and skin like pearl. She had bangs and wore a headband. I wrote to my mother about her: "She is the biggest sweetheart and would do anything for anybody." I also wrote that Laura had invited me to her house in Yorba Linda for Thanksgiving, and that's where I wound up, throwing a football on a wide street with her little brother, then eating at a long table with more food than I had ever seen in one place. At home, Mom and Marzelle and Jack had turkey and mashed potatoes at the local Perko's.

I bunked in a fraternity house with a guy named Ramon who also stayed around campus for the holiday. He was one of two guys in a house of a hundred or so active members who professed a devotion to Jesus Christ. It was Ramon, on the day after Thanksgiving, 1988—a day I was scheduled to work the dinner shift at Islands—who would not let me leave our room until I was wearing his motorcycle helmet. He insisted. He blocked me from getting out the door. The roads were wet, he said, and oil had percolated to the surface under the influence of rainwater.

I took his helmet and strapped it under my chin. "Happy now?"

He said he was happy; he said he would see me after my shift.

"What about you?" I said. "Won't you need it?"

He said he didn't think so. He said if he went anywhere, it wouldn't be far.

I rode the back route out of Westwood, up steep Strathmore Drive, an ascent that filled me with expectation, like the clackety climb of a roller coaster. Both sides of Strathmore, normally jammed with cars parked bumper-to-bumper and wheels turned into the curb, were eerily vacant, the students all home for the holiday, back to their old neighborhoods and warm autumn tables. At Strathmore's peak, I stopped and used my coat sleeve to wipe rain from the face shield. I overlooked for a moment the expanse of pricey apartment villages, verandas clogged with bicycles and Weber grills and empty pizza boxes, places where four students squeezed into two bedrooms and were never happier. It was so still and quiet that day, misty, and sitting up high like that, at the neighborhood's highest point, I felt like I was inside a cloud.

I shifted into low gear and toggled my hand brakes. I rode downhill past the apartments and back-row frat houses until I picked up Veteran Avenue, a left turn, and a straight shot south to Wilshire Boulevard. Station 37 of the LAFD was on my left, and on my right, the Los Angeles National Cemetery, where one afternoon during a blue streak, on a day when I'd needed perspective, I laced up my sneakers and took a long walk through white headstones and read the names of fallen soldiers.

It was near four-fifteen and my dinner shift started at four-thirty. The rain was light and there was a fine sheen on the asphalt as I approached the intersection. I had a green light, a strange bit of luck at a place I normally would have stopped to wait for a long line of cars onboarding the 405 at Wilshire. Ahead of me, I saw headlights and a left turn blinker on a silver coupe of some kind. The car was moving into the intersection. I remember having time to consider this, and I began to see the outcome before it happened. I flashed my headlight—high, low, high, low—as a warning that I was coming through. *Stay put, silver coupe. I am on my way.* I opened up the throttle, picked up speed, and did the one thing you should never do on a motorcycle in traffic: I got aggressive. As I did, the driver of that silver coupe leaned into a left turn—a quick, sloping parabola—the kind of turn you make when you're in a hurry, when you know it's going to be a close call but you feel sure you can make it through without a collision because the other guy will tap his brakes and probably his horn, but he will pass behind you anyway, a little ticked but safe.

Here's what I saw: a Honda emblem centered on the grille, a white laundry basket overflowing clothes in the passenger seat, a silver door and side view mirror and a rear wheel with a missing hubcap. It was blurry, like a photograph in which someone had moved. I squeezed my brake handles and my bike slid out from under me, skidding left as though on ice. I cannot explain how I wound up more than sixty feet away from where my slide began, how my body came to rest on the lawn of the Federal Building and my bike wound up on the other side of Veteran Avenue on the sidewalk. How I shot one way and my bike shot another in a near perfect *V.* I cannot explain this because I was not there, not in a conscious state anyway, for the chemicals that flood the human brain before death had gone to work in me. My brain had embarked on a journey independent of my body, and my closing moments of consciousness unfurled in gradual motion. In those moments, I saw Marzelle—who would not be dead for another three years—and she beckoned me. She hovered in the foreground of a gray sky and extended her arm. How is it that a woman still alive was calling me into death? I saw, too, the family I would never have; there was a wife and three children, but they existed only in shadow, their faces washed out by a brilliant light. This one I can explain: my deepest desire manifesting as the last cognitive experience preceding death. If you could have one thing in your life before you die, what would it be?

Marzelle, though, I can do nothing with.

There is a gap in the narrative, a void of about fifteen minutes I would guess, where I remember nothing. I can offer a fiction here, something not too far-fetched that will get me back to memory. But before the fiction, a fact: A police report exists somewhere among the keepsakes of my life. There are just two details I recall from that report: an officer's sketch of the intersection in which X marks the spot where my body came to rest, with "V1" showing the same for my motorcycle. On the sketch, these designations are not more than two inches apart; in life, they were more like forty feet, but I can't know for sure, because my eyes weren't open to see it. The other detail I remember is a sentence. This one has burned in my brain for three decades: "Vehicle 1 collided with the street." That is it, essentially the sum total of the LAPD report: Motorcycle crashes into street. There is no mention of a Vehicle 2, which now exists for me only as a symbol of my closest call.

Because this all happened in plain view of LAFD 37, I can surmise they were first on the scene. Someone had to get me from the Federal Building grass to a gurney in the UCLA Medical Center, my mouth bleeding down my neck, my right arm shattered and coursing with sharp, torrid pain. My own cries brought me back to consciousness. I remember this, and I remember questions I could not answer: *What is your name? What year is it? Who is the President?* A brain in trauma does surprising things. Here's what I did say: "Call my manager Mike at Islands and tell him I won't be in for my shift. Here's the phone number." Then, "Call my girlfriend Laura in Yorba Linda. Here's her phone number." And finally, "My father lives in Long Beach. His name is Ken. Here is his phone number." That was the order: my boss, my girl, my dad. My brain and its confounding electricity could generate number sequences and the names of others who would need to know what happened, but it could not recall my own name, the year, the President of the United States.

To this day, I don't know why I asked for my father.

But before that, in the void, there was a rescue, a firefighter or paramedic trained to stabilize a body in trauma, someone who knew what to do with oxygen and a backboard, and another someone to ride alongside me in the ambulance, take my vitals, put the needle in its proper place and read the blips on the monitor. Someone practiced in defibrillation in the event the green line went flat and the tone went constant. I have no idea how close I came to that flat line. It is strange to consider that there is a block of my life, maybe only a quarter of an hour, during which my soul may have departed my body.

The two large bones in the human forearm are the radius and ulna. There are muscles there, too, the *pronator radii teres* and the *supinator longus,* which allow you to do things like lay your hands flat or turn your palms up. The biceps play a part, too. When there is a fracture of the radius, muscle tension draws the broken bone upward and inward. Anyone with a copy of *Gray's Anatomy* can tell you that, but only if they do some digging. If you're lucky like I was, that bone doesn't tear through your skin under tension from those muscles. Not that it would have mattered for me. I still wound up after hours of surgery with a six-inch keloid scar on my inner forearm that over the years I have attributed to shark bite and a back-alley knife fight, even though the truth is just as exquisite.

My surgeon told me the procedure went well. He had gray hair tucked into a blue cap and wore his surgical mask under his chin. He explained to me what he did to put me back together. I was still groggy, but I remember most of it. My radius was shattered, so he went in with what he called a "little strainer" and fished out the bone fragments. That image has always stayed with me, this picture of a miner panning for gold. He filed down the sharp, exposed ends of the bone and left a clean gap of somewhere near two inches, give or take, a chasm that would need to be filled with other bone, in this case from my right hip. This was the graft, he said. He took just enough bone from my hip to bridge the gap in my radius, then he sistered it all together like a floor joist, flat metal plates on both sides of the mended bone and thirteen screws to hold it all together.

"I hope you're not superstitious," he said. There was not a hint of sarcasm in this. My surgeon was matter-of-fact and serious and looked up from his notes as he spoke to me. I still think about him when I find myself in really cold places, on trips to the snow with my family, for those are times when my forearm aches most as the hardware he installed inside me freezes.

I also learned from him that my range of motion would decrease significantly, even with six weeks of therapy. *Gray's Anatomy* puts it this way: "In treating such a fracture, the arm must be put up in a position of supination, otherwise union will take place with great impairment of the movements of the hand." I have found this to be true; my right hand no longer moves like it once did. It pronates just fine; I can turn my palm downward with little effort. I can still dribble a basketball. I can manage a computer mouse. But there is only partial movement the other way. Supination just doesn't work any longer. Unless I lie on my back, my right palm will never again turn heavenward. Without contorting my shoulders, my right hand cannot accept change from a cashier, and getting food to my mouth with utensils is awkward. I cannot eat cereal without dribbling milk down my chin, and I will hover my face over my plate in the expectation that food will drop. These are basic executions in which I feel the metal plates in my forearm stop progress at a midway point, right at the place I might shake another man's hand. I can do that. And I can pick up a suitcase and throw a baseball and sign my name just fine, and because I can do these things, I feel like I have lost nothing.

There were other things my surgeon told me. Every four hours I could call for morphine; that would help with the pain I felt all over my body, but most acutely in my forearm and hip. I measured my days and nights in these increments, hailing nurses with my call button thirty minutes early in case they were running behind. When I could stand it no longer, I used my voice: "Nurse! Nurse!" and they came, and they checked the bags that gave me fluids, and they emptied the bags that received them. They held syringes to the light and flicked them with their fingernails before plunging them into my IV. Warmth was instant and comfort soon followed. I could rest for at least three hours until the hurt started leaking into my body again.

There was nothing I could do for myself. When she was there, Laura held the straw close to my lips and gave me lollipop sponges soaked in lemon water because my mouth tasted like coins. She held her compact in such a way that I could examine my face. I was inflated all around my eyes and over the bridge of my nose, and there were stitches in my chin and upper lip and forehead, twelve in all, four in each cut. My right arm was plastered from wrist to shoulder and hung suspended above my bed from cables hooked to a trapeze. My right hip was bandaged and throbbing, and when a nurse changed my dressing, there were staples in my skin and a small, hollow pocket where once there was bone.

Laura scratched under my cast with a wooden dowel when the itching was too much to bear. She talked with my mother as I slept, as I wandered in and out of consciousness. Another girl was there, my mother's helper, a sixteen-year-old named Richelle, the first of probably thirty helpers we would hire in twenty-odd years, girls who cooked and cleaned and shopped and clipped coupons and helped my mother work the VCR. They came as part of my mother's in-home disability package, funded by Fresno County at something like eight bucks an hour. If we were lucky, they were helpers who actually enjoyed being with sick people, and Richelle was one of those. She liked my mother so much that she drove from Fresno to Westwood so Mom could sit next to me for a few hours and stroke my forearm with her arthritic fingers and wear a look of grave concern.

My surgeon visited every day to check on me, to ask about pain levels from one to ten, one being comfortable, ten being unbearable. I always said eight, nine, or ten in hopes he'd be magnanimous and up my morphine dose, which he did not. On one of those days, when I was alert, he brought Ramon's helmet in a clear plastic bag. He set his clipboard on the bed at my feet and extracted the helmet from the bag. There was blood inside, but it was dried and brown now. Seeing the helmet gave me a chill. It was white and blood-spattered. I could see where my blood shot through the mouth vent then sprayed the sides. My surgeon held the helmet before me. He turned it one way, then the other, the way you might appraise a vase or a piece of abstract art. *My kid could do this with finger paint.* He tapped the crown of the helmet with his knuckle. The face guard was shattered and jagged like a broken window, which explained the stitches in my chin, lip, and forehead. He said he thought I might like to see the helmet, and I knew why. I asked him anyway. What would have happened to me without it?

His face turned stern, and he looked at me like this was a silly question. How could I not see it? Wasn't the evidence right there before my eyes? "You would not have made it," he said. "We would not be talking right now."

Eleven months after the crash, I bought a black NIV Study Bible at a Christian bookstore in Westwood. On the presentation page, I inscribed the date: October 1989. I had my name embossed on the cover next to the secret ichthys. Now I know: If I ever come upon a stranger in a desert, I will draw one arc of the simple fish in the sand; if the stranger completes the drawing with the second arc, I am in good company.

I started hanging out with a guy named Derek. He was a stranger to me until he appeared at my bedside a few days after the accident and asked what he could do to help. Were there professors he could visit for me? Were there assignments I needed turned in? He said he had heard through the grapevine about me, that all of fraternity row was talking about the accident, and that God had put me in his heart. Derek had people praying for me, and I said that was nice, thank you, that I could use all the prayer I could get. He left me with C. S. Lewis's *Mere Christianity,* which taught me not to be surprised to find myself in a rough place; apparently, there would be more, and greater. I should expect that God had in mind for me situations in which I would need to be much braver than I would ever dream of being, but that somehow, this was a good thing, part of a great plan God had for making me the man I was meant to become.

Derek had a cleft chin and a receding hairline. He drove me to church at Bel Air Presbyterian on Sundays, where I once shook hands with Ronald Reagan. Derek told me that the person he most looked forward to seeing in heaven was John Wayne, who had a deathbed conversion and was welcomed into the church two days before he died. This is the same man who was married three times and kept Marlene Dietrich and Maureen O'Hara and a stable full of other girls on the side. He also drank a whole lot and smoked five packs of Camels a day, just like my Uncle Jack. Derek's point was that it was never too late to come to God, even if you had spent your life drunk and unfaithful.

There's a whole parable about this in the New Testament, where people hired to work a few minutes in the field get paid the same as folks who worked an entire day. Long before John Wayne, there was a penitent thief who hung on a cross next to Jesus, and as they hung there in agony, their arms outstretched and their organs failing, that asphyxiating thief after a life of crime and debauchery accepted Jesus as Master, right there at the zero hour. With his dying breath, just before guards broke his knees and took him down, he said Lord, remember me when you come into your kingdom, and Jesus said sure thing, you will be with me in Paradise.

Once I learned this, I remember thinking I was just like that thief, but instead of hanging on a cross next to Jesus, I was in a hospital bed. My body was broken and strung up. There were times I cried out to God, when I said, "Lord, remember me," and sure enough, a ministering spirit who looked a lot like a nurse showed up. She brought forth salvation, and I received it, and in moments, as it worked its way through my blood and body, I too saw Jesus, and He said, "Welcome, Chuck, Welcome." He said, "You can be with me in Paradise."

In my final year of college, I was living in a one-bedroom apartment called Club California on Roebling Avenue, splitting the $1,200 monthly rent with a pre-law student named Mike. I spent the summer working two jobs. I was still at Islands, but I also had a side job working security at movie premieres. Once, I stood with my back to the stage at the Hard Rock Café while Dennis Quaid and Jerry Lee Lewis dueled one another on baby grands for the opening of "Great Balls of Fire." By this time Laura was gone, this sweet girl who cared for me until I was well enough to break things off. I told her she could do much better.

The apartment I shared with Mike came with two parking spots in an underground garage, one of which I used for Mom's Corolla. Mike drove an old Porsche. In the months after the crash, I managed to repair the motorcycle and sell it, but not before having to ride it one more time, on the 405 south to a bike shop in Westchester, where a mechanic gave it a once-over and told the buyer to steer clear, not because it was a bad bike but because "motorcycles are dangerous." The guy took it anyway. Mike drove behind me in the slow lane and brought me back to Club Cal once the deal was done. I had two months' rent in my pocket.

Mike had a neat-nik girlfriend named Kelly who was also pre-law. She hung around a lot and it was like the three of us shared the place. I didn't mind. I liked her there. We had a kitchen full of useful things like noodle strainers and wire whisks and muffin pans, because Kelly liked to bake. She tidied up and fluffed throw pillows. We had Tupperware for our left-overs. It always felt like Kelly was practicing to become a wife and mom, and the joke around our place was that she had come to UCLA for her *MRS degree*. She put the kibosh on that right away, since Mike and Kelly were high school sweethearts and she had not come to college just to find a husband; she had found him years before at Tustin High, "thank you very much." She called him "honey" and he called her "Kell," and there was an air of domesticity in our apartment.

Sometimes she was there when I got home, and Mike would come in with the mail, wearing a suit from his internship and toting a briefcase, and they gave each other a kiss at the sink where she was drying a dish. And even though they did the best they could to include me, I always felt like an interloper in their American Dream.

Mike's dad Dave was once a major-league pitcher. In 1989, he was still the last pitcher in Red Sox history to throw a no-hitter, before Hideo Nomo did it in 2001. Dave's no-no came in 1965 against the Indians at Fenway, and I had a kind of pride-by-association about this: My room-mate's dad threw the last no-hitter in Red Sox history. It was much sweeter than what I had to offer of my own dad, whose greatest accomplishment was an epic poem he'd written called "I Am Old Glory," told from the perspective of the American flag in which she narrates her trek through pivotal points in US history: "I was there in a place called Pearl Harbor on that terrible day of infamy . . . December 7, 1941." It was somber, overdramatic, anthropomorphic, and in some places, rhyming, precisely the type of patriotism you might find in a newsletter produced by the Benevolent and Protective Order of Elks, which is exactly where it wound up in the spring of 1982, courtesy of the Bellflower Lodge #2003.

On warm afternoons, Mike and I took our gloves to the intramural field and played catch, a little hum-baby, and the sun was always out and the field was clogged with students playing soccer and flag football. These were afternoons of luxurious freedom in a place I would leave several months later. I would stand in cap and gown at Drake Stadium in June of 1990 with my parents in the bleachers, Mom with Richelle, and Dad with Loose-Wheel, who was decked out in a muumuu and lei. Later that afternoon, with everything I owned packed in the Corolla, I would drive out of Westwood for a job as a summer camp counselor in the High Sierras, just sixty-five miles from Stuccoville, on the shores of Huntington Lake. But before that, when I was still a student, there were those afternoons playing catch with Mike. It was then I discovered a wicked curveball I didn't have before the accident, some oddity in my reconfigured right arm that generated sharp breaks away from right-handed batters. I also fashioned a knuckleball with a dizzying wobble. There was some joshing about how my arm was now bionic and I should try out for the Bruins' baseball team. Dave could give me pointers. Mike was amazed by it all. He said he'd never seen a breaking ball like it. It was like it fell off the edge of a table. He told me I would be a revelation. Coaches would be astonished by me. They would say, "How is it we have never heard of this kid?" They would say, "Where on God's green planet did he come from?" and God would answer them. God would say, "He is a whole new creation, this kid, but he has been here the whole time. He has been here all along."

16

About as Popular as Anyone

"Mom,

On our trip to see Dad the clouds were fluffy, the snow on the ground and the skies above were white.

You may not know it, but you are in the seat next to me.

I got you started on your way to Heaven. God will take over now."

—Note from Jack to Marzelle, April 1991

THE REVEREND MORRIS WILLIAMS OF THE FIRST CHURCH of God officiated Marzelle's memorial service on April 2, 1991. Frank and Nancy were there, along with Mom, Jack, and me. We were the only people left in the world who knew Marzelle, along with her nephew Harold and his wife Beulah back in Clinton, Indiana. It was Harold who'd sent us Marzelle's obituary neatly clipped from *The Daily Clintonian*, "the only newspaper in Vermillion County." On the backside there was a recipe for chicken and cheese souffle.

In life, Marzelle's folks were Bruce and Eva. Her middle name was Viola, and everyone called her "Vi." Her yearbook credits include Literary Editor, Chorus and Junior Class Play, along with this senior quote: "About as popular as anyone." She graduated from Indiana's Hillsdale

High School in 1931 with her soon-to-be husband, Lloyd. They had been in school together with the same twelve classmates since they were in primary at Summit Grove School, kids with stalwart, unimpeachable names like Opal Harper and Fred Steffy and Philbert Stewart. The gal she spent the most time with was Ethel Plank, who was voted most likely to become the first female President of the United States, selecting Marzelle as her private secretary. My grandmother would instead become a real-life Rosie the Riveter. During the war, she assembled B-24 Liberators at Willow Run Airplane Factory near Ypsilanti, Michigan. I have artifacts from her time at Willow Run: a Liberator lapel pin and a necklace with a gold B-24 at the center of a crystal, five-pointed star.

For the memorial service, Jack chose "That Wonderful Mother of Mine," a popular song from 1919, when Marzelle was six. The five of us sat in folding chairs in a small room at the Tinkler Mission Chapel on the corner of Broadway and Belmont in Fresno, and we listened quietly as it played: "The moon never beams without bringing me dreams of that wonderful mother of mine." The recording must have come right out of Tinkler's library of standard funeral tunes, because Jack wouldn't have owned a record like this. Perhaps he picked it because he liked the title. The song itself sounded old-timey and staticky, like it was piped through a gramophone.

Reverend Williams stood before a table in a dark suit and held open a Bible. When the song ended, he read the Twenty-Third Psalm. My mother held her hand over mine. She always did this at big moments, during times she felt unmoored, as though she wanted to make sure I wasn't drifting away from her, too. The Reverend said a few other ceremonial things in his capacity as rental clergy, things I can only paraphrase, but his message was along the lines of Marzelle resting in eternal glory with a new body free of the afflictions that beset her in life. I wondered where the Reverend Morris Williams got his information. Other than an overactive thyroid and emphysema, Marzelle didn't suffer much in the way of afflictions. She was smoking a Lucky Strike the day before she died of respiratory failure at seventy-seven, so her total time in affliction was less than twenty-four hours.

When Jack, Mom, and I showed up in Marzelle's room with the hospital priest, she knew her time had come. Her already buggy eyes grew wide as saucers and had she been able, she'd have shed her blanket and run from her room screaming for one last Lucky Strike, one final Colt 45 before the journey to the Sweet Hereafter.

Reverend Williams spoke low and tonelessly, his lips moving in ovals on his elastic face. There was a gap where the drapes almost came together behind him, through which I caught flashes of cars sweeping by. The occasional pedestrian peered inside. To one side of the reverend, there was a piney table stained blond. On it, there were just three things: a bouquet of white flowers wrapped in yellow ribbon; an heirloom Bible, which Tinkler threw in as part of its Love and Remembrance Package; and Marzelle's ashes in a bronze urn overlaid in walnut with praying hands. The urn wasn't very big—maybe slightly larger than a brick—but it struck me that even though Marzelle was a slight woman when she died, her sum total in ashes ought to have amounted to something more than what rested in that box, on that piney table, just a few feet in front of the last people she knew. She was sturdy, my grandmother, pleased to giggles by small things like roller derby and my big toes.

Marzelle's good life, hard-lived, had come down to a few data points some folks would remember but soon forget, her body now residue that would fill a pickle jar and ride shotgun with Jack for thirty-two hours—from Fresno to Hillsdale and her place of final disposition—Helt's Prairie Cemetery in Vermillion County just west of the Wabash, which in Miami Indian means "water over white stones" and sounds like a peaceful place to wind up. For a $150, a man named Bernard Lake opened Lloyd's grave with a spade and placed Marzelle inside. I wasn't there, but I imagine that once Mr. Lake settled her remains, he filled the hole with the same snowy earth he'd just disturbed, tamped it down a few times with the bottom of his boot, and uttered something sacred that would serve as a kind of epilogue to Marzelle's journey, maybe a prayer or holy sonnet, *Death be not proud*, reuniting my grandparents in the same town where they met as children at Summit Grove, which means my grandmother made it full-circle, and that her flawed life, in the end, was pretty perfect.

At the time Marzelle died, I was living in a second-floor apartment at the northernmost edge of Fresno, just a mile or so from the San Joaquin River. In less than ten minutes, I could bike to a quiet spot lined with cottonwoods and watch the water slip by. On the other side, there was woodland filled with mule deer, reclusive creatures that emerged at dusk to drink. I remember a kind of vanilla-scented wind flowing through the channel as I stood barefoot to my kneecaps in the frigid river, water that began its journey as snow at ten-thousand feet in the Ansel Adams Wilderness, and more than a hundred miles later collected in my cupped hands, which I lifted to my face.

I was twenty-three. I had my own kitchen and bedroom. I had cable television and a sofa and a particle-board coffee table I'd assembled with an Allen wrench and a dozen hex bolts. I had a brass dinette with a glass top, and that's where I kept my typewriter, the one I used to write my very first paper for my very first class in grad school, a class in nonfiction prose for a professor named Dr. Zumwalt. The assignment was to render an incident in our lives that served as a turning point, something that took us from one path and put us on another. Just a few years removed from my motorcycle accident, I felt like this assignment was made for me. I would write about the crash and how almost dying changed my perspective on things, how it transformed me from reckless, abandoned boy to mature man of letters. I would throw in the bit about seeing Marzelle on the other side of the veil, even though she was still alive at the time. There would be this whole supernatural element then, and what reader doesn't love a ghost story? It was perfect. Death would be my milieu.

My essay was called "The Caterpillar," and it was three pages long. I thought the metaphor was muscular and original: a caterpillar who becomes a butterfly! The night before it was due, I hammered at my typewriter keys and zipped the pages from the platen with artful aplomb. I stacked my three pages on my glass table, ran a staple through the corner, and went to bed that night feeling as though I had just finished my magnum opus.

I carried that feeling with me for a week, straight into the second meeting of Dr. Zumwalt's class, when I walked in and saw my essay in front of every student. My classmates were thumbing through it as I took my seat. We were going to "workshop" my writing, Dr. Zumwalt said, and this sounded so literary to me. We were going to talk about what was working in the narrative and what was not. I sat back, smug, waiting for adoration and praise. That there might be something *not working* in it seemed outlandish to me.

Dr. Zumwalt solicited initial reactions. "Do you feel like you know anything about the writer?" he asked. He had a soft voice with some gravel to it. His hair was gray and unkempt, and he had a mustache. He spoke from the position of a gentle soul. "What was he like before the crash, and what was he like after it?"

I remember a shuffling of paper, of my classmates looking concerned and thoughtful, like they were all just a breath away from uttering something insightful, something that might reveal how I had gotten them to think in unique and marvelous ways. I glanced from side-to-side as my classmates underlined sentences and circled words and scribbled notes in the margins, but no one spoke up.

"Well?" Dr. Zumwalt said. "Anyone?"

Then, Dr. Zumwalt asked another question: "Has anyone ever heard the term pathetic fallacy?" I remember that question; I remember hearing only the first word: *pathetic*. There were a few thoughtful nods. I did not know the term, and none of my classmates seemed to know it either. Dr. Zumwalt said pathetic fallacy is when you give human qualities to inanimate objects. It is the lie of imparting emotions to things that cannot emote, he said. He pointed to the second paragraph of my story.

"See here," he said. "Mr. Radke on a rainy day has the sky 'crying'. And here," he continued, flipping the page, "his broken arm 'wails' in excruciating pain."

Skies cannot cry. Arms cannot wail. These things should have been self-evident to a graduate student.

There were other examples, too, along with clichés: the road "hit me like a ton of bricks," and I found myself "knocking on Heaven's door."

There were transparent attempts to overwrite, to impress with figurative language. In the hospital, my tired eyes became "leaden," my head "heavy as a medicine ball," the muscles in my neck like "springy rubber-bands." When Laura spoke to me, she did so in "motherly, dulcet tones."

"If you are writing with a thesaurus on your desk," Dr. Zumwalt said, "throw it away." My writing called attention to itself; it "snapped the reader out of the dream." Toward the end of the essay, I had my mother tell me to "be strong and heal," but I couldn't just attribute her words with *she said*. No, I wrote that my mother "implored in a strong whisper," because I wanted my reader to feel the impact of her words. Dr. Zumwalt counter-implored in the margins: "Don't tell your readers what you want them to hear! Show them!"

After the final line of my paper, in the bottom margin, Dr. Zumwalt left this handwritten note: "Those bastards at UCLA were derelict in their responsibility in teaching you how to write."

Bastards. Derelict. At least Dr. Zumwalt was straightforward with me; I appreciated authenticity then. I needed people who told me like it was, who let me know straight-up there was no reason for me to waste my time with things like writing. His words seemed to lay it pretty bare for me. I should do something more practical. I should do something that made sense.

When Jack came back from Indiana, I helped him take his things from the apartment he'd shared with Marzelle. At some point in college, I found out from Mom in a letter that things with Jack and Gayle had "gotten ugly." Those were her words, and it was pretty easy to figure out the ugly part. After a short stretch masquerading as the perfect husband, Jack started revealing the chinks in his armor, and there were plenty. I suspect there was a point at which Gayle's older son, a star athlete, may have told Jack to get his hands off his mother or he'd kill him, and that Jack mouthed off in a wild-eyed stupor, "I can touch my wife where I damn well please."

From there, I further suspect that Gayle, a godly woman, had gritted her teeth and said "You are no longer welcome here, not if you keep drinking, God help you," and that Jack eventually burned through his second chances until one day the locks were changed and he had nowhere to go except back to his mother, who lived alone and drove herself to the grocery store in a brown Dodge Dart and managed just fine with her instant coffee and Colt 45s and now, once again, her derelict son.

Jack rented a mobile home around the corner from Mom, in a trailer park called Sunset West, which was right off Highway 99 and had a flea-market-sized parking lot out front for sleepy truckers. Next to that lot was the Astro Motel and Bar, stumbling distance from Sunset West. It had a tall light fixture on top like a party hat. Against the dark sky, the light moved upward in wands and exploded through sequentially animated neon rings. On Saturday nights, the big parking lot was full of rigs and from Mom's mobile home, we heard bar noise from the Astro, mostly laughter and vague chatter above a jukebox playing country music and classic rock. Sometimes we heard deep-voiced drunk men wailing "Simple Man" into the night air.

Mom and I helped Jack get settled in his new place. I was driving a pickup by then, and I was on my third or fourth trip with essentials that smelled like smoke and old newspaper. Jack threw nothing away. I carried boxes and dusty furniture inside while Jack smoked a cigarette under his carport and leaned against the hood of his inherited Dodge Dart. His eyes were bloodshot and teary, his face overrun with whiskers. He looked bewildered by it all. He kept watching me go inside then come out. "Put the boxes anywhere," he said. "I'll sort through them later." Mom said she could help. She said the two of them could go through it and throw away things like old receipts and medical bills and that Jack could get a new start. Her plan was for the two of them to sit in lawn chairs, drink iced tea, and slowly unpack Jack's life. They would divvy up the keepsakes—Lloyd's signet rings for Jack, Marzelle's necklaces and brooches for her—and they would get organized and reconnect over their shared history; they'd go on walks through Sunset West against the backdrop of highway noise. "People might think they were a married couple at first, and wouldn't that be funny," Mom said. "No, not married," she'd say, "just a brother and sister from the Midwest by way of Hollywood." She tried to reminisce with Jack, but he seemed to have no interest in the past. He seemed to have lost the ability to be reflective.

Inside his mobile home, he paced nervously and hung his head and nudged things out of his way with his toe, only to nudge them back again on his return trip through the narrow path he had cut for himself. Mom talked and talked and said this unpacking chore was no big deal, that they would eat the elephant one bite at a time, and time was something they both had lots of now. She stacked plates and bowls in cupboards; she washed utensils by hand and arranged them in a plastic drawer caddy; she had me set the Crock Pot on the Formica countertop and told Jack he could put a chuck roast and onions and a can of broth inside and cook it on low for eight hours.

"It's easy," Mom said. "You can throw red potatoes in there, too, and they'll just fall off the fork." Jack walked in and out of his mobile home; his screen door slammed every few minutes. My mother looked across the small, dim room at me and shrugged her shoulders. She told me Marzelle's death was hard on both of them, but Jack seemed to be especially out of sorts, "more so than usual, even."

At some point in the early fall of 1991, Jack asked me for money, and I gave it to him. The figure I have in my head is seventy-five dollars, and I want to say he needed it for fishing gear. I was doing all right for myself moneywise, so seventy-five wasn't much of a stretch. I worked nights, waiting tables at Tony Roma's and the place was always packed; shifts where I walked out with less than a hundred dollars were a disappointment. During the days, I was a substitute teacher. Jack said he would pay me back once he got his Social Security check.

Over the summer, Jack replaced the Dodge Dart with a small Chevy pickup. It had a trailer hitch and a camper shell, and he towed an aluminum boat from Fresno to Shaver Lake a few times a week to drop a line in the water. This was good for him, Mom said. It gave him a hobby, something to keep his mind off his troubles. Jack outfitted his truck bed with a raised, carpet-covered piece of plywood, and he stowed his fishing gear underneath. He would sometimes drive into the high country, to a tiny fishing lake called Cortwright, and drink Budweiser and eat potted meat and smoke Camels, not coming back until he got hungry or ran out of beer and cigarettes.

We saw very little of Jack. When I drove by his place on my way to Mom's, his carport was always empty, and his drapes never shifted on the rod. I would sometimes stop and nose around. I would walk the perimeter and look for a sign that he'd been there, a drop of fresh motor oil in the carport, maybe footprints on the dusty steps to his porch, all in the hope I would catch him home and recover the money he owed me. But I did not see him, not once, until the first week of October, Friday the 4th, to be exact, when I saw his pickup and walked up the carpeted ramp to his aluminum screen door.

I peered through the screen door and called his name. "Jack?" The television was blaring. I could see that Jack had unpacked nothing in the months since Mom and I moved him in. The boxes he told me to put anywhere were still everywhere. I poked my head inside and looked toward the kitchen and called out again. The Formica countertop where I had put the Crock Pot was overrun with empty Budweiser cans; hundreds of them littered the kitchen and floor, window ledges, overflowing two garbage buckets. There were beer cans that doubled as ashtrays. There were more beer cans stacked in a tower atop the television, which was tuned to a cop show.

That I know the date was October 4th is not a product of memory; it is, rather, the date written neatly into box 27A of Jack's death certificate by attending physician M. Margaret Hadcock, the date the *decedent* came under her care. On the following day, October 5th, Dr. Hadcock performed a subtotal colectomy on my uncle. She removed part of his colon to stop the bleeding inside him. This is also on his death certificate.

I called out a third time. "Jack," I said. "You home?" I pulled open the screen, stepped over the threshold, and let the door bump closed behind me. The inside air was hazy, and bits of dust floated glacially through a strand of sunlight breaking through the drapes.

I called out one last time: "Jack?"

Where the carpet was visible, it was dirty and worn. The floor was clogged with open cardboard boxes disgorging crumpled, yellowed newspapers, fake plants, and framed pictures of family, long dead. Jack had started to unpack, but lost interest and tossed things aside. *Strewn* is the word that comes to mind. Jack's mobile home was *strewn* with garbage, papers mostly, carbons and invoices in dog-eared file folders on top of more file folders with handwritten words on the tabs: Bills, Receipts, Check Stubs, Social Security. There were pill bottles, overturned. There were spill stains and cigarette burns. The air was thick with smoke, but it wasn't fresh, floating smoke like you might encounter in a bar. It was smoke you had to break through to move from one side of the room to the other. I stepped carefully over piles. I passed Jack's orange chair. I navigated my way to the back of the trailer. To my left, a bedroom: an unmade bed, piles of clothing. To my right, a dim, narrow bathroom, and that was where I found my uncle.

He looked beyond saving. He was on the floor huddled-in on himself wearing nothing but soiled boxers, and all around him there was black, bilious blood. I may have gasped, but I remember not being surprised. I had seen Jack like this before, and by now, I was used to Death coming around every so often, just to remind me who was boss.

I remember first thinking that Jack had been murdered, that he was into someone for a lot more than seventy-five bucks, perhaps someone from the Astro, someone who dealt in drugs or hookers. I thought that were I to turn his body with my toe, I might see a bullet hole in his forehead, or maybe in his chest or gut, a hole from which Jack's insides had leaked.

I knew enough not to touch him. Perry Mason inspected dead bodies with nothing more than stern curiosity.

I also remember the smell. It didn't hit me until I saw him up close. It was the odor of a body that had decomposed from the inside out. My father, when I was a boy, used the word *putrid* to describe me when I came in from playing outside. He was a show-off when it came to words: "What's that putrid smell?" he would say. It was his roundabout way of telling me I needed to bathe. He got this from Grandpa Leo.

But my dad's idea of putrid was nothing like this. This was an old meat smell. It was a smell I have often attached to maggots. When the company has been right and the conversation has taken a morbid turn, I have shared this story, and I have said the same thing every time: "The bathroom was splattered with bile. My uncle's liver exploded." I now know that was not true. M. Margaret Hadcock cleared things up for me: "Cirrhosis and lower GI bleeding." That's from box 25, "Significant conditions contributing to death." The blood vessels leading to his liver were blocked, causing them to burst. And that's what I saw. Blood from burst vessels pooling on the bathroom floor. Not an exploded liver.

Despite all of this—despite the blood and putrescence—I was wrong about Jack being dead. I knew I was wrong when I saw, almost imperceptibly, his ribcage rising and falling. He was breathing. Jesus, my uncle was still alive. I didn't know how that could be possible. It was easier thinking he was dead. Dead I could handle. Dead didn't necessitate urgency. Almost dead was a whole different story. Almost dead meant I had to find a telephone amid a thousand Budweiser cans, and when that didn't work, it meant I had to jog to Mom's trailer—through her metal-sided, wrought-iron, plastic-grass neighborhood—and bang on her locked door and wait for her to let me in, a pocket of time that felt interminable. Her phone was easy to find because everything had a place. Her telephone had its own table, and I used that phone to do what you are supposed to do when you walk into a smoky trailer and find your uncle bleeding-out on his bathroom floor.

I remember what one of the paramedics told me as he rolled Jack into the back of the ambulance. He said it was lucky I stopped by when I did. He said a couple more hours and Jack would be heading to the morgue instead of the ER. At that point, though, one was just as good as the other. I'm no doctor, but I didn't see a future in which Jack recovered from this. Hours later, after M. Margaret Hadcock repaired his insides, he continued to rot away, most visibly around and inside his mouth, which had contracted some kind of infection the shift nurses covered in salve. Jack began seeing people who weren't in the room, and he spoke to them, the words from his shriveled mouth mostly indecipherable. Days before he died, my mother had to start introducing herself. "Jack, it's your sister." She'd say, "It's me, Barbara," and he'd nod like he knew her. "And that's your nephew. You remember Chuck?" I stood at the foot of his bed and waved, and I wondered if he knew me. I wondered if he remembered he had once taken me to a Dodger game or that he owed me money. Judging from his blank stare, it was clear he did not. It was clear that his declining brain sought things to eliminate, and one of those things was me.

Box 21A lists Jack's immediate cause of death as pneumonia—boggy, bacteria-filled lungs—an affliction he had for a week and succumbed to on the seventh day. Like Marzelle, Jack wanted to be cremated, so the good folks at Tinkler handled this for Mom, along with the arrangements for his final resting place, three miles off the coast of San Francisco, at nearly the exact spot in the ocean where, in 1954, he had been a signalman in the United States Navy aboard the USS Helena. Jack was dishonorably discharged, so I didn't understand why he would want to end up where he was not wanted. His ashes were to be sprinkled over the Pacific by a man named Allan Vieira, who owned an airplane and got paid seventy-five dollars a pop to deposit human remains in the big blue ocean.

Jack's death wasn't as tidy as Marzelle's. His loop didn't close the way hers did. Why should it have? Why shouldn't you reap what you sow? More than six years after we committed his remains to Allan Vieira and provided my uncle the most fitting and dignified disposition we could manage, Mom got a letter from the Tinkler Funeral Chapel & Crematory, which I still have. It is two full pages, typed, single-spaced, on soothing, cotton-bond stationery. It informs my mother that Tinkler's long tradition of excellence, as she may have heard, had been compromised by Mr. Vieira, who fatally shot himself on a remote hillside when it became known that instead of scattering the ashes of dead souls over the ocean, he had simply stockpiled them in a couple storage lockers and an airplane hangar. There was a list of loved ones put out by the county sheriff's office—more than five thousand sets of remains, it would turn out—and Jack was among them.

Vieira was dead two weeks before his body was found. He had driven fifteen miles on a two-lane road off Highway 49. That road became rutted earth as it climbed into the foothills through an area left blackened by wildfire, skeletons of burned pine trees standing amid new growth emerging from the ashes. Vieira found a secluded spot with a view, parked his car—which still held the remains of eleven people— and walked some two hundred yards through poison oak and manzanita thicket before putting a snub-nose .38 revolver to his temple and pulling the trigger. If Vieira's aim were true, once the bullet turned his skull to powder, it would have burned through the medial temporal lobe and the hippocampus, which rests atop the brain stem just above the ear and is the structure most often associated with memory. The bullet would have pulverized the hippocampus and actually erased Vieira's memory moments before it erased his life. Thus, before he died, he would have forgotten everything.

Allan Vieira was identified, the coroner said, by dental remains. A body becomes unrecognizable quickly when there is no one to tend to it, when it is left to warm in the sun with only vermin and vultures for company. It returns to Mother Earth, to its most primitive state, to simple organic matter, to nothing but pulp and bone.

17

It's Not Too Late to Change Your Mind

"Currently in an acute hospital in critical condition. Will transport to SNF if she survives illness."

—Adult Day Care, Participant Cancellation Form, B. Radke
State of California, Department of Aging
January 26, 1994

AFTER JACK DIED, I MOVED MOM OUT OF SUNSET WEST into a nice apartment complex not far from me on the north end of town, one that had yet to meet its quota of government-subsidized renters. Her place had one bedroom and a shaded back patio with a view of the gated, sparkling pool. It was "real uptown," she said, "like living in a resort." I don't know that I had ever seen her so happy, and all it took was a view of a pool and a canopy of lush green trees with heart-shaped leaves. She decorated the place nicely with cute stuff she ordered from Harriet Carter and Fingerhut, and before she knew it, she had five-grand in credit card debt, most of it sunk into wall art and throw pillows and a white wicker bedroom set, along with regular teeth cleanings for Reggie because his breath smelled like canned tuna. Mom loved that dog like a child; no expense was too great for him, even when she didn't have real money.

While I was looking after Mom, my friends were growing their own lives, getting married and starting families. They had entry-level jobs with benefits and wives with teaching credentials. They had mortgages and married parents who wanted grandkids. They lived near public parks and had started contributing to retirement funds. As for me, I was languishing in grad school, not in much of a hurry, because school served as my excuse for not doing more with my life. I paid rent and tuition with money I made as a waiter and substitute teacher, both augmented by wages I earned as my mother's helper. I hate to admit this now, but there was a time when the County of Fresno paid me just over eight dollars an hour to ensure my mother's basic needs were met. It seemed to me I should have been doing this anyway.

The other part was we couldn't find good help. One woman we hired stole my mother's painkillers. Another had a difficult time making it to work because she often missed the bus. And yet another had a young child who came along for the job then banged incessantly on Mom's glass coffee table. I had to let all of them go. I even had to fire the last woman while she held her child in her arms. I got tired of it, so I took over. I seemed like a logical choice: I was trustworthy, close-by, unattached, and needed all the financial help I could get. It would also be much easier, if need be, to fire myself.

So, when I wasn't subbing or slinging ribs, I went to Mom's place and cleaned and cooked and shopped for groceries. I did her laundry and arranged her closets and drawers. I clipped coupons and organized them by category in a Velcro wallet. I did this over and over and over again. Once a week, I sorted her pills into Dixie cups. I lined them up on the counter like little soldiers; Mom took the lip of the cup in her fragile talon and brought the pills to her mouth. She threw her head back and swallowed them all at once with water drawn through a straw. I made simple meals and put them on paper plates covered in plastic wrap. Each day, I carved out five minutes to swing by and empty her bedside commode. I carried the bucket to the toilet and flushed it. Mom had trained Reggie to do his business in the bathtub, so I gathered his poop in a wad of toilet paper and flushed that, too. I poured a spot of bleach into the tub then washed it down the drain with hot water.

Since Mom slept late, I tried to get all of this done in the morning so I could have the rest of the day to write stories for school. I was working on a collection called "The Primitive Streak," which is a term I'd learned in *Gray's Anatomy*: "the first traces of the embryo are seen as a faint streak, *the primitive streak*." I viewed my stories as embryonic, written from a narrow reservoir of experience. One of them was about a girl who went to the circus with her mother and watched a tightrope walker fall to her death. I wrote, "She watched her white boots rotate strangely around her straggling black hair, her sequins explode toward the netless, hay-strewn ground." Brenda Cuttin's death still haunted me, and so I wrote about it. I thought if I could wrap my arms around her death maybe I could make sense of it.

In the meantime, I was also grappling with life. My mother's life, in particular, but also my own. On those mornings I visited and did my chores, I tried not to wake her. In fact, I tried to avoid her. It wasn't that I didn't love my mother; I was just ashamed of myself and where I was in life. I felt like I should have been doing other things at twenty-five, things that did not include the daily cleaning of my mother's bedside toilet. There were thoughts I couldn't help thinking, and these thoughts filled me with guilt. My life would be easier without this extra burden, I thought. I would be farther along if she were just normal and healthy like other moms. She was holding me back. I resented my mother for being so sick for so long, and I resented my father for leaving me to deal with it all.

Then in the fall of 1993, there was a job available, "an exciting opportunity with a magazine startup," a chance to join a "small, dynamic team of industry professionals." There were other words in the pitch, in that tiny square in the *Fresno Bee* classified ad, words like *creative* and *independent* and *work from home*. The biggie for me, the one that really sold it, was *publishing*. I imagined myself like Robert Redford in *All the President's Men,* a world of deadlines and black coffee and a salty editor who growled things like, "Have it on my desk by noon." I imagined meeting a dark-suited source in a diner or parking garage, some guy in a porkpie hat who whispered "this has to be off the record" as he cased the scene with steely eyes. In my mind, it all seemed so mysterious and appealing.

This felt like the grown-up opportunity I was looking for. I could start telling people I was in publishing and they might just say, "Wow, how interesting." They might say, "That sounds really cool." I might just hold my head higher.

I applied and landed an interview with a young woman named Wendy. She gave me an address over the phone. It was not an address for an urban, downtown loft or glassy office building. It was to her home in a gated, North Fresno neighborhood. She told me what number to punch in on the keypad. Turned out, Wendy was not a salty, cigar-chewing editor-in-chief. She was a stay-at-home mom and the publisher of a new family monthly, which she envisioned would one day find its way into every doctor's office waiting room in the San Joaquin Valley, right along-side the tattered board-books and *Highlights* magazines I remembered as a kid. She had yet to print a single issue.

We sat at her dining room table, her "home office," she said. There was a child I could not see mewling from the other side of a safety gate. Wendy had pale skin and black hair in a bob and this sly, funny way of talking from one side of her mouth. That's not a metaphor meant to paint her as some kind of snake-oil saleswoman. She literally had a strange nerve thing going on, maybe Bell's Palsy, something I had myself while in college that paralyzed the right side of my face. I woke up on the day after Thanksgiving—exactly one year after my motorcycle crash—and I could not speak clearly or blink. In the mirror, the whole right side of my face seemed to sag from my skull like melting wax. I thought I was hav-ing a stroke. I was alone in my apartment and half my mouth wailed at my own reflection. Something was terribly wrong. You could have stuck a sewing needle in my cheek, and I would not have felt it. I got myself to the UCLA Medical Center, where a kind physician assured me that I was not dying. Turns out there had been trauma to my seventh cranial nerve—the facial nerve—the one that signals muscles in our faces to do things like smile and blink and smirk and make a moue. Eventually, he said, the facial nerve would recover, and I would feel things again, but I should carry a hankie because it was likely I would start drooling without realizing it.

During my interview, Wendy murmured. Her words slipped from her mouth as though she spoke with a cigarette between her lips. She asked about my "expurrience in sells," and I told her that out of college, I had sold long-term benefit care to small business owners in Long Beach. What I left out was that in the three weeks I spent with the company, I failed to make one sale.

"I am really interested in the publishing side," I said. "I'd really like to write."

Wendy said she was looking for an "Ad Man." I should have stopped her right there. I should have stood up from the table and said, "No thank you," that because of my father, any job having to do with ad sales was a major trigger for me. There was enormous potential for despair and addiction. Instead, I said nothing. I needed a job and selling advertising seemed more career-minded than waiting tables and less perilous than substitute teaching. In an eighth-grade wood shop class, a student once threw a padlock from the back of the classroom that buzzed past my ear and rattled off a bank of metal lockers behind me. It could have killed me. I knew I had to find something different.

So, advertising sales was it. I started to wonder if despite my efforts to avoid it, becoming my father was inevitable, a genetic code I could never reconfigure. Wendy said she would put "Sales Manager" on my business card, but that didn't mean I couldn't keep my ears open for a story, maybe a book fair at the local library or advice for parents on how to choose a summer camp, that sort of thing. "You can be a guest contributor," Wendy said. It wasn't the kind of gritty scoop I was looking for, but one of my professors told me that whenever you can get paid to write, you should, no matter what it is.

Wendy also said that if any of my ideas had traction she would let me draft a story. If I was too busy with all my selling, she would farm my stories out to Carey, the staff writer, a woman with thick glasses who told us every week at the staff meetings Wendy held at her dining room table what she had in the hopper. Wendy, who got excited about nothing, said that content drove sales, that one needed the other. This is how it worked in the world of magazine publishing, she said. Meanwhile, her unseen child threw soft blocks into the kitchen from the other side of the safety gate. Every so often, they just tumbled onto the floor, leaving me to wonder if there was intent behind them, maybe some kind of discrete distress signal. Maybe side-talking Wendy with the pale face and black bob and Eeyoric temperament had swiped a child from a public park and was holding it hostage in her formal dining room. Maybe if I collected the blocks and arranged them, they might spell out HELP.

My mind had a way of wandering during staff meetings with Wendy and Carey.

I started on a modest salary, something like three hundred a week, but the ultimate goal was straight commission. Wendy said she had analyzed the local market and knew there was money to be made. If I hustled, I could make double that in just a few months and she could wean me off the salary. It was hard to be enthusiastic for a woman who was strikingly gloomy. The bigger problem was an established player in the free family magazine space that Wendy wanted to invade. And then there was the fact that I was not a hustler, at least not for someone or something I couldn't believe in.

Still, I tried. I called on specialty shops and quaint bookstores with names like Kids' Kloset and Petunia's Place, alliterative boutiques that smelled of cinnamon run by chirpy women with acrylic fingernails. They all said the same thing: their ad dollars were already tied up in the competition. It didn't help that I had tender feelings, so I gave up politely without effort, *thanks for your time,* and after just a few months of contributing very little, I quit on Wendy. I don't think she was sad to see me go, but it was hard to tell with her. For me, there was never a worse fit jobwise, and Wendy was drowning because I wasn't a home-run hitter on the sales side. Or maybe it was just that Carey's stories were lousy. Content drove sales, after all. Maybe discerning advertisers took one look at the headlines—"Sanity and the Stay-at-Home Dad" or "Raising Confident Readers"—and didn't see the return on investment. Maybe they thought, like I did, that Wendy's magazine was fish wrap.

But here's the thing: I can't just cast aside those few months as a waste of time; nothing ever is. There is value in everything, even the stuff that seems worthless and painful when you're in the middle of it. What I realize now is that I *had* to be there, in that lousy job I was ill-suited to perform. I had to be there, not because it showed me a path that would have shackled me to a life of self-doubt and misery—my father's path—but because had I never been in *that* job, then I would never have found myself in Mom's neighborhood on a Wednesday in mid-January, 1994, calling on a piano teacher who worked out of her home and had expressed interest in a quarter-page ad in our upcoming issue. Wendy gave me the lead. My task was to convince this piano teacher that her money would be well-spent, that her quarter-page ad would reach the very people she needed to reach, and there was value in locking-in long-term: fifty-percent off the normal rate for a six-month placement, a professional favor from the publisher, because this piano teacher was Wendy's friend, someone who, in just a few years, would be teaching Wendy's block-throwing hostage-child "Yankee Doodle Dandy" and the dotted half-note.

It was a gray, cold day. My appointment was for 11:30, and I wore a brown string tie with a dress shirt, cotton slacks, brown leather shoes, and a tan barn coat. I sat across the street in my pickup until my watch said 11:29, then I walked to the front door. At exactly 11:30, I rang the bell and stood a respectable distance from the threshold with my leather planner, a gift from my mother, tucked under one arm. Even though I had been at this for a few months, I felt sick inside. It was the way I felt every time I stood before strangers knowing that my first job was to make a great impression, and my second job was to convince them why parting with their hard-earned money was a good idea even though I could not prove it. It felt smarmy. Imagine having to stand still while worms crawl all over you. It felt like that.

A minute later, I rang the bell again and stood rocking on my heels. I whistled and blew into my hands. The house was quiet and unlit. It had the feel of being empty. The whole block had that feel. There were very few cars on the street. The yards were tired and brown. I began to wonder if I had my day and time right, or even the place. The houses in this neighborhood were nondescript, most of them some variation of tan. Mom would have said they were beige. It was possible I was standing in front of the wrong house on the wrong street, all of which were named for trees: Maple, Fir, Pine, Elm. I opened my leather planner. It told me I was where I was supposed to be, when I was supposed to be there. I had numerous flaws at twenty-five, but being disorganized was not one of them. My shoes were lined up in my closet, my shirts hung lightest to darkest.

I went back to my pickup and waited where it was warm. At 11:45, I drove across the street to a pay phone in front of a grocery store. First, I called Wendy to double-check the details of my appointment. She said I had everything right. Wendy wanted to know if I was sure she wasn't there. "Did you try knocking instead of ringing?" she asked. "You know, sometimes people with small children disconnect their doorbells." I was sure, I told her. I could hear the bell ring. It was the kind of doorbell that played a tune. Wendy said you might expect that from a piano teacher.

"Call and leave a message," she told me. "Then have some lunch. Maybe drop by after you eat. You never know what might have hung her up. Could have been anything." I called the piano teacher and left a message. Then I stood there in the cold with extra time on my hands.

The grocery store with the pay phone happened to be where Mom shopped. There was a pharmacy inside where she got all her prescriptions filled. Next to the grocery store there was a hair stylist, a bagel place, and a pet supply store. There were two sub shops and a pizza joint; there was a postal annex. Mom used to say that she had everything she needed right in her own backyard.

After I hung up the phone, I walked to Mom's apartment. There was a path between the bagel shop and the hairdresser, and that path led to employee parking and an alley for delivery trucks. On the other side of the alley another path led to an opening in a cinder-block wall. Mom's apartment was on the other side. It was a two-story complex painted gray with slate blue trim. One building over from my mother, on the second floor, a Hmong tenant had recently been evicted for keeping two live chickens. The woman directly above Mom had a black cat, which eyed me suspiciously through wrought iron railing as I walked up just before noon.

My mother was still in bed. This was not a surprise to me. She often didn't stir until 11:30, just in time for the midday news. Her apartment was dark and, as usual, smelled faintly of urine. Like the piano teacher's house, it felt empty. I flipped on the lights in the front room and kitchen, and I went about the business of getting Mom ready to face the day. There was coffee to be brewed, so I got that started. I took off my coat and hung it over a chair. I loosened my tie. Mom liked to see me dressed up a bit, so I didn't take it off. Plus, I was going back to the piano teacher's place, so why bother.

There was a small fry pan on the stove with a layer of butter fat in the bottom and a plastic spatula in a spoon rest. When I got behind on meal prep, as I was then, my mother fried hot dogs in butter. She left the ketchup on the counter next to a bag of buns. Guilt surged through me. I felt it in my face and in my throat, which seemed to close in on itself. I had done nothing last night except sit on my couch, drink, and wallow. I could have come over and done something nice for my mother. I could have sliced an apple, or opened a can of chili, or grated some cheese. I could have sat with her while she ate; she would have offered me a hot dog.

In Mom's bedroom, Reggie was curled at her hip. He slept when she slept; after so long together, they shared bio-rhythms.

"Wake up, you two," I said. "Rise and shine." Reggie lifted his drowsy head. I gave him a tummy rub and he thumped his tail, then he stretched. Mom was on her back, asleep with her mouth open. I turned the blinds open. "Mom," I said. "Good afternoon." Some time ago, Medicare had funded a hospital bed for my mother. Normally, she used the up button to lift herself. Once she got comfortably upright, she would turn her legs and take hold of her walker. She had the strength to stand on her own, but not on that gray Wednesday. I told her she must have stayed up late the night before. I asked, "Did you party-hearty?"

I stood next to her hospital bed and raised her into a sitting position. She opened her eyes. "Hey," I said. I jostled her shoulder. "You having a hard time waking up this morning?" There was an oval mirror in a white wicker frame on the wall. I had lifted her so she could see her reflection in it.

My mother turned away from me to look into the mirror. She said, "My eyes."

"What about them?" I said. "What about your eyes?"

And then, as though charged by a current, her body bolted upright. Her legs swiveled over the edge of the bed and for an odd moment she sat with perfect posture; her body had moved with urgency and ease. It was like nothing I'd ever seen. There was an energy moving through my mother and she wore it, for just a moment, like an aura, like a glowing crown. She looked straight ahead into that wicker mirror and said again, "My eyes."

And again, I said, "What about your eyes?"

"They're crossing," she said.

I stood looking into the mirror, into my mother's eyes reflected back at me, and as soon as she said that her eyes were crossing, that's what they did. Her eyeballs converged on the bridge of her nose, and then the shaking started. She dropped to the carpet. I stepped around the foot of the bed, and right there in front of me, my mother's charged body quaked and seized and flopped in ways she could not have managed were she in control of her own movements. Right in front of me, my mother's face turned blue and she gurgled and gasped. I thought this was the moment I had known was coming since I was a boy. This was the way people passed from this world to whatever comes next, and I knelt close to her and took her head in my hands to keep it from banging into the wall. I cried. I said the kinds of things people in television dramas say when they sit on the brink of a loved one dying: *No, no, no, don't do this to me not now please please please oh God what is happening mama no not now oh please God.* I wailed as my mother shook. Somehow, I had the wherewithal to turn her head to one side as her tongue rolled from her foaming mouth.

When the seizure stopped, I held my mother's face. Her eyes were open and she was breathing heavily. She wore a necklace with an emergency response pendant, and I took one hand from my mother's face and pushed the button. A moment later, through a speaker on my mother's phone, a voice came through the line: "911, what's your emergency?" The best I could, I explained my emergency, my mother's emergency.

I explained the shaking, the contortions, the uncontrolled spasms, the whole thing about my mother's tongue and the foam slipping from her mouth onto the carpet. An ambulance, the voice said, was already on its way. She said to stay where I was, next to my mother. Tell my mother it was okay and that someone was coming to help. I didn't need to move, she said. There was a lock box on the doorknob, and this was all part of the emergency response procedure. I knew this. I knew there was an apartment key in that lock box, and the paramedic would have access to it, and I didn't have to worry. I could just hunker there next to my mother with her face in my hands and wait for the help to arrive. I could just give her comfort and tell her that everything was going to be okay, to just hold on and breathe and be calm because someone was coming. Someone was most surely coming.

That is what the voice told me.

In the hospital, shift nurses looked after me. Mom was in the Critical Care Unit, hooked up to a ventilator. There was a tube in her mouth sending oxygen to her lungs. I had a chair next to her bed. The first two days, nurses brought me soft drinks and packaged sandwiches and told me they thought it best if I leave for a while. Go home and shower, they told me. There is nothing you can do here.

I did as I was told. I left for a while. I went to Mom's apartment and got Reggie. I took his dog dishes and kibble. I put him up at my apartment and showed him where the bathtub was. I left him extra food and water in case I wound up being gone more than two days. Reggie was glum about the whole thing. Dogs know. I scratched his head and told him it would be okay. I held his face in my hands and looked into his black eyes, which at some point had started to go milky.

Days passed. My mother would not wake up. She had been placed in a "relaxed state," which was necessary because of the tube in her throat. In the afternoons, I sat next to her bed and talked her through game shows. One of the nurses said this was good for Mom, the talking. "She can hear you," the nurse said, and I asked how she knew this. "There have been studies," she said. The nurse told me that Mom could hear me with her ears and she could hear me with her soul. "We have different ways of hearing," she said, "so keep talking."

So I did. I talked her through Oprah and the evening news. I read to her from magazines I found lying around the waiting room. When I got tired of that, I read Flannery O'Connor stories, because I had brought a collection from my apartment. I read parts of "Good Country People" out loud. I read the part of Mrs. Hopewell with a higher pitch—"If you can't come pleasantly, I don't want you at all." I also told Mom how Manley Pointer reminded me of Jack. I told her I wouldn't have put it past Jack to trick a woman out of her fake leg. Then, because it seemed as good a time as any, I told her about the day I was cleaning Jack's trailer after he died and found an application he'd completed for some kind of death benefit from Marzelle. It might have been Social Security, I don't know. Jack had written on the form that my mother was dead, despite her being very much alive. "Can you believe that?" I said to Mom. "He tried to bilk you out of your share." My mom just lay there, her chest rising and falling under the influence of the ventilator. But if what the nurse said to me was right, Mom heard me. Why did I think she needed to know this about her brother? What good did this do?

I began staying long hours, and one nurse let me clean myself up with a warm cloth and a tub of soapy water. She brought me hospital-issue deodorant, a razor, some shaving cream. When I said I wasn't going home that night, she brought me a blanket and pillow. I slept on the couch in the waiting room, but it was fitful. The next day, I went to Mom's apartment and got a couple Vicodin and the following night was much better.

People came to see me. There was a social worker who talked about hospice and said that at some point I might want to consider managed comfort with morphine. There was a grief counselor, a nice woman who held my hand and told me that I had done well, that I was a good son. Because this was a Catholic hospital, I got a visit from a priest, who prayed for my mother and then for me. When he was finished, he made the sign of the cross and brought a gold crucifix to his lips to kiss the agonized Jesus.

There was another visitor, a sharp lady in a pressed skirt, and she carried papers for me to sign. "I know this is hard," she said. "I'm sorry." She asked how far the doctors should go to save my mother's life. I told her I wanted them to do everything they could. She handed me some papers on a clipboard. "Full-code then," she said.

"Damn right, full-code," I said. The fuller the code, the better. I initialed boxes and signed on lines and then initialed and signed again to indicate I understood what I had initialed and signed.

A couple more days passed before the conversation turned to ventilator withdrawal. The word I kept hearing was *extubation*. There were so many people talking to me. It was the sixth day and fatigue had long since taken hold. There was a doctor and a nurse, and I sat on my sofabed in the waiting room and listened to them tell me that my mother had lost the ability to function. The situation was grave, they said. It looked to them like things were *imminent*. This made me cry some more. It made my shoulders heave. The doctor and nurse said that with the right mix of medication and equipment, they could remove the tube and Mom could die peacefully. I could be there with her, right by her side, just as it should be. Mother and son to the end. I put my face in my hands and blubbered. There was a decision to be made and it was left to me to make it. I lifted my head and looked around the waiting room. I realized I had no one in the world with whom to consider this. And because I was so tired, because I had started harboring thoughts about a new life in a new city after all of this was over—awful thoughts I couldn't help thinking—I agreed to the extubation. I told the doctor and the nurse to go ahead with it.

By then, there were others in the waiting room. The social worker was back. So was the grief counselor. There was a chaplain instead of a priest. On some piece of paper I had written the word Presbyterian, which would explain the clergy swap. The chaplain would be there with me to pray us through the process of Mom's dying. The people in the waiting room began to bustle. They made whispered preparations. I remember what I said to myself: "She never got a chance to be a grandmother." That was my greatest regret, my biggest failure. This made me feel deficient, and even worse, I thought of myself as a murderer. "I just signed my mother's death warrant," I said.

The social worker told me I did no such thing. She held my hand. My body filled with anguish. "You did everything you could," she said. "Your mother is so proud of you."

"I just killed her," I said. Fatigue had rendered me irrational. "How could she be proud of me?"

I buried my face in my hands.

Then, another voice. A different nurse, one I had never seen. She knelt next to me and spoke softly. "It's not too late to change your mind," she said. I lifted my face to hers, but I cannot remember what she looked like. I can sketch her out, but it would be a caricature, nothing more. I could say she had a plump face, auburn hair pulled into a bun, a small mole on her upper lip, green eyes. I could say she smelled like hand lotion, that her high cheekbones had a sheen, that her chin had a barely perceptible cleft. I could say she wore a cameo pendant. She seems like someone I should never forget, but everything about her has vanished from my memory, everything but her words: "It's not too late to change your mind."

So, that's what I did. I told this nurse who I cannot remember that I had changed my mind. "Please," I said. "It was a mistake." She said she would get to work on it, that the tube would not come out that night. It was a Saturday night, the 29th of January, and it may not have been late, but it was dark. I walked outside without a blanket around my shoulders. I was alone and sat on a concrete ramp somewhere on the hospital grounds. Fluorescent lights glowed in bars over my head and whatever warmth there had been in the winter sun had gone, replaced by chill.

I considered my standing with God. I had been a lousy believer. I figured this was my punishment. I figured the source of my troubles was my recalcitrance, my last few years of kicking and screaming. Whatever faith I once had eroded to almost nothing, but what I remembered that night on that concrete ramp was this: all I needed was a mustard seed. All I needed was that much, and I had that, so I pulled my knees up to my chest and I closed my eyes and I prayed out loud.

I am certain I told God that I was bad and had no right to come before Him and ask for a favor. I likely made promises He knew I wouldn't keep, something that sounded an awful lot like, "If you just do this one thing for me, then I'll . . . go to church every Sunday. Quit drinking. Stop entertaining impure thoughts." There were so many things I could have put in that blank. All I can offer for that part of my prayer is context, a paraphrase, but I do remember the angry part, the bit where I said, "If you're going to take her, just do it already! Either take her tonight or give her back to me!" I remember saying, "I can't take it anymore!" I had been talking to my mother for seven days and had gotten nothing by way of response. It was enough to make me crazy.

After my rant to God, I didn't feel a whole lot different. There was no sudden, bright light, no comforting voice. It was just me with my back against a cold concrete wall, my tired eyes closed. Me, lifting myself off the ground, walking back inside the hospital, through the long, sterile halls to the waiting room, my sofa-bed and knapsack containing pilfered Vicodin. An old friend of mine once called it a "religious drug," because when he took one, he saw God. That's what I was hoping for as I swallowed a pill with day-old soda. I lay down under my hospital blanket and fell asleep.

Morning came, and with it a nurse, another new one who shook my shoulder. "Mr. Radke," she whispered. "Mr. Radke?" I'm afraid I don't remember what she looked like, either. I won't venture another caricature, because what is most important was her voice, and the words she spoke as she ushered me awake, words that I heard with my ears, that I heard with my soul: "Your mother is wide awake and she wants to see you."

18

What Does Poor Look Like to You?

"Dear Mom,

I hope you are making wonderful walking progress and that you aren't feeling so much pain. Remember, your goal is to get lots of exercise and learn to walk with a cane."

—Card to my mother, February 18, 1994

I DON'T KNOW HOW IT WAS ALL RELATED. THERE WAS A stroke, a gran mal seizure, pulmonary aspiration, pneumonia, all happening at once, over the course of several hours. I don't know how that's possible. It was explained to me, but I had been sleeping fitfully on a waiting room sofa for a week, taking expired Vicodin. It seemed like there were a thousand people talking to me at once. And I had been negotiating with God. That makes me unreliable when it comes to reporting details of a medical nature. I remember the words for what went wrong but not the sequence. I do remember I wasn't surprised. My mother was a life force; her body could fail catastrophically in many ways and she could always pull through.

At some point during her perfect storm, Mom inhaled food into her lungs. Her epiglottis got lazy and let pieces of hot dog pass into her windpipe. Hot dog, of all things. I found a way to blame myself: If only I had gone to her place the night before I found her. If only I had made her something better to eat. *If only I had, If only I had.* I ruminated constantly. I beat myself up for being self-absorbed, and since beating yourself up is a kind of self-absorption, I was doubling-down.

There was a young doctor. He looked barely older than me, maybe thirty, and he'd been in the critical care unit for a few months. He came from the UC Davis School of Medicine in Sacramento. His name was Dr. Thompson. He had straight black hair, a dark, flawless complexion, a boyish face and wire-rimmed glasses. He was the guy who saved my mother's life. Dr. Thompson fished out the aspirated hot dog. Because of that, I couldn't resent him, but in any other circumstance, I would have. He seemed superior to me in every way, and when I sat with him, I felt purposeless.

Dr. Thompson tapped the glass, then slid back the door of Mom's room. He walked in and eased the door closed behind him. "How's the patient?" he asked, and I said something insipid: "As good as could be expected."

He leaned close to her face, settled a thumb on her cheek, and shined a penlight into Mom's eyes. Then he asked her to open her mouth. She did. He used the penlight to look into her throat. Hours earlier, some skilled folks in blue scrubs had extubated my mother. Her throat hurt. She had a board in her lap with magnetic letters that she used to communicate things. She slid the letters into place to make words. Before Dr. Thompson came, when it was just the two of us, Mom brought her left hand to her throat. There was pain in her eyes.

I said, "I know, it hurts." I told her I was sorry. Then on her letter board, with the same hand, she spelled FIRE. Her throat was on fire, she said. She pushed a red button and a nurse came with an eye dropper filled with codeine and squeezed it into the side of my mother's mouth. She suckled at the eyedropper. This was how it worked. A nurse came when my mother pushed a button and gave her things to numb pain. My mother craved this numbing. She pushed the red button with her able thumb every half-hour. She slid letters into place on her board: PAIN, WATER, THANK YOU, SLEEP, things like that.

For Dr. Thompson, my mother spelled TIRED.

"I expected that," he said. "You had a close call." He perched on a stool on one side of her bed. I sat on the other side. We looked at one another over my mother's body as her face drew up in worry.

"Barbara," Dr. Thompson said. "You won't be able to go home for a few months. In fact," he said. "I've asked your son to look into nursing home placement."

When he said that, my insides went hollow.

When my mother was a young girl, Lloyd and Marzelle referred to the county nursing home as the "poor house." It was where old folks who couldn't care for themselves—who weren't lucky enough to have kids to take them in—were sent to live out the rest of their lives on the government's dime. One of these homes was on the outskirts of Joliet, Illinois, where Mom grew up. It sat at the end of a long dirt drive with nothing behind it but a blank horizon. There was a lonesomeness about the place. My mother believed it was filled with wistful spirits trapped in the attic, the souls of the unloved. On Sunday drives, Lloyd pointed out the home as a general point of interest. "There's the poor house," he would say. "You don't want to end up there," and my mother never forgot this. She told herself she would never end up in the poor house. She said she would rather die first.

That's why the words "nursing home" sent her into tears. It's why it filled her gut, and mine, with emptiness. I had been wondering how, after her stay in rehab, I could take her in. I had thought about buying my own house, putting Mom in a back bedroom or a cozy cottage with a big yard, then hiring a real nurse to manage her care. And maybe that nurse would be young and attractive and single, and we would fall in love. Maybe once Mom nodded off for the night, this young, attractive nurse could join me on the sofa in the living room and we could drink wine with something mellow in the CD player, maybe Miles Davis, and we could talk about our days and everyone would feel safe and be loved. And this nurse would carry out these duties with a joyful heart, without an ounce of resentment, because it was her life's calling to care for the elderly. She would say things like, "Your mom is such a joy to be around." She would nuzzle my neck and whisper, "You're such a good son." She would tell me there was a special place in heaven for me. My mind went to places like this all the time. It was exhausting. I imagined scenarios in which I was dutiful and wealthy and married and guilt-free, and Mom was close by, not in a nursing home, not in the poor house. It wasn't realistic, not a bit of it.

"Barbara," Dr. Thompson said. "Have you thought about a nursing home?" She turned away from him and looked at me. I have only seen that look one time since: the day I took my infant daughters to get their first shots. One at a time, they smiled at me from the exam table until the instant the needle went in, then their eyes filled with hurt as though to say, "How? How can you look so kind and loving but still betray me?" They looked at me as though I were the agent of their pain. That was how my mother looked at me.

"How?" she seemed to say. "How can you look so kind and loving but still betray me?"

She looked away from me to her magnetic message board. She snuffled. She spelled NO. Then she found two more letters. Next to her first NO, she spelled NO again. She was yelling at me. She turned the board so Dr. Thompson could see it. She was yelling at him, too. If there were exclamation marks on this board, she would have lined them up like fence pickets. Nursing home was not an option. My mother was only fifty-five, and nursing homes were for old people.

Dr. Thompson grinned. He liked Mom's fighting spirit. "You will have your work cut out for you, then," he said. "There will be long days."

I told Dr. Thompson what my mother could not. "She can handle it," I said, but it was kind of late for me to swoop in and testify to her grit. In her mind, I had already lined up her final residence.

"You will have to show miraculous progress," Dr. Thompson said.

My mother arranged her letters into the word FINE. She made sure both of us saw it. She was yelling again. She would have loved nothing more than to stand up and march out of that fish tank and threaten us with her knotted fist and scream, "I'll show you both!" But the truth was her situation was dire. She was attached to things that were keeping her alive. The young doctor was right: It would take a miracle.

Days later, Mom was discharged to a rehab hospital. She had a room of her own with a nice television and shiny Pergo floors. She had her own valet, someone who came every morning to push her to physical therapy, then occupational therapy, then speech therapy. My mother re-learned things. She learned to stand up and sit down. She learned how to lie in bed, then move to a sitting position. She learned to brush her teeth and hair and write using a pen in a fat foam sleeve. She learned to eat with curved utensils, to squeeze putty, to say "how now brown cow."

In the three months she was in rehab, I paid rent on her apartment as though she were there. I went in and out of her place. I collected her mail every couple of days. When her neighbors saw me, they asked after her. They said, "I haven't seen your mom and her dog around," and I told them she was under the weather but doing fine, just fine, thank you. I told them she'd be up and about again soon.

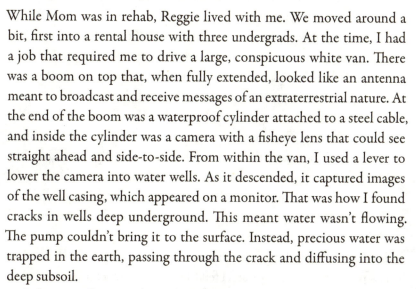

While Mom was in rehab, Reggie lived with me. We moved around a bit, first into a rental house with three undergrads. At the time, I had a job that required me to drive a large, conspicuous white van. There was a boom on top that, when fully extended, looked like an antenna meant to broadcast and receive messages of an extraterrestrial nature. At the end of the boom was a waterproof cylinder attached to a steel cable, and inside the cylinder was a camera with a fisheye lens that could see straight ahead and side-to-side. From within the van, I used a lever to lower the camera into water wells. As it descended, it captured images of the well casing, which appeared on a monitor. That was how I found cracks in wells deep underground. This meant water wasn't flowing. The pump couldn't bring it to the surface. Instead, precious water was trapped in the earth, passing through the crack and diffusing into the deep subsoil.

I drove to farms and ranches in the Central Valley and met with farmers having trouble with their water wells. We drank black coffee and hitched our feet up on the van's front bumper and talked about things like nematodes and drought resistance and pump capacity and flow rates. They catalogued their difficulties and I did my best to stomach their coffee, which one farmer called "coffee you could chew." They would climb into the passenger side of the van and navigate me to the source of their troubles, holes in the ground no wider than a Frisbee that gurgled brown mucky-muck and did nothing to sustain their crops, which would suffer further unless I could find the problem.

It was a job that didn't last long. The guy who owned the van sold it. He gave me a small severance for my troubles, enough for me to leave the raucous rental and find a place of my own in a forties-era fourplex downtown. My place was on the second level, upper left as you looked at the front of the building. There was hardwood throughout, a Murphy bed, and a screened-in sun porch where I drank coffee and wine, depending on the hour, while reading the likes of Raymond Carver and Alice Munro. Every morning, Reggie lounged in the bars of light that stretched across the sunroom floor. This was my writer's hovel. I felt especially like a writer because I had hardwood floors and a Murphy bed and a dog that bathed in sunlight by my feet.

I was working two jobs. A few nights a week, I tended bar at a packed nightclub near my place. People threw bills around, people I should have cut-off, but they parted so easily with their money, much of which wound up in my tip jar. After last call, I found these people asleep in booths. I worried they were dead. I poked at them with a broom handle. "Hey," I'd say. "Time for you to go." I jabbed them until they lifted their heads and assessed their situations, the house lights up, our barmaid collecting empties from cocktail rounds. "Time to go," I'd say again. When they slurred at me, when they'd manage to ask, "Can you call me a cab?" I couldn't help myself. I was sober. I was snarky. I was tired. I'd say, "You're a cab."

By day, while working on my master's degree, I was a TA in the English Department at Fresno State. I felt like a grown-up. I taught Freshman Composition, and on the first day of class, I gave my students a diagnostic. I remember telling them that I was like their writing doctor. I needed to draw blood from them and run some tests and see what was going on inside, to see if something was wrong. I had been around so many doctors with my mother that the metaphor was comfortable. The assignment was pretty elementary: "Describe the person in your life who has had the greatest influence on you." I gave them fifteen minutes to freewrite on this influential person, not a long time, but neither are blood tests. In return, I was given platitudes: "My mother was always there for me" or "My father was my rock." I was given this one, too, about a best friend: "She has always been my partner in crime." None of it showed me anything of these people and their influential personalities.

The following week, in an effort to fix this problem, I talked about the difference between abstract and concrete. We analyzed a piece of microfiction called "Cheers" by Jayne Anne Phillips. I read the whole story out loud in two minutes. I read the words "Row of skinny houses on a mud alley" and I said, "See how the words paint a picture? Do you *see*?" Some of my students nodded as though they really did see. I felt like I was reaching a few of them. I explained that "Row of skinny houses on a mud alley" is a vivid picture of a poor neighborhood, an image that carries more weight than, "The sewing woman was poor." The first shows you poor; the second shows you nothing because people have different pictures of *poor*. I asked my students, "What does poor look like *to you*?" To Jayne Anne Phillips, poor looked like a row of skinny houses on a mud alley. "Now you try it," I said. "Use your words to show me *poor*."

Only my students from poverty understood this assignment. One wrote that *poor* was a broken refrigerator on its side in his front yard. I remember this. I thought it was sad that as a kid, he walked by that refrigerator on his way to school in the mornings. Another kid wrote about his father's work clothes draped over a fence, drying in the sun. And there was a girl who described her red, swollen feet, the product of having to wear shoes that were too small. I felt awful over this assignment. Maybe they didn't want to reflect on their poverty and there I was, holding their faces right up to it.

Then there were the students who didn't like *poor,* as an image, that is; they wouldn't—or couldn't—visualize it. "Can I choose another abstract word? Lonely or beautiful? Can I choose rich?"

I said, "Have at it." I told them to show me lonely or beautiful or rich. Just don't use the words *lonely* or *beautiful* or *rich* when you show me.

"You have ten minutes," I said.

I would have loved a full paragraph, but I would have settled for an image, something like the broken refrigerator on its side in the front yard. These kids who didn't know *poor* tapped their pens against their teeth. They stared out the window and yawned. They put their heads down. They didn't write anything until I said, "One more minute," and then they wrote whatever came to them. They wrote furiously. I said, "Let's hear what you came up with," and this is how most of them began: *Words cannot describe...*

"But that is your job," I said. "Your job is to use words to describe."

And that's when it hit me. I have only anecdotal evidence to support this, but I believe it nonetheless: Poor kids are better at seeing. Two years later, as a Freshman Comp TA in Miami, I would witness it again, this time with Cuban refugees, who wrote heartbreaking essays about cramming aboard homemade boats bound for Florida and having to toss their dead loved ones into rough seas. Their English was barely functional, but their descriptions were vivid and pure, because they wrote from a place of real pain. Here's my theory: The poor see things better because they have much less to see. And this led me to something more: When I was a kid, the adults around me—teachers, mostly—always said how observant I was. They said, "Wow, I never noticed that." It was never anything earth-shattering, maybe a chip in a coffee mug or a wall clock that didn't hang quite right. I was fussy over detail, even then. I was also poor. I operated constantly from a position of discomfort and worry, something I managed to displace temporarily by focusing on minutiae, through seeking out and finding tiny faults in my surroundings, little fissures that told me brokenness was everywhere, that it wasn't just me.

In the spring of 1996, for her fifty-eighth birthday and fortieth high school reunion, I bought Mom a round-trip ticket to Chicago. Her best friend Jan from the Joliet Township High Class of '56 met her at the airport and looked after her for a week. They scuttled about town to Mom's old house, to their school, to Caterpillar, where Mom once worked. She wrote to me about it: "Saw all, and I do mean ALL, of my old stomping grounds yesterday." They went to the reunion in the high school gym and reminisced with old classmates and said things like "You haven't changed a bit," and "Where have all the years gone?" She was eating well and sleeping well and "having a very nice life right now," she wrote.

I stopped on that phrase, "a very nice life right now," and I thought about what it meant to Mom at that time, after her big scare, when she was told she could lose her apartment, when Dr. Thompson said it would take a miracle. What might she have said were she one of my students and I had asked her to show me what "a very nice life" looks like? She would not have said "Words cannot describe . . ." Instead, she would have offered something visceral, because she was so good at seeing and feeling. She would have offered me the vivid, the simple, the pleasant. She would have offered images that neither of us would have taken for granted because she taught me how to see. She would have shown me what "a very nice life" looked like to her: a patio with a pool view, a small black dog in her lap, a plastic spatula in a spoon rest.

She would have shown me things just like that.

19

The *Potato Quarterly* Is Where You'll Stay

"Dear Chuck,

I'm having a great time here in Jolietland and don't know
how I've survived these past years in an apartment in Fresno,
California."

—Letter from my mother, June 28, 1996

THERE WAS A CATHOLIC CHURCH JUST DOWN THE STREET
from my fourplex in Fresno. It was called the Shrine of Saint Therese,
named for a young French nun from the late 1800s who struggled with
depression and what, at the time, were known as *scruples,* causeless and
sometimes overwhelming feelings of guilt. I could identify with Saint
Therese. Every day, I felt sad and guilty for no reason. When people
were upset, I thought it was because of something I did. I told myself I
could write a book on feeling sad and guilty. That's what Saint Therese
did. It's called *The Story of a Soul,* an autobiography that covers her brief
life under heaven; she died at twenty-four after a painful struggle with
tuberculosis. Still, she managed to write a best-seller before she died.

Here's what Saint Therese, the "Little Flower of Jesus," had to say about
God Almighty: "He allowed my soul to be overwhelmed with darkness,
and the thought of heaven [. . .] now became a subject of conflict and torture." *Conflict and torture?* A nun wrote this. Did she not think she was

good enough to please God? She wrote that you have to pass through a dark tunnel to understand its blackness. Springsteen said something similar, only instead of a tunnel, it was a dark grove of trees with the River of Life somewhere on the other side. In his metaphor, Bruce said he stood paralyzed by fear until he was rescued by a gypsy woman, and I imagine it was the same for the virgin nun, only without the gypsy. One day, Saint Therese hoped, she might be set free from the land of darkness and released into that River of Life, but her writing suggests she was sad and doubtful to the end. Here's the sentence that resonates deepest with me: "He knows that I try to live by Faith, though it does not afford me the least consolation." It didn't matter how faithful Saint Therese was; in her mind, she wasn't good enough and she remained mired in anguish.

I was still tending bar and making crazy money. One-fifty in tips was expected, and this afforded me opportunities to do things on a whim. One time, I did. On a Monday, I bought a round-trip plane ticket to Chicago for that Friday; a spirit beckoned me there.

I had a bizarre, unfounded love affair with Chicago. Maybe it was that my mother spent her young life in Joliet. She graduated from high school, did some secretarial work, and before she lit out for California in the summer of 1958, she graduated from Chicago's Patricia Vance School of Charm and Modeling. She earned a certificate, which I still have. It's inside a keepsake chest along with a stack of letters bound in a black velvet ribbon from her first boyfriend, a doctoral student in pharmaceutical chemistry named Jim Muren, who was studying in Madison, Wisconsin, and was clearly over the moon for her: "The frequency with which I make the trip to Joliet will depend more or less on how much encouragement I get from you, young lady!" he wrote.

My mother was apparently coy and a bit evasive. She was also sick. Lovestruck Jim Muren, in another letter, wrote that he was developing a drug called "Barbaramyacin" meant to help my mother through constant bouts of fatigue; she was just nineteen. Jim Muren worried over her. She "seemed so tired all the time," he wrote. This is a man who would go on to have an enormously successful career at Pfizer, where he was VP of Manufacturing for thirty-four years. He spent his life making drugs for sick people. The irony is almost too much to bear: If there were one person in the world who could have helped my mother, it seems to me it would have been Dr. Jim Muren, maker of drugs.

In Chicago, I stayed in a hotel on Lake Michigan. I watched a Cubs doubleheader at Wrigley on Saturday and drank a dozen Old Styles in the left field bleachers with a guy named Pumpkinhead and his coterie of drunken friends. By the seventh-inning stretch of game two, we had our arms draped around one another like European soccer fans. We sang along with Harry Caray. After the second game, we went bar-stumbling in Wrigleyville. I had all of these new best friends, and it just so happened that Pumpkinhead was looking for a third roommate to live in his brownstone. I could live there, he told me. He would get me a job at the tire place where he worked. It was a sales job, but everyone in Chicago needed tires, so it was good work. I told him I had spent a little time in sales. "You need to move out here," he said. "I'll take care of everything." It was all settled then. I would pack my things and move to Pumpkinhead's Chicago brownstone and sell tires with him. At that moment, I didn't want to be anywhere else but Chicago. We sealed the deal with a shot of something that lit my throat on fire.

Then came Sunday morning, when I rode the elevator down to the lobby with John Larroquette, and thought I might puke on his shiny shoes. All the way to O'Hare, I hung my head out the window of the smoky cab. I was sweating beer on the plane ride back to Fresno. Before takeoff, I kept the airsick bag open in my lap and waited for the little vent overhead to start hissing cool air, which took an unreasonable amount of time.

After my visit to Chicago, I made my life intentionally predictable. I worked every day and most nights. I locked up the bar every Saturday, which meant Sundays were for sleeping, except at the Shrine of Saint Therese, where the campanile tolled before Mass and Catholic families said their Our Fathers and remembered their sins and asked for mercy. That was as close to God as I got in those days.

Sundays were also for reading. I read hundreds of short stories. It was a genre I could handle. I could flirt with the short story, whereas novels required commitment. So, I stuck with stories. I read Tobias Wolff and two Jameses: Joyce and Salter. I read William Trevor and Susan Minot and T. C. Boyle. I went through a Nabokov phase, and then John Cheever. I read every story in the annual *Best American,* and I dreamed of one day seeing my name there.

I wasn't just reading; I was writing and sending my stories out. I collected rejection slips by the dozens. I aimed high—*The New Yorker, Atlantic, Ploughshares*—because one of my professors told me that if I only sent stories to the *Potato Quarterly Review,* then I would forever be a *Potato Quarterly* kind of writer. He was a Southerner, a writer with gorgeous talent and slim, tapered fingers and a fashionable drawl. I wanted to be Southern, too. In our writer's workshops, he made Southern sound so relaxed and warm. "If you only send stories to the *Potato Quarterly,* the *Potato Quarterly* is where you'll stay," he said.

So, I aimed high and took pride in my rejection slips. On workshop nights, my classmates and I brought them in like show-and-tell pieces. We passed them around the table and admired one another's failures. They were mostly prescriptive quarter-sheets letting us know our stories were not what the journal was looking for. I taped my own to one of the windows in my sunroom and arranged them in a hierarchy, *The New Yorker* on top. In fact, that *New Yorker* rejection slip featured *actual* handwriting from an actual *New Yorker* editor: "Nicely written, but not what we're looking for at this time." *Nicely written!* My classmates were impressed. It was a story called "Seeking Dust" about a forgetful old woman, a widow, who rummaged through her artifacts to construct her personal history. It began the way so many recollection narratives do, with the woman sorting through old pictures, then pausing to meditate on a photo of her glum-looking parents, her high-collared mother seated at the hip of her father in a dark wool suit. I used the picture to evacuate the old woman from her present to her happier, albeit impoverished, past; I used it as a key to unlock her memories. I am quite certain the word *sepia* appeared in this story, likely multiple times, because when a young writer describes an old photograph, *sepia* is the one word that strikes him as indispensable.

My businesslike approach eventually paid off. In the fall of 1994, I entered a contest for unpublished writers—the AWP's "Intro Award"—and I was one of eight winners whose work would appear in the Fall 1995 *Hayden's Ferry Review,* a student-run literary journal out of Arizona State. I was proud; I felt as though I was on the verge of something much bigger. My newfound confidence was out of proportion to my talent, but I would not have believed it then. Later that year, with a publication under my belt, I audaciously applied to the Iowa Writers' Workshop because I thought I could write like T. C. Boyle, whose title story in *Greasy Lake* featured a strafed, hauntingly familiar landscape and a narrator who wanted to be bad but at his worst was nothing more than a low-level delinquent.

Iowa turned me down. I cried when I read the letter. My writing samples weren't strong enough. I wasn't the kind of writer the program was looking for at the time. I had been hearing that a lot, it seemed. I suppose it was kinder than saying "Your writing stinks."

Hayden's Ferry Review took six poems and two short stories by unpublished writers for Issue 17, which featured a still-life of two pears casting long shadows on its cover. My story was called "Alaska" and its point-of-view character was a guitar player in a predictable relationship with a barmaid. I set the story in the Astro Motel and Bar, right there near my mother's old trailer, because in workshop one night, our Southern professor gave us some advice: "If you write a scene in downtown At-a-lanta that takes place at a Burger King on Peachtree Street," he drawled, "in real life there had better be a Burger King on Peachtree Street in downtown At-a-lanta."

So, I chose the Astro, a hundred yards from the Golden State Highway between Shields and Dakota avenues in southwest Fresno, an easy walk or wheelchair ride to the mobile estate park. Those nights I languished outside with Mom at Sunset West, those nights she sat with Reggie in her lap and stroked his neck with her crooked fingers, I conjured settings I felt must be more appealing than the place I actually found myself. I could not have imagined at the time that anyone would have taken interest in a slummy bar next to a trailer park and a trucker's highway, but as it turned out, that was exactly what I needed to imagine. In my award letter, the judges applauded my use of place, my sense of detail, my location skills. I had made them see what my characters saw. The word "acute" was in that letter; I believe it was attached to the word "observations."

The story itself wasn't as impactful. It was a take on the Boy Loses Girl archetype featuring the aforementioned guitar player and barmaid, two characters loosely based on my parents, though my mother was never a barmaid nor my father ever a guitar player. I made the guitar player a weak man with a choice to make: the safe woman who wouldn't hurt him or the free-spirited floozy who filled his head with visions of adventure in far-off lands like Alaska or, as long as I'm making real-life comparisons, Montana. This would make the floozy my dad's girlfriend Patty, who before she ran off with someone else, convinced my father that life would be much more exciting with her, something he believed in the deepest part of his soul, and that made him just one more in history's long, long line of stupid, shortsighted men who followed a pretty predictable pattern.

I was paid in contributor's copies, which I have jettisoned to a cabinet in my garage where they molder with similar paychecks from *Gulfstream Magazine* and *South Dakota Review* and a few dozen paperbacks I cannot bear to give away. On the back cover of that *Hayden's Ferry Review,* I am listed alphabetically after Alexander Pushkin, who wrote a poem called "Romance" in 1814 while he was still in high school and which was subsequently translated and republished over a hundred and sixty years later by a writer named Lee B. Croft. Pushkin's name listed above mine is nothing more than an alphabetical anomaly, which over the years I have trotted out as cocktail party fodder when mentioning that once I used to write: "See, there I am. Right under Alexander Pushkin."

But here's the more interesting part, at least for me. I said there were two short stories published in Issue 17 of *Hayden's Ferry Review,* the issue with the two shadow-casting pears. The second is called "We Take Care of Our Own," and by sheer coincidence, it's by a writer who shares my mother's name: Barbara Lewis. The story covers some pretty familiar ground: It's about an eighty-four-year-old Jewish woman named Helen Grossman who suffers from arthritis, from "useless throbbing fingers," and who relies on a young homecare worker from South Africa named Bertha. Helen is bound to a wheelchair and takes so many pills that she has lost track of what Bertha gives her. The two learn to tolerate, then even care for one another, but when Bertha forgets to fill a prescription, Helen's daughter Carol gives her the heave-ho. The title drips irony: Carol does not take care of her mother, not even close. But she thinks she is taking care of her when she fires Bertha: "I don't know how they treat family where you come from," she says, "but in this country, we take care of our own." She says this while her large, manicured hands cover Helen's tiny shoulders.

Mom eventually graduated from the rehab hospital and went back to her apartment. She returned better than she was before, and she was now doing things like scrapbooking and water therapy. In fact, the apartment manager installed a contraption on the pool deck that lifted her into and out of the shallow end. I had to take Mom to buy herself a swimsuit, which took approximately four days if you tallied up all the hours she spent trying on suits in the JC Penney's dressing room while I brought one after the other from the old lady section and handed them over the curtain. She eventually settled on one that looked like something from the 1920s, a black number with fringe and bloomers.

I laid back in a chaise longue with a book while Mom held on to the side and performed these little scissor-kicks under water, first one leg, then the other. This caught the attention of the rental agent, a sweet, middle-aged woman with round eyeglasses and a mean ex-husband. Her name was Pam and she had a swimsuit and she told me she didn't mind watching over my mother while she did her exercises. She got right in the pool with her and the two of them scissor-kicked in the shallow end and grew chummy. Pam sold Shaklee and had the inside track on a bunch of bee pollen, which Mom wound up buying and spooning into her yogurt because Pam said it increased energy and decreased inflammation. "You should try it," Mom told me. "Honest to God, I've never felt better." Pretty soon, Pam and Mom were spending so much time together swimming and swallowing bee pollen that I offered to pay her.

I said, "You're here anyway, you may as well make some money," and sure enough, Pam took every one of the eighty hours a month the county allotted for Mom's in-home care, and I was out of a job.

Reggie was back in the apartment, too, though I could tell that his body was shutting down. He survived until the night before Thanksgiving. Mom and I sat with him as he refused food and water. He lay on his side and threw up. I put him on her bed in his basket and let her scratch his muzzle until he fell asleep. Then she said I should take him, so I did. I carried him in his basket to my pickup, then I drove him to an emergency vet who gave me the option of very expensive kidney surgery in northern California, which may have bought Reggie six more months. My other option, the one that had me walking into Mom's apartment later that night with an empty dog basket, cost me seventy-five dollars. My mother burst into tears.

Six weeks later, we drove into the foothills in response to a classified ad in the *Fresno Bee*. There were teacup poodles up that way, a whole passel of them. On a Saturday morning during Christmas break, I drove my mother to a small ranch house turned puppy mill. Inside, there were poodle puppies scampering about the living room behind plastic safety gates. The woman in charge told us the puppies couldn't be outside. "Up here," she said, "there's predators." She said there were hawks, coyotes, foxes, snakes, and any one of them could make off with a puppy in seconds, though it might take longer for the snake. I told her I saw her point. I told her that would be an awful thing to witness. "Oh, I seen it happen," she said, but before she could go into detail, I cut her off.

"It's okay," I said. "We believe you."

"So now they all inside," she said. "Every last one of 'em. They all nice and safe."

Despite every puppy outfitted in a newborn diaper, the carpet was badly stained. The stench choked off air to my lungs. I was wheezing within seconds of being inside. Imagine all those puppies in diapers, none of them looking as though they'd been changed that day. Mom and I wanted to take them all. We wanted to tackle the puppy mill lady and spring the safety gates and scream at the puppies to make a run for it, but that would only be worse. It would be like that episode of *Tom and Jerry,* the one where Tom tries to lure Jerry into a mouse-sized hotel, the door of which happens to be Tom's open mouth. We wouldn't have wanted to send the puppies into a coyote's open mouth, so we rescued just one, handing over a stack of cash in exchange for a black male teacup in a diaper along with what I am sure must have been phony AKC papers. It didn't matter. Mom loved that little dog, and living alone like she did, she needed the company. She needed his warmth in her lap and his black eyes to look into and his tiny pink tongue to lick her cheek. She named him Sammy, after Sammy Sosa, who at the time was hitting thirty to forty home runs a year as the Chicago Cubs' right fielder. This was in keeping with her pattern: first Reggie Jackson, now Sammy Sosa.

The road to the puppy mill took us through the small town of Friant, which sat at the base of a concrete gravity dam. Were that dam to break, it would be curtains for the town's 509 slow-footed citizens. We drove by Cliff Finch's Topiary Zoo, Acme World Auto Sales, and after that, a fish hatchery, and all of those places wound up in my second published story, "Fish Talk," about a warden whose daughter goes away to college—to UCLA—but comes back in the spring because she's pregnant and wants to be home to have her baby.

The story is kind of a caper, really, but it's not too difficult to figure out. The warden has this young assistant, a down-on-his-luck Hispanic kid named Jimmy, and after the warden's daughter Meredith comes home, Jimmy skulks around the hatchery full of nerves and electricity.

The warden goes so far as to drive his county-issue Ford Taurus with a whip antenna down to UCLA because he thinks he'll be able to find the father of his grandchild and drag his no-account tail back to Fresno to own his responsibility. He's been given one clue. The father of the baby, Meredith tells him, is an Italian fraternity boy, first name Michael, last name Angelo. The warden scribbles this name on his pad and peels out for parts unknown, returning in time for the birth of the baby, who sucks the warden's pinkie finger and turns the old man soft, and that's when the solution to the mystery reveals itself. The warden looks into the baby boy's eyes, at the slope of his nose, at his black hair and dark complexion, and every bit of this baby screams Jimmy, who by the time the warden gets back to the hatchery, has fled and left the gates open for the feral cats to devour the fishes.

All-in-all, the story wasn't bad. Probably my best yet. There was narrative drive and acute observations, both of which got the attention of the grad student editors at Florida International University's *Gulf Stream Magazine*, who passed it up the chain to the faculty editor, who found a place for it in Issue #12, the 1997 Green Issue. I had first submitted the story with my MFA application in the spring of 1996, and it was strong enough to get me admitted, which also came with a TA gig and full fee waiver.

Finally, I was just the type of writer someone was looking for at the time.

The invitation had been tendered: Come write with us in Miami for a couple of years, teach our students, and it won't cost you a thing, except for rent and food and beer money. Mom was all for it. She said I needed to go, that I would regret it if I stayed, and she was doing okay, especially now that Pam was around. She had her water therapy and bee pollen and scrapbooking, and what was there for me in Fresno, anyway? I was a young man. I needed to see things. "I don't want to be the reason you stay," she said. She would write and call, and I would fly home for the summer and for Christmas, and the two years would go by fast because that's what years do no matter how hard we try to slow them down.

Mom was nostalgic that whole summer before I left; memory was pleasant for her. She talked about how nice it was to visit Joliet and drive along Cowles Avenue, through her old neighborhood, to see her house again, still the same color blue, the same stone steps that led to the sitting porch where there were now white wicker chairs. She recalled evenings sitting there herself as a girl, watching the fireflies hover over a bramble bush. She talked about the people she once knew, and she wrote cards to these people, and she put stamps on envelopes, and she put them in the mail slot. She loved to send letters and she loved to receive them. She kept them all, and they are now with me, bound by ribbons and full of stories.

20

My Life Felt Too Small to Give a Name

"I've gained about 6 pounds. I'm going to have to pull myself together, lose the 6 pounds, get my hair done, and stop thinking so much."

—Letter from my mother, September 8, 1996
(my 28th birthday)

I SET OUT FOR FLORIDA IN A TWO-CAR CONVOY WITH MY soon-to-be-roommate, a guy from a small town in Massachusetts who graduated with his MA from Fresno State the same time I did. I'll call him "Bob," because the last thing he did in Massachusetts before he came to California was break-off an engagement to an Italian girl whose father, Bob said, "had mafia connections." The wedding date had been close, very close, and at the time Bob called it off, expensive, non-refundable things had been purchased and rented. Schedules had been cleared. As a result, Bob was sick with paranoia during the years I knew him. In both Fresno and Miami, he kept a sealed envelope in his top dresser drawer. Once we became roommates, he instructed me to open it in the event he wound up hacked to cat food in his bed or floating in a canal with a bullet in his brain. Within that envelope, he said, were instructions on how to find his killers. "Just give it to the cops," Bob said. "They'll know what to do." What he didn't seem to realize, but I certainly did, was that roommates of mafia targets never survive a late-night mincing. They don't get to stick around and clean up afterward. This made me just as paranoid as Bob. I considered writing my own letter, which I would seal and put in the top drawer of my dresser. It would read, "If I wind up dead, look for the sealed envelope in Bob's dresser. Tell my mom I love her."

Like me, Bob was a young writer who had been admitted to FIU's MFA program. Our apartment was on Van Buren Street in Hollywood, and Mom thought this was a wonderful coincidence, that she once lived in Hollywood, and now I would, too, like mother, like son, albeit different cities on opposite sides of the country. Bob drove a black and silver van from Fresno to Miami, along with his girlfriend—I'll call her "Bev"— his computer, and dozens of Elvis Costello and Tom Waits bootlegs. He was one of those guys who traded concert recordings through the mail within a clandestine network of music pirates. If the mafia didn't get Bob, a posse of angry, violated musicians would.

At summer camp the previous season, a friend gifted me a copy of *Blue Highways*, the traveling memoir of a guy named William Least Heat Moon, Bill Trogdon, for short. I thought of Trogdon and his van, Ghost Dancing, as I drove alone in a U-Haul: "Quit trying to get out of the way of life. Chuck routine. Live the real jeopardy of circumstance." On seeing a flock of snow geese moving north across a deep sky, Trogdon said to follow spring as they do, "darkly, with neck stuck out." He drove Ghost Dancing all over the country on the map's blue highways, on the roads less traveled to little towns that barely made it on the map, if they made it at all: Remote, Oregon; Simplicity, Virginia; New Hope, Tennessee; Why, Arizona; Whynot, Mississippi.

But my U-Haul was no Ghost Dancing, and this was no journey into the crevices of America. Rather, it was three-thousand miles of bland, dead-red interstate, almost a third of that in Texas, a state I cursed for its bigness, for its ornery headwind, for its lunar desolation between watering holes. I cursed it for the way its oppressive heat turned the U-Haul's air conditioner into a hair dryer. I cursed it, too, for its mockery. The highway mileage sign on I-10 as I slipped into Texas from New Mexico let me know I was 18 miles from El Paso and 852 from Beaumont. In

May of 1998, on my way back, I left Louisiana and saw nearly the same sign in reverse: Beaumont 23, El Paso 857, with nothing in between, with no smaller, more achievable goals like Fort Stockton, San Antonio, or Houston. At the rate I was driving, with no wind at my back, I'd be crossing Texas for fifteen hours, which felt like an entire, motionless summer.

Still, I drove "darkly, with neck stuck out," a US map open on the seat next to me and my Ford pickup on a tow-dolly behind. Thanks to a governor on the gas pedal, my top speed was sixty. I was forced to creep along deliberately, like a cargo ship, and watch the tedious landscape slip slowly behind me. I might appreciate the beautiful view as one of life's simple pleasures, today, but back then it struck me as a barely tolerable disappointment.

Along with the road map, I drove with a microcassette recorder, which I chattered into as the hours passed: Arizona, New Mexico, Texas—almost three days in the Southwest under the perpetual illusion that the road before me was one long sheet of water. Then five hours in boggy Louisiana, where the late afternoon sun glimmered golden on the swamp-split freeway and I puzzled over place names like Atchafalaya and Calcasieu; over an hour in the southern Mississippi panhandle, where I bought a vending machine Pepsi and read a PSA on a rest area bulletin board that warned against wandering amidst nearby decayed tree stumps that housed venomous, burrowing snakes. Another hour in Alabama, through the space-age George Wallace Tunnel, beneath the Mobile River, then out the other side to the Jubilee Parkway, a word I've always been fond of—Jubilee, not Parkway—because, like *clinker*, it's fun to say.

Jubilee. Jubilee. Jubilee.

Then, Florida.

Years later, I came across that microcassette recorder and rewound the tape and pushed the play button. For about five minutes, I listened to the twenty-seven-year-old me trying to figure out who I was and who I wanted to become. My recollection of what I said is hazy. That's because shortly after I heard my former, hyperbolic self complain about being lonely and unwanted, I tossed the tape. It was unlistenable, at least to me, not something I wanted my wife or kids to hear after I am dead. Do they really need to know *everything* about my life before them? So, the tape is gone, and all that is left is the memory, now over two decades old, which means the boundaries between what I actually said and my imagination are murky.

I didn't start my narrative until I was well into the California desert, somewhere between Indio and Blythe, after the exhilaration of beginning the journey had faded into drudgery and I came to realize just how many more miles were ahead of me than behind. These weren't even the middle-miles and already I was exhausted by a landscape that constantly reminded me of my place in it. It didn't help that I was forced to drive slowly, so Bob and Bev cut me loose somewhere after Joshua Tree, which is when I started talking into my recorder.

Throughout the trip, but particularly in the Southwest, I was anxious about the temperature gauge, and I said so on the tape. I monitored the needle's approach to the danger zone, that small red wedge on the gauge face, and mused over the very real possibility that the U-Haul would overheat. I pulled over whenever I found shade, which was not often in Arizona or New Mexico, and hardly ever in Texas. I read the dashboard warning sign into the recorder, which went something like this: "To avoid overheating, turn OFF the air conditioner." I did this, and by God's grace, over dozens of slow miles and a few pit stops, the needle backed off to about half-way, out of the red wedge. I know I commented on this. I sang praises to Our Lord into my recorder: "Thank you, God, for not leaving your child to have vultures devour his eyes in the desert." I believe a man's faith is more acute when faced with the prospect of having to roam a hot, howling wasteland in search of water; his faith is strengthened when spared from that by the Miracle of a Cooling Engine in a desert. I thought of Moses, who was a badass and wandered the desert for forty years—between the ages of eighty and one-hundred twenty!—but he was a prophet who founded a nation. I had no such resume. I wouldn't have lasted forty minutes out there.

So, I was very, very careful. I drove most of the way going no faster than fifty, with the windows down, stopping every chance I got to rinse my face in truck-stop bathrooms, drink a cold soda, and scold sign makers for plurals-made-possessives, which was a problem all along the Interstate: "Over 10,000 *Video's* for Truckers!" "One-dollar *Taco's*!" "Cash only. No Credit *Card's*!" On the highway, I remained as long as I could in the shade of passing semi-trucks. At one place, I bought a Styrofoam cooler and filled it with ice cubes and soft drinks, which made the U-Haul more tolerable but forced me to pull over more than I would have liked.

In East Texas, I stopped to rest and sat at a sticky, concrete picnic table. I took off my shoes and socks, stretched my toes, and let my feet breathe. Nearby, stood a tall pole, at the top of which billowed a state flag the size of a log cabin. There was a gas station with one pump, and one tree that cast a welcome shadow over the picnic table. Still, the concrete was hot to the touch. The bench scalded the backs of my legs. I had purchased a fountain drink in the gas station. Out of boredom, I took one ice cube from it and left it to puddle on the tabletop. The ice cube pooled quickly, and then I felt foolish to have let it go for a moment's entertainment. In Texas, in August, one should not waste ice cubes.

I sat beneath that meager tree and stretched my back one way, then the other, and I looked for meaning in the rippling, oceanic desert. The longer I looked, the more this desert and its refracting, wavy light held me spellbound and seemed to give something back, an odd, unnerving clarity that I had not sensed during the fifteen-hundred or so miles I'd driven to get there. It was as though this were my final destination. It was as though this Texas desert awaited my arrival, waited for me to sit down at that lonesome concrete picnic table with my fountain drink and settle in for a revelation. It said to me, "You are trapped in an in-between place. You are stuck in a seam." It said, "You cannot move forward or go back." It asked, "What are you going to do?" We can, of course, see a mirage, but can we also hear one? That hot, muggy afternoon, I thought I did.

I sat there with no sense of forward movement, no notion that an apprenticeship in Florida would somehow help define me and who I wanted to become, and I was not to the point in my travels where the promise of the journey's end had renewed my energy for the stretch run. Instead, I was in a lonesome stasis, outside the world that shaped me. The desert will make you feel that way. I said things like that on the tape: "I feel small. I feel disconnected. I have never felt so alone." In the movie *Grand Canyon,* while sitting on the edge, Danny Glover's character Simon says he feels "like a gnat on a cow's ass." That in comparison to the ancientness of the canyon and its rocks, one man's time on the planet is "too small to give a name." That about covered it for me. Out there, my life felt too small to give a name.

The desert prompted self-reflection. I asked myself, "What am I doing?" Actually, I asked myself, "What *in the hell* am I doing?" The whole enterprise seemed ridiculous. Moving to Florida? To write? It was folly. It was impractical. This wasn't like going to college straight out of high school, four hours from home. This was different, much bigger somehow. I was ten years older, for one, and much more capable of rational thought. What I sensed on that hot Texas roadside—my life stuffed into a recalcitrant U-Haul—was that I had intentionally disconnected myself from my own story. That's what the desert seemed to tell me. "Your story is behind you," it said. "It is in California. It is in Fresno. It is in all the places you have ever lived." Mostly, though, it was with my mother. That's where my story was, braided to her story, ropelike. One depended on the other to survive.

And when the desert told me this, I felt scared and unbraided.

This scared feeling came upon me suddenly in the sticky solitude, but it was something I could name because I had lived with it for so long, like an old horse that knows the way: I believed I would never see my mother alive again. I was afraid she would die while I was gone. This fear became much bigger to me that day, at that moment, in Texas. I was numbed by it. I found myself unable to move. I felt selfish for leaving my mother, even though she had told me to go. And now, I was too far gone to go back. I knew I had to move forward, and that was my answer to the desert: "I'm going," I said. As much as I may have wanted to turn around, I could not. My ancestors buried their dead children in shallow graves under rocks in a land just like this. They prayed over their small bodies, then moved on, and that's what I had to do. I had to bury my fear under a rock. I had to put on my damp socks and sneakers. I had to climb into the cab of that U-Haul and finish the journey, one that carried with it my mother's blessing.

I sat up straight. I turned over the key in the ignition. I watched the temperature gauge climb halfway, no further, and I made my way to the interstate, driving east. I held my tape recorder against my cheek and felt its cool, soothing smoothness. With inexplicable confidence out of character for me, I held down the red record button and told myself I was going to be a writer. Maybe the heat had finally made me delusional, but here's what I said: "That's it. I am going to be a writer, and the reason I am still alone is because writing is lonely."

That's what I remember saying. Something just like that.

I lived in Florida from September of 1996 through March of 1998. While I was away, Mom wrote me letters, one or two a month. This was a painstaking act of love, given the condition of her fingers. She could not use her right hand for much of anything. It was a small, purplish fist, its shade the product of little to no circulation below her wrist. Every so often, I had watched her lift it to her nose—at the same time she bent her nose to her thumbnail—in an effort to scratch an itch. Otherwise, it just rested in place against her stomach. The fingers on her left hand were fully curved, a process that had started in the early 1980s. Her knuckles hyperextended, but her fingertips bent towards her palm. Her thumb was in a similar fix, only without the benefit of a middle joint, it persisted in the shape of a towel hook. It was with this hand she turned on lights, brushed her teeth, pushed the buttons on the TV remote. And typed.

As she had when I was an undergraduate ten years earlier, Mom sat slumped over her typewriter, hunting down letters one at a time with a doo-hickey that looked something like a small turkey baster. Attached to its business end was a pink rubber eraser, the kind shaped like an *A* or a *V,* depending on its orientation. She squinted through reading glasses balanced on the tip of her nose and wrote with the television on so that she could report news items as they happened: a pipe bomb in a local elementary school, one grocery chain looking to buy out another, the weatherman expecting his third grandchild. Mom reveled in facts, no matter how dull, because they were real and un-nuanced. Facts were soulless. She did not have to interpret facts the way she did people's actions or words, which confused and often hurt her. When this happened, she blamed The Stroke, which she said had twisted the wires in her brain. Other times, she called it hormonal. When Pam overlooked a chore, Mom thought she was taking advantage of her passive nature. It didn't occur to her that Pam had simply forgotten. "I guess I have a complex," she wrote. "Believing nobody can like me for myself—motive, everyone has a motive."

In Florida, I read these letters and saw in them my mother's battle with self-doubt and paranoia. I worried that without me there, she might just lose her mind altogether. She would become Jack without the drinking. She would hoard newspapers in stacks that would eventually fall over and trap her beneath. She would eat cornmeal with weevils and peaches with mold and let the whiskers on her chin grow. She would never change out of her nightgown. Her carpet would become a minefield of dog turds, her countertops repositories for cockroach eggs that would bring forth Kafkaesque insects, which would grow to the size of men, bugs Mom would pelt with apples to show her disgust. This would all happen after she fired Pam and completely shut out other humans who were sure to take advantage of her, everyone but me, the only person in the world she could trust.

Maybe I was the one losing my mind.

There was one spate of letters in which Mom was convinced Pam was plotting to get hurt on the job and go after Worker's Comp. "She is complaining about an injury to her elbow," Mom wrote. "She is starting to have trouble lifting things." There were things I would have to do for her when I came home for Christmas, she said, things she could not ask Pam to do. She wanted some gravel in her yard, for one. There were also some storage bins in the closet with things she wanted to give me for safekeeping, things of value, family heirlooms no one should know about. These would turn out to be silver coins and postcards made of cowhide and a ruby glass cup from the 1904 St. Louis World's Fair bearing the name "Vilena," in cursive, Mom's grandmother.

Then there was the autographed Elvis portrait, which she had been hauling around for thirty years. Seems Mom saw one just like it on a PBS documentary about Wayne Newton. It was on the wall of a Las Vegas wedding chapel, and Mom caught the name of the place—Graceland—so she picked up the phone and dialed information in Vegas and got in touch with a man named Bill, the guy who ran the chapel. For some reason, she thought he might have a sense of the portrait's value, a "ballpark," she said. In her letter, she wrote that Bill was "a gentleman." She told Gentleman Bill all about her Elvis portrait, how she came by it, how big it was, what the King had written. "I could hear his ears perk up," Mom wrote. I was not sure how this was possible: How can one hear such a thing? It was her way of saying she had a feeling, some fluttering in her gut that made her suspicious of Bill. She worried that she had said too much and he would come looking for her. Could Bill trace her phone number and pair that to her home address? "My suspicious mind," she wrote. "I should be a mystery writer." This gave me one more thing to do when I came home for Christmas: Find a hiding place for Elvis. Maybe in the back of her closet, covered by a blanket, behind her dusty winter coat. Until then, she wrote, "Be careful who you tell that I have this picture, or I may have a robbery." She thought Elvis was worth thousands, a million, maybe. She thought she was sitting on a gold mine.

Sometimes it's difficult for me to reconcile this paranoid woman with the young, hopeful girl I see in the pictures I keep—her senior yearbook photo and her graduation portrait from Patricia Vance. In both of them, she is looking ahead toward her unknown future, to that dark grove of trees, to the belief that on the other side flows the River of Life, the River of Joy, the River of Happiness, to that side where I am nothing more than an idea to her.

21

I Brought My Own Pen

"I didn't use to be the way I am now. I used to have a mellow, easygoing personality. It was the strokes that messed with my mind."

—Letter from my mother, November 4, 1997

MY FINEST STORY AT FIU WAS ABOUT A MAN WHO VIS-ited farmers and drank their chewable coffee before lowering a camera with a fisheye lens down their broken wells to reveal their hidden problems. I titled the story "Well-Watching." Because the story was also about a man looking after the well-being of a boy—a kid who didn't belong to him—I was particularly proud of the title.

The story opens in the predawn fog when my protagonist pulls back the curtain over his sink and sees a car parked at an angle in his driveway behind his white van. He recognizes the car as belonging to a woman friend, who it turns out has had a dust-up with her drunken lover, and she has a swollen eye to prove it. On that foggy morning, she has her five-year-old son with her, and she asks if she can leave the boy for a few days for safekeeping while she deals with the abusive drunk at home. My protagonist turns this over in his mind a bit, but he takes the boy, and the story winds up being about their relationship: this boy who needs a father and this man who yearns for a family, and both of them are me.

It's a stranger-comes-to-town story; there's a revelation brought about because the man and the boy come together. For this one, I was trying to work out the problem of loneliness in my mind, not just where it came from and why I seemed to suffer so badly from it, but also what I could do to fix it.

"Well-Watching" came from an assignment I got from a poet-professor, a high-strung redhead, who had at various times worked his own strange jobs. I remember reading in one of his "About the Author" blurbs that he had driven a taxi in some big city and wrestled alligators—not at the same time—and these kinds of experiences became fodder for his poems, mostly having to do with American popular culture. I don't know that he did either of these things, but it does make the book jacket more interesting.

I remember this poet as a young man who spoke faster than I could think. I also remember him telling us once in a workshop to write about a job we'd held because work is always full of material, but instead of writing a poem, I wrote "Well-Watching," which I later submitted to a contest put on by the National Society of Arts and Letters. The Boca Raton chapter liked it so much they awarded me first prize and two-thousand dollars and announced I was getting an all-expenses paid trip to the national convention in Ann Arbor, Michigan, where my story would go up against other regional winners. Following this announcement, I shook hands and took photos with generous donors and supporters of the arts at a party on a bay full of swanky yachts. (This was my second swanky yacht bay party since I'd been in Florida; the first happened just after I'd arrived, when my status as an MFA student at FIU gave me the carte blanche needed to attend an after-party for the writers-turned-musicians supergroup, The Rock Bottom Remainders, during which I got pickled alone and waited for Stephen King to toss a cocktail napkin I might fetch from the trash.)

I had a sponsor from Boca Raton who treated me like her grandson. Her name was Ruth. She was a classy woman with pewter hair and white pearls, a philanthropist who called me often to ask if there was anything I needed. Ruth was a bit like my mother, only able-bodied and well-to-do and at least twenty years older. Together, we flew to Ann Arbor and walked around the UM campus. We stood at the top of the football stadium and imagined it full of people. We ate dinner and she picked up the tab, and then I fell asleep in a hotel room I had all to myself. The next evening, we mingled with other sponsors and writers and judges, and I wore a blue blazer and khakis and drank red wine because it was floating around in the white-gloved hands of bow-tied stewards and didn't cost me anything. I felt like a guest at Gatsby's West Egg mansion.

I was giddy and light-headed at first. I made small talk with other contestants and a few judges, chatter that came easier because of the wine: *Where are you from?* and *Who are your biggest influences?* things like that. After more wine, the small talk grew heady and we pondered bigger issues like minimalism's place in contemporary fiction and the inimitability of Raymond Carver, only I called him *Ray,* because as my wine buzz swelled, so did my belief that Carver and I were best friends. That's when I lost my filter altogether, when I started prattling on about myself, which is something I did as an insecure, peripheral person when I got wasted on red wine—on anything, for that matter—because I wanted so desperately to be impressive and admired. I felt it happening, but I couldn't stop it until—about the time the chandeliers began to look like disco balls—the master of ceremonies called us to order and we shuffled back to our chairs. I sat next to Ruth and fought the spins by keeping my head steady and my eyes closed, just like when I got car-sick as a boy.

I remember wishing Ruth had been next to me all night to drive her heel into my foot, to let me know that my self-adulation and navel-gazing were turning me into a person one could absolutely *not* root for. That the one thing you cannot travel without through a national awards ceremony is humility. I needed that kind of wisdom then, much more than I needed free wine, but since the free wine was within reach, I took the road more easily traveled. By the time the master of ceremonies began reading names, I was wishing for the event to be over. My only recourse was to sit quietly, applaud when prompted, and practice sentences in my head that painted me gracious in loss, *Happy to be invited, but more happy to meet you because you are going places, I can tell, you are really going places. I'll keep my eye out for your book, you can be sure of that.*

I tried to pay close attention to the master of ceremonies. He worked his way alphabetically through all the contestants—reading brief bios, story titles, represented regions, judges' comments—and these were followed by polite applause. Up next was the letter *P,* and I thought it was my turn, because even drunk, I still knew my alphabet and there are so few surnames that begin with *Q.* But rather than stopping on *R,* the blue-suited master of ceremonies moved right over to *S*—from Paulsen to Simmons or something like that—and I took this to mean that my story was so bad as to not even earn a mention. I began to wallow and chew the inside of my cheek. I felt my life's purpose was irrevocably gone, and I pondered career options for has-been writers because, let's face it, I was washed-up before the age of thirty and not only had my story stunk, I had been forgotten.

But then, the master of ceremonies said there were four more contestants to announce—"the top four according to the judges"—and the prize money was one thousand for fourth, three thousand for third, five thousand for second, and ten thousand for first. Ruth put her arms around my shoulders and gave me a squeeze and said, "This is it, you're in the top four," and my wallowing turned into something quite different, whatever is the opposite of wallowing. I was now fighting upstream to bring myself back to a place of coherence. I sat up straight. I could not grasp what Ruth was telling me, but the essence of it was this: I was a winner.

Fourth-place was announced, and it wasn't me, and then third-place, also not me, and these two circumstances made Ruth especially gaga, because of course, that meant I was second or *God-forbid first!* and I'd be taking home some real money, and real recognition for the Boca Raton chapter, but I was so sauced, I couldn't understand what was happening. It was like trying to stop a spinning top with my fingertip. My name came next, along with Ruth's sparkling eyes and her arms wrapped about my shoulders like a shawl, then a feeling of misplaced love for her. The two of us stood and walked forward to one side of the podium. She nudged me in the direction of a man holding a check—not one of those big replica checks, but an actual check—and on it was my name and in neat cursive, *Five thousand dollars.* I stood still and held that check and looked in the direction of a camera, Ruth on one side and the Society's Grand Poobah on the other, but all I wanted at that moment was a chair because the possibility of me falling face-down on the ballroom floor was high, which would have been quite a picture for the Society's national newsletter.

A week later—June 15, 1998—a small article in the "Local News" section of *The Fresno Bee* told of my accomplishment (and my prize money): "Fresno man receives award." Later still, in the winter of 1998, came publication in *South Dakota Review.* My mother was ecstatic because her boy was Fresno Famous and had made more money on one story than she made in half a year from Social Security. I think she was secretly more thrilled about the money. That I had won it, of course, but also because anyone who read that little article in the *Fresno Bee* would find out I won it. Ours would be a rags-to-riches story people could really feel good about. In fact, once the article came out, Mom sat back and waited for her phone to ring. Because this was a time when people still read the newspaper, there would surely be interest, maybe even from the local TV stations, someone wanting to sit down with her for a kind of Barbara Walters' interview, this permanently disabled mother of the Next Great American Author, a local hero right here in Fresno. She had Pam collect that day's *Bee* from every neighbor's recycle tubs, then the two of them clipped the newsbyte, which Mom sent to people she still knew, including her pals in Joliet. "He is on his way," she wrote Jan. "My boy did good!"

Before these good and wonderful things happened, though, I struggled through periods of homesickness and depression, which began after I got to Miami in August of 1996. Mom said I needed to keep busy. I couldn't do that without money, so I applied for a job at Tony Roma's. For a few months after I'd gotten to South Florida, I'd driven by it almost daily on my way to the FIU campus on Biscayne Bay, where I was teaching and taking classes. The restaurant was in Hallandale on US-1, across the highway from Gulfstream Park, which on any given afternoon was home to what had to be the largest population of French-Canadian senior citizens in the world. This was a fact I'd recently learned about my new, temporary home. Nearly six months out of the year, more than a million snowbirds flocked south from Quebec to clog the beaches, byways, food courts, and lawn bowling clubs in and around Hollywood and Hallandale. I remember *Je me souviens* on long lines of license plates and couples perambulating on the Boardwalk in unflattering swimwear. They lived life unashamed, and who wouldn't want to live like that?

At four o'clock each weekday, those couples and their friends and their friends of friends piled into booths at Tony Roma's, a confederacy of tank tops and sun visors, the whole lot of them *parlez-ing* ardently and smelling of sweat and coconut oil.

That's what I walked into one afternoon in the fall of 1996, desperately in need of a job, since my summer money had run out and my teaching gig at FIU, while appreciated, was a subsistence assignment at best, one that covered the rent, cable, and a grocery list of milk, cereal, pasta, and jarred tomato sauce. I ate a lot of bread and butter, too, and remembering my boyhood—those days when Mom was too debilitated to cook—I took comfort in tomato and mayonnaise sandwiches and the occasional frozen beef pot pie, which the local Publix offered at two for five bucks.

A stone-faced waitress met me at the door. She was a round, older woman, her dark hair pulled back, her eyebrows painted on in tall arches. She wore glasses with gold frames and violet lenses and a name badge: Katrina.

"Just one, hon?" she asked, but before I could answer, she suggested I might get served more quickly at the bar, which at four in the afternoon was surprisingly empty and, not so surprisingly, dark. There were a couple televisions tuned to horse racing, presumably a live feed from across the highway, with a couple more showing Dolphins' highlights.

"Actually," I said, "I'm here to pick up an application."

Katrina looked surprised, then doubtful. She wore a heavy coat of rouge on her cheeks. "In that case," she said, "you *definitely* want to go to the bar." Maybe she thought I needed a drink to reconsider. She pointed me in the direction of the bartender, a man with long, silver hair in a ponytail. He had a matching silver mustache and wore a leather bolo cinched by a polished turquoise stone. He was slicing lemons when I interrupted him.

"Katrina said I should see you about a job application," I said.

The bartender continued to slice lemons into half-circles, cradling them in his palm and running the knife through their pulpy hearts.

"Not me you need," he said. His voice was deep and native. He looked at me and I saw darkness in his eyes, maybe a history he never spoke of. He set his knife on a cutting board and wiped his hands on a bar towel. Moments later, he reemerged with a young woman who introduced herself as Carolina—pronounced "Caro-LEE-na,"—an exotically accented shift manager who led me to a booth in a corner with closed, wooden blinds. It was ashy and thick in that corner. Carolina lit a cigarette.

"You smoke?" she asked. She was pretty, with long, dark hair and brown eyes. I would guess she was in her mid-twenties, a bit younger than me. But like the bartender, there was a visible disquiet about her. She blew smoke from the side of her mouth, the way my mother used to do.

"I don't," I said. I smiled at her. "Those things'll kill you." There was an immediate, intriguing tension between us that could not be ignored. I went with it. I was playful and flirtatious, which was unlike me, and I was confident, which was also unlike me.

Carolina's eyes seemed to flicker. She moved the ashtray, like a chess piece, toward the outer edge of the table. "We all die of something," she said, and this reminded me of a poet I knew in Fresno, a smoker, who once told me that each cigarette he smoked took seven minutes off his life. True or not, he saw this as a glass half-full: Those were seven fewer minutes he'd have to spend in a nursing home. And who could argue with that?

There was small talk. Carolina sat up straight and coughed over her shoulder, then she asked me about my work history and where I came from. I told her Fresno, and she cocked her head to one side. "Halfway between Los Angeles and San Francisco," I said, well-practiced, since I had been doing that often for the folks I met in Florida. Fresno was off the map for many of them. I also told her about Tony Roma's in Fresno, how I knew the menu, the difference between baby-back and St. Louis-style, what went into a Roma's appetizer sampler, and how much sauce to provide with an onion half-loaf. She said I probably knew more about the menu than the people who worked there.

"I don't know if that's good or bad," I said, and she said it was good. Definitely good.

"So," she asked, "how did you wind up *here*?" I remember the question, because attached to the end of it, though left unsaid, was this: *of all places?* It suggested that South Florida was the last hope for people who had exhausted all other options, kind of like Stuccoville, the bottom of the funnel. I had felt that way about Fresno, too. It's the way people regard places they think they can never leave.

"Miami's not so bad," I told her. I remember saying the word "cosmopolitan," which to me had become synonymous with clothing-optional beaches. I also told her it was a nice place to live for a while, but I couldn't see spending the rest of my life there. There was the humidity, for one. And the hurricanes.

"Anyway," I said. "I came here to write. I am at FIU studying to be a writer."

The way she looked at me, I remember feeling like an unexpected windfall, like someone sort of famous. My chest swelled. Carolina mashed out her cigarette and fanned the blue smoke toward the bar.

"A writer," she said. "A *real* writer." She leaned forward and propped her chin in the palm of her hand.

"As real as it gets," I said, and by this I meant what was likely the opposite of what she imagined. Had I told her that by *real* I meant ramen noodles and repeated failure, maybe her sparkle would have faded, but I doubt it. There was real electricity there.

"What do you write about?" she asked.

"People," I told her. "That's what most of us real writers write about. We write about people. Especially people we don't know very well."

Carolina found this curious. "Why do you write about people you don't know?"

I told her it was simple, really. "Because we want to know them better."

She nodded as she considered this. "Maybe you will want to write about me," she said. And then, "Ha, ha, I'm just teasing." She reached across the table and tapped my hand. Just as quickly, she pulled it away.

"Maybe," I said. "But I guess if I'm going to do that, you have to give me a job."

Carolina narrowed her eyes at me, as though I had somehow tricked her, but we both knew I wasn't leaving there without a job, and ten minutes later, she hired me.

"You still have to fill out the application," she said. "But that shouldn't be so tough for a real writer."

I told her it wouldn't be tough at all. I told her I brought my own pen.

22

I Dance Like an American

"I think often about your current sacrifice, letting me come here to Miami to better myself."

—Letter to my mother, November 4, 1997

CAROLINA WAS FROM ARGENTINA. OVER THE SCRABBLE board, Bob and I had fun with that: "Caro-LEE-na from Argen-TEE-na." She danced tango for a hobby and corrected me when I said "tango" like a white man.

"It's *tong-o*," she said. "Not *tang-o*." Like bong, not bang. She took me to lessons and I danced like an American. I know this because Carolina said so: "You dance like an American."

"That's because I *am* an American," I said.

For a while, this was okay, me being an American. It was a novelty. I didn't even have a name. Among her friends and family, I was "Carolina's American boyfriend." At tango lessons, South American women giggled at my clumsiness. The young men thought I was a buffoon. I would find out later that one of these young men yearned for Carolina, and in the auditorium where these tango lessons took place, he eyeballed me with silent fury and plotted with his friends to drive me out, first by threat and, if need be, by other, more physical means. This was a machismo I didn't understand, what with me being an American, and Carolina told me to forget about it. "It's all talk," she said. "That's just the way of South American men."

So, that's what I did. I tried to forget about it. I tried to forget about it on Thanksgiving that year while, with Bob home in Massachusetts, I sat alone in our apartment watching the Detroit Lions. I tried to forget about it later that day, too, when I watched Robert Downey Jr. in *Home for the Holidays* on the VCR because Carolina thought spending the day with her family might be awkward. They started drinking early, she said, and nobody spoke English. "It might not be so fun for a *yanqui*," she said, which sounded like "junkie" when it crossed her lips. And while the real writer in me was intrigued by the idea of being a fly on the wall at an Argentine Thanksgiving, my basic human need for survival won out. It was best for me to stay away from drunk, South American men within arm's reach of carving knives.

Working with Carolina in the restaurant was a lot like tango. She always said we had to keep things "hush-hush," which made for a kind of titillating charade that lasted for months. At the food line, as I waited for plates, she came up behind me. I could feel her hot breath on my neck. Her knees brushed my knees. Her hip grazed my hip. She reached over my shoulder to fetch an onion loaf, getting so close our cheeks touched. There was electricity in her fingertips, which she raked through my hair and over the small of my back. This literally brought shivers; made me weak in the knees. The line cooks loved it. "*Ay, gringo,*" they said. They smiled knowingly. It was fun for me.

Not as fun were the hours between four and six in the afternoon and the daily rush of early birds, all there for the dinner special, which was painted on the front window, bright enough to be seen from Gulfstream Park. Back then, six-seventy-five got you a half-slab of baby backs, a baked potato, coleslaw, and a tin dish of rainbow sherbet, along with a beverage, which for the early birds was always a cup of coffee alongside a glass of water with lemon, no ice. Because I was new, this became my regular shift. I called it "quarterback hour," which was actually two full hours of French-Canadian chaos, of niggling over menu substitutions and separate checks, of warming up coffee that was never hot enough, of badgering the silver-haired bartender for more lemon wedges, only to be left with seven sweaty, one-dollar bills and the expectation of change, one *quarter*, which if I was lucky, I got *back*.

I wrote about this for a fiction workshop at FIU in the spring of 1997. I called it "In the Weeds," which was the euphemism we used on the floor when we were so busy, we didn't know what to do next. The idea was, when someone was in the weeds, you jumped in to help. You fetched drink refills, you ran food, cleared plates, anything to help the waiter in the weeds see more clearly. Only in my story, my protagonist gets no help. He is abandoned in the weeds, and his guests are the senior citizens who line up pre-meal pills the size of poker chips on their placemats and cough phlegm into napkins. They are cantankerous and bossy, and no matter what my protagonist does for them, they cannot be made happy. One couple sits at his table for two hours and leaves him seventeen dollars on a sixteen-dollar, ninety-four-cent check. "Since they sat for two hours," I wrote, "he earned three cents an hour."

The story didn't work, overall. I was writing from a place of frustration and in the workshop, the general consensus was that I was whining on the page. My protagonist was self-absorbed and chippy, and I hadn't mined the emotional experience like I could have. "I don't care about him," someone said. "And if I am going to read a story, I have to care about the characters."

The old folks in the restaurant were caricatures. They growl at my protagonist: "Make sure there's nothing on the potato," one man says. "Make sure it's cooked all the way through!" "If the potato is cold," he warns, "I'll send it back." Ho-hum. My classmates said mere description wasn't enough. They wanted to know what made him that way.

But it wasn't all bad. Toward the end of the story, there is one glimpse of an elderly man who, after dinner, sits waiting while his wife is in the bathroom. She has left her purse—"a white wedge with arched handles and a gold clasp"—on the table. The old man takes her purse and rests it on his lap. "He passes the time," I wrote, "by clicking the clasp open and shut, open and shut." I can hear this. For me, the clicking clasp sounds like a ticking clock. It is the sound of time passing. There is a hint in the

gesture that the old man knows this. He is of an age where he can measure his moments in clicks. There is a melancholy about him. He knows
Death can come for him or his wife at any moment, maybe even *that*
moment, in *that* restaurant.

Click. Click. Click.

After six, once the full dinner menu prices kicked-in and the early birds
gave way to real tippers, there was solid money to be made. I was a hard
worker, which helped, and I stayed until closing for servers who wanted
to take off early. In this way, forty dollars in tips became eighty or ninety,
and I found myself in a place of relative comfort. I had money to pay my
bills and I had money for fun, which often meant beer drinking until the
wee hours at beach bars, usually with Carolina.

I worked with interesting people, too, and I swore at the time I would
write about them. I scribbled notes on order pads and napkins and my
coworkers said, "You better not write about me." Sometimes, though,
they said things like, "Make me rich and pretty." They said, "Put me in
a big house by the water." I said I would do that, and for good measure,
I asked them what else they wanted. To a person, each of them said this:
"Psh. To be anywhere but here."

Besides Katrina and Carolina, there was a stripper-mom named Tif-
fany, who was astonishingly dark and beautiful and who taught me to
never ask a stripper-mom (or any stripper, for that matter) why she strips;
it's dumbass and insensitive. "Why do you write?" she shot back, and at
the time, my answer was pretty self-evident. "Because I have to," I said.
"Because I can't quit."

"Well, there you go," she said. I believe that was the last time we ever
spoke.

There was also Dave, the other young shift manager, a balding man
who brooded over Pearl Jam's "Black" on the jukebox in a Hallandale
beach bar that reclaimed a chunk of my tip money after work. Dave
reminded me of my father with the way he closed his eyes and fell into

rapture over the lyrics, especially these, which had been haunting him after a break-up: "I know someday you'll have a beautiful life, I know you'll be a star, in somebody else's sky, but why oh why can't it be mine?"

After the bar closed, I'd walk with Carolina toward the ocean, and that's where we'd find Dave, on his back in the sand, his fingers clasped behind his head, staring into the braille of stars. We'd lay down next to him, three of us in a quiet chain, like paper dolls. We might lie there until the sun reddened the horizon line, nodding off to the sound of waves. It was always Dave who sat up first and said we had to go. Dave who stood and brushed sand from his black restaurant trousers and rubbed his eyes with his chubby fists, eyes gone dark and swollen with longing for the woman who made him this way.

While Home for Christmas in 1997, I shared stories with my mother. I told her it was an eleven-minute drive from my apartment to Pro Player Stadium. For ten bucks I could watch the Florida Marlins play baseball. I told her I had started playing golf at a course not far from our Hollywood apartment, and that little alligators were known to emerge from water hazards and steal golf balls from the fairways. I went to readings at bookstores and ate authentic Cuban food, and before classes I sat in the sun on Biscayne Bay and looked for manatees, which at the time, folks in Miami had been talking lots about because they couldn't swim fast enough to avoid boat propellers. She said it sounded like I was having fun. She said I had to keep doing fun things in Miami, because soon it would be over and I wouldn't want to feel like I missed anything.

"Live it up," she said. She was adamant about this. "You only have a few months left, and then. . ."

She left it hanging there, so I said, "And then *what*?"

"Then you'll have to figure out what to do with your life," she said.

"I have figured it out."

"And?"

"I'm going to write."

We were sitting at her kitchen table over coffee. She looked at me, and in her hazel eyes I saw something like dread. Maybe it was just unease. It was enough to make me look away from my mother, because this thing she felt, I felt it, too, and it was a truth too terrible to confront.

Somehow, I knew that twenty-five years ago, at a kitchen table over coffee, in a yellow house in Stuccoville, my father must have told her the same thing.

Once I'd returned to Florida in January, 1998, I drove to Key West alone one weekend and checked-in to an opulent, two-story Victorian ensconced in palm trees. I slept in a four-poster canopy bed with a mosquito net. It felt veiled and gauzy, which was appropriate because I was deeply wounded, nursing a Hemingway-sized hangover after a Friday night at Sloppy Joe's when my goal had been to drink a mile in Papa's shoes. I was hoping for Hemingway-by-osmosis, for an unconscious assimilation of ideas that would only happen if I settled in for the long haul, several hours, at least.

I got the unconscious part right. I woke up in my room the following Saturday, in my clothes. For all I knew, I'd been delivered there on the shoulders of Hemingway's ghost.

I had come to believe that the success of great writers was irrevocably tied to consumption, and that many did their best work when drunk. Faulkner kept his whiskey within reach, Cheever drank with the homeless, Joyce wrote *Ulysses* while drunk (that explains a lot about *Ulysses*) and Hemingway downed a quart of whiskey a day. Writers were drinkers. I was a writer. Ergo, I was a drinker.

But there is something about bad hangovers following blackouts that will hurl a person into deliberate self-examination. The Saturday after drinking myself unconscious, I wondered what I was doing it all for. It seemed so silly. Drinking myself blind wasn't going to make me Ernest Hemingway any more than using his typewriter would. There was no such thing as Hemingway-by-osmosis, and the truth that began to emerge for me was this: I wasn't drinking because I thought it would make me a better writer; I was drinking because I knew I wasn't anywhere near the writer I wanted to be. There was no way I'd make a living at this, which made my prospects after graduation dim. I would be thirty soon, and my friends at home were married, had children, and held down steady jobs. For years, they had been building real lives. They had started small businesses, gone to dental school, practiced law. Many of them went into sales and had done quite well for themselves because they hustled. Grandpa Leo had been right. There was money in paper bags.

My real life looked a lot different. In a matter of months, I would be back in Fresno with a sick mother to look after. I would have three university degrees hanging on my wall to remind me I wasn't marketable. And then on that dreadful Saturday, on that day when I felt like such an awful, unaccomplished failure, I figured something out: The reason Mom kept urging me to have so much fun in Florida was because she knew what I was coming home to.

On Sunday in Key West, I showered and had a fine breakfast at the B&B. I felt nourished and whole. I took a walk to a big concrete buoy marking the southernmost point in the Continental US. I have since learned that this is a fable, that the actual southernmost point is an island ten miles south of Key West, a place called Ballast Key, and even with that, there might be some argument. No matter. I found myself at this buoy with my camera, at this southernmost point, wearing a gray shirt and blue shorts and a ball cap. Digital photography was not a thing then, so I set the timer on my film camera and positioned it on a sea wall. I stepped to the buoy and leaned my right forearm against the concrete, right above the "ST" in the word southernmost. To the right of my face, in yellow, were the words "90 Miles to Cuba." I smiled into the lens and waited for the red light on my camera to count down, then for the shutter to open, and the mechanism to click. Before it was a word, I had taken a selfie.

A few days later, I had the film developed at Publix. I was disappointed to see that my self-portrait in front of the buoy was blurry. I sent it to Mom anyway, and she put it in an album she made about my Florida adventures. In it were pictures of me inside Hemingway's house on Whitehead Street, next to the desk where he wrote "The Short, Happy Life of Francis Macomber." There were pictures of me in the town of Seaside, in a community park, in the shade of a gazebo that would later make a cameo in *The Truman Show*. There I was, too, on the beach in Hallandale, a sea of colorful umbrellas in the background.

On every one of these, I wrote something on the back so Mom would get a better idea of what she was seeing. That's what we used to do then: We wrote captions and dates on the backs of prints and when those pictures showed several people, we wrote their names in order of appearance, left to right. I have a great number of photographs from my mother and grandmother, and they are mostly of dour-looking folks in wool clothing. Sometimes, written on the backs, are question marks where a name should be, because at the time they were documented, that person had been lost to memory.

On the back of the buoy photo I wrote this for my mother: "I have gone as far as I can go."

In the lobby of a performing arts theater in downtown Miami, I held Carolina's hand. We were at the intermission of the touring musical "Forever Tango." We stood next to her family: her older brother, her mom and dad, several cousins. They were all chatting in Spanish about the first act. Carolina translated. "He said the orchestra is beautiful," or "She said the dancers show great passion." I remember Carolina whispering to me. I remember her breath in my ear as she shared these things in a language I could understand. It felt like we were eavesdropping, and despite Carolina standing with me, I felt out-of-place.

At the time of this performance, I was a few months away from returning home to Fresno. I would graduate from FIU soon, and Mom was anxious for my return. Carolina knew this, and there had blossomed between us an odd, nervous tension. It was in the form of a question: Would I be going back to California alone? It was something we'd danced around, but only as a kind of joke. I might say something snarky about how she wouldn't last two months in Fresno, and she might shrug and say, "Try me." She was waiting for the words, "Okay then, come to California," but it was an invitation I never offered.

At times, though, this appealed to me. There was something genuinely romantic about going off to South Florida for two years and returning with a vivacious Argentine tango dancer. Think of the scuttlebutt! I'd be a real man about town. I'd be *worldly*. Carolina would have come with me, too. She'd have jumped into my pickup with nothing but a suitcase. She'd have cranked the window down and ridden shotgun with the wind in her hair. She was a drop-of-the-hat kind of girl.

In the Spring of 1998, as I was driving from Miami to Fresno, I found myself missing Carolina. I missed her electricity and broken English. I even missed the dry aroma of her cigarettes, which after a few weeks of dating, she disguised with spearmint gum and a fragrance that smelled of hyacinth and lilac. All along the interstate, I asked myself, *What would have been so wrong with spontaneity? What was it that stopped me?* I spent much of that drive second-guessing myself. Westbound on the mesmerizing highway, I fantasized turning around, driving back to Tony Roma's in Hallandale, and sweeping Carolina away forever. And then I reminded myself of what had happened later that night in the theater lobby several months back. I reminded myself how during the intermission, as Carolina was translating for me, holding fast to my hand, her mother had sidled up next to her in what I believed then to be a purposeful diversion.

Carolina turned away from me to talk with her mother. This lasted only a minute, but it was long enough for her brother to catch my attention. He said nothing, but held my gaze while his eyes narrowed to slits. Those eyes, sharp as blades, bore into me, and as they did, he slipped his index finger beneath a gold chain around his neck. He ran his finger the length of that chain. He pulled it taut so there was a crease in his skin, so that flesh folded over the chain, then he twisted it into a loop that cinched around his fingertip. Had he held it there, his finger would have purpled. But he did not hold the loop. He let it drop and the chain fell back to his neck. He parted his lips so I could see his teeth, white and even.

Then, it was over. Carolina's brother looked away from me. He turned his attention to his father and his cousins and joined them in their animated Spanish, words lost to me. Carolina's brother smiled his charming smile. He put his hand on his father's shoulder and said something lighthearted, something that doubled the two of them over in laughter. I can only imagine what he said, what the son said to his father to make him laugh like that. Honestly, this is something I can only imagine, because though I have had a chance to be many things in my life, one thing I have never really been is a father's son.

The whole production might have lasted thirty seconds, maybe less. And maybe what I saw was nothing more than a handsome Argentine man with perfect teeth adjusting a gold chain hanging uncomfortably around his neck. As for Carolina's mother, maybe she just wanted a moment of her daughter's time.

Maybe, maybe.

But here's what I think his message was that night in the lobby. Here's what I believe he wanted to tell me in the twisting and tightening of that gold chain: "You are not welcome here. Take my sister to California, and you die."

Let's say I'm right. Let's say my suspicion had some basis for truth. How did it come to that? I believe it must have started with Carolina's mother, who when I first met her struck me as deeply intuitive. She was cordial, but discerning, and if I'm right, she must have shared her intuition about her only daughter's *yanqui* boyfriend with her husband, the quiet patriarch, the man Carolina said knew no English, her excuse for why he never spoke to me. She must have told him what Carolina had told her: I was a writer from California, an only child raised by his sick mother, no other family to speak of. Blond, fair-skinned, English-only. All of it painted me as unwantable and unfit. To Carolina's parents, I was *sin valor*. I was *indigno*.

In my mind, my conjecture takes on a scenic quality, a fiction: I see Carolina's parents in a Miami restaurant, a table for two with candlelight and white linen napkins and a waiter in a bow tie. This waiter pours a fine Argentine wine, and Carolina's mother whispers across the candle glow, "*Carolina seguirá al americano.*" Carolina will follow the American.

Her father, I imagine, takes some wine to his lips and narrows his eyes in a look that suggests he has grown deeply concerned. Later, after dinner, he and his wife go home, and the wine has made Carolina's mother lightheaded, so she turns in early. Her father is too disturbed to sleep. Instead, he picks up the phone to call his only son, Carolina's brother, and though it is late, he knows he will be awake. This night, as fortune would have it, he catches his son at home. They talk on the phone, and it is short and perfunctory. The father says, "*Carolina seguirá al americano.*" On the other end of the line, the son grinds his teeth.

"*Manejarlo,*" his father says. "*Hazlo.*" Handle it.

His father places the receiver softly in the cradle and walks from the kitchen to his bedroom. He wears fine silk pajamas. He is slow and deliberate, walking with his head down, as though in thought. Of late, Carolina has been a wildcard, out of control, improvising through life as though it is one of her tangos. She is not one to follow tradition, and because of this, she has become her father's greatest burden.

In the bedroom, it is warm, balmy, so he flips the switch on the ceiling fan and crawls into bed next to Carolina's mother. She is breathing softly, her eyes closed. He pulls a cool sheet over him and nestles into the mattress. The bedroom, this late at night, is gunmetal, almost blue. There is moonlight seeping in, enough for the fan to unfurl slow, waltzing shadows on the stucco ceiling. It is into this bare, dancing light that the father whispers, loud enough so Carolina's mother can hear.

"*Se hace,*" he says. It is done.

And after he whispers this, his wife rolls over, so her face nuzzles the crook of his neck. She stretches her manicured fingers over his broad chest, then they move to his face, where her fingernails graze his whiskered cheek. There is a charge in them, something that sends a current the length of his spine, something that inflames his noble blood.

"*Familia,*" he whispers—into the shadows, into the slow fan—and then, once more, before he turns toward her and closes his heavy eyes for sleep: "*Familia.*"

23

I Sighed My Way Through All of It

"Count down! I'll try to stop giving advice to you as of now. I know you have things under control. I guess I feel like I can get you here faster if I toss out suggestions."

—Letter from my mother, March 25, 1998

IN APRIL OF 1998, I WAS BACK FROM FLORIDA. I WAS ALMOST thirty years old, and I had moved into the same apartment complex as my mother. Pam arranged the whole thing. She had the walls painted and carpets cleaned before I moved in. In the days leading up to my leaving, Mom called me in Florida to give me progress reports. "I saw the painter go into your new place today," she said. Days later: "The carpet cleaners were in your apartment. Did you remember to mail your deposit?" She had other questions: Had I remembered to have my mail forwarded? What about the cable, the PG&E? Had I called to have them turned on? And the phone? What about the phone? Did I have a number yet?

She knew about the comings-and-goings of workmen into my apartment because she could see my front door from her back patio. Mine was the next building over, and my place was on the second floor. After she had the landscape man trim a Photinia, she had a perfect unobstructed view. Mom sat in her patio chair and looked up at my front door for weeks before I moved in. She dreamed of me being so close. From the window in her dining area, she could see my covered parking spot. From her bedroom, the window next to my front door. There was no vantage from her place that didn't permit some view into my daily life, and if she wasn't sleeping, she was always watching. We may as well have lived together.

This closeness didn't bother me at first. It only became awkward when I had things to hide. "You were out late last night," she'd say, or, "Who was that going up the stairs with you?" Sometimes, my telephone would ring within a minute of my walking in. "Glad I caught you," she'd say, "I need a favor." Could I run over real quick and get the mail? Sammy had an accident on the carpet. There's a spider in the corner. Within a month, I was hiding from my mother. I parked in guest stalls so she wouldn't see my truck. I scampered up my staircase taking three steps at a time, thinking she might blink and not notice me. I sat inside with my lights off and blinds closed, hoping the TV flicker wouldn't give me away. These were terrible things to do, and I felt like a terrible person for doing them.

"I won't bug you too much," she promised. "I will let you live your life."

In her heart, she meant it, but there was so much she needed, so many little things I could do in two seconds that would take her a half-hour. One night, after I'd been home a couple of weeks, she called me. She caught me in a grouchy mood, which was common. "Can you come down and open a can of soup?" she said. "I'm hungry." I said I would be right down. I let myself in and went to the kitchen and opened the can of soup. From her wheelchair at the dining table, Mom watched me in the kitchen. I left the open can on the counter.

"Anything else?" I asked. This was petulant of me; I was behaving childishly to foil her passive-aggression.

"If you could just pour it in the saucepan," she said. "If you could just turn the heat to low."

I sighed. I meant for her to hear me.

"Maybe you can stir it a little? I hate it when the soup sticks to the bottom. Just stir it a little, then you can go. I don't want to be a bother."

But I could not just go. The hot soup was not going to pour itself into a bowl and float over to her placemat, so I stayed and prepared her soup.

I opened a sleeve of saltines and fanned them out on a napkin. I sighed some more. I opened a can of Pepsi, I put a straw in the can, and I slipped the can inside a plastic coffee mug with a handle. Mom had long ago lost the ability to wrap her fingers around a Pepsi can.

For years and years, this is how little things became bigger things, and I sighed my way through all of it, every little favor turned bigger, because life got knotty and my heart filled with resentment.

"How about some soup?" she said.

"No thanks," I said. "But I'll wait here with you while you eat."

Sigh.

My apartment had a nice view of the crystalline pool. This was what Mom was most excited about; we both had a pool view. "We've really made it," she said. "We are really uptown."

It was kind of like living in Hearst Castle, only without the square footage, terraced gardens, fanciful Gothic study, and the sculptures of Neptune and the nereids. I had an overlook, a small balcony enclosed in wrought iron, where I kept a charcoal grill and a small glass table next to a deck chair. I could drink a beer there and grill a steak with a ballgame on inside, so in those ways, it was real uptown.

On the downside, my balcony was west facing, so by mid-afternoon between June and September, my vertical blinds were hot to the touch. Plants other than cacti didn't stand a chance against the sunlight, which concentrated all of its twenty-seven million degrees onto my concrete slab and rendered outdoor sitting useless until dusk. By then, I was at the computer anyway, writing, because I had not spent the last two years in Florida to sit in my apartment watching TV. I meant to ply my trade, only now it was a more serious business, especially with my advanced age and extensive education. I had three college degrees, and this was supposed to be my livelihood; it was what I had trained for. Teachers taught, bankers banked, and writers wrote. It seemed like a pretty straightforward formula.

I turned my front room into an office with a huge prefab computer desk against one wall. Next to that stood a tall bookcase where I shelved everything I had read in the past five years, books I referred to when looking for inspiration or when trying to make an impression: *Gray's Anatomy, The Westminster Dictionary of the Bible,* the *Collected Works of William Shakespeare.* Also, there were *Tristram Shandy, Lolita, Tom Jones,* and *Robinson Crusoe.* There were short story collections by the biggies: Cheever, Nabokov, Carver, O'Connor, Munro. And fine novels: Steinbeck's *East of Eden,* Hemingway's *For Whom the Bell Tolls,* and Faulkner's *Light in August,* keeper of my favorite character in all of fiction-dom, Joe Christmas, a flawed, brooding loner without an identity, a man who wanders unprofitably, looking for a place to belong.

There were also two phone books—one from Fresno, one from Broward County—which I'd learned during my time in Miami were a valued commodity when it came to naming characters. A successful published writer I knew swore by this; he wrote stories longhand with a stack of phone books by his kitchen table. Somewhere out there, in small towns throughout the southern US, are real people named Billy Sykes and Alvin Lee. There are folks named Earlene and Dolphus and Dencil and Mr. Fox Ruston Ledbetter, Esquire. Jerry Meachum, Dessie Rae Odum, Royal Landry, Lurleen Dooley and Marzell Swan.

So, I started collecting phone books, because I thought that's what successful published writers did. They drank a lot and they collected phone books. They also kept their ears open. They jotted things down for later use. They kept small, spiral notebooks in their hip pockets and pens behind their ears; they knew that everything was material: a road sign, a cereal box, a book of matches on a barroom floor. Everything was fodder for a good story, even something as simple as a name.

I lived in my new apartment for two months before taking a job an hour away at a children's summer camp, a winding drive into the High Sierra, where I worked on an island in the middle of a lake. It was a summer job, ten weeks or so, and I was there to oversee a waterski outpost, a sub-camp off the main camp twenty miles away on a separate, higher lake. Every two-and-a-half days, kids came down from the main camp to live on this island. When their time was up, we swapped groups. Fifty clean kids arrived as fifty dirty kids left, and there was this two-week loop of them, clean kids coming and dirty kids going.

At this outpost, we taught kids to waterski. It was my job to get full boats with ski instructors out on the lake, four times a day. I was able to take this job because Pam agreed to stay with Mom for the summer. When my job was done in August, so was Pam. There was an assignment waiting for her as a classroom aid, and the pay was good, better than what the county gave her to do Mom's laundry and empty her bedside commode. So, at least for the summer, I was free of it: the laundry, the commode, the constant watch.

On the island, I made sure we all had food to eat and water to drink and a place on the beach to lay our heads. Sometimes, I drove boats or played cards with kids. Sometimes, I helped cook and serve meals. I talked to kids who were homesick. I told them the time would go by fast, and the next thing they knew, they'd be home with their moms and dads. "The secret was keeping yourself busy," I said. The secret was keeping your mind off your homesickness by getting in a boat or playing in the water or reading a book with the sun on your face.

"Believe me," I said. "I've been there."

At night, I told stories by the evening campfire, spooky ones about old prospectors in log cabins and rats that only came out at night, and only on the island, where they rattled pots in the kitchen and scavenged jars of peanut butter, which they could open with mutant forepaws like giant monkey hands.

I told children these stories into their firelit faces. I spoke just above a whisper. "And the rats grew to the size of beavers," I said. "If you're quiet, you can hear them in the manzanita." At night on the island, hundreds of toads crept through bushes, the crackle of dry leaves beneath their webby feet. "So, keep your heads covered and your toes inside your sleeping bags, because these rats-big-as-beavers have been known to eat just about anything." At this point, I would hold my hand to my face in the campfire glow, my index finger bent at the knuckle, hidden in my palm. "Including fingers!" I'd howl. Some children squealed happily and some cried. For those who cried, I sat with them afterward and told them that the sounds in the bushes were cute little toads. I rummaged through the manzanita until I pulled one out. "See?" I said. "Just a toad." I also showed them that I did, in fact, have a finger, that it had not been gnawed to the knuckle by a mutant, beaver-sized rat, stuck for eternity on this island with others just like him.

On the island, we had no electricity or running water. There was a gas-powered generator that kept a refrigerator and freezer cold enough to refrigerate and freeze. We drew water through a pump from the lake, which filled a bleach-treated tower and ran by gravity flow into a kitchen sink where we rinsed our pots and pans. As the director, it also fell to me to ensure the daily maintenance of our pit toilet system, two Port-o-Potties that filled up quickly when there were sixty or more people living and eating and defecating all day, every day. Over the years, these toilets had acquired a crude nickname, KYBOs, a euphonic acronym meant to encourage quick, efficient visits: Keep Your Bowels Open.

Each morning, first thing, I treated the tanks with a thick blue solution meant to degrade solid waste. I stirred the mixture into a slurry with a kayak paddle, then forced it toward an open drain that emptied into a fiberglass coffin underground. I wore long rubber gloves, sunglasses, and a painter's face mask to protect against splash-back. There were days I couldn't bring myself to do it, so I delegated. Part of it was the smell and the way I felt on any given morning. But part of it was due to the bigger picture, the heavy burden of doubt and fear I carried around that summer before my thirtieth birthday.

I didn't write at all that summer, but I thought about it. I lived in a ten-by-fifteen tent on a wooden platform that overlooked the lake, west-facing like my apartment, but much cooler in the evenings as the sun dropped below the piney horizon line. Inside, I had a bed, crude table, gas lamp, and a chair. I told myself I would sit by lamplight and put pen to paper just like Thoreau. I had my primitive workstation all set up. One day, tourists would visit and see the empty chair before my table made of planks and cinder blocks, my yellow legal pad and box of Bic ballpoints and say, "That's the *very spot* where he wrote . . ." I would write at night, into the late evenings, with the tent flaps open to the black sky and the holy host of stars. For ten weeks, I would write the old-fashioned way, just like my forefathers, wearing an ink-stained notch into my middle finger, just left of the nail, the vestige of hundreds of handwritten pages.

But all I managed to write were letters to my mother: "Dear Mom, I am sitting at my table writing by lantern light . . ." That's how most of them began.

The counselors and instructors were all eight to ten years younger than me—kids, really—so naturally they wanted to know what I did for a living. What was it that allowed me to leave my "real job" for ten weeks during the summer to live on an island? Those words "real job" always chilled me. I had this conversation a hundred times.

"You must be a teacher," they said.

"I'm a writer," I said, which didn't sound at all like a "real job," but it was a cool thing to say to these kids, who were full of romance and wanderlust and idealism. They all seemed to have the same plan. When they graduated from college in two years, they were going to start nonprofits in Sydney or Paris or Oslo.

"What do you write?" they asked.

Fiction and short stories, I told them. "Someday, a novel. I know there is a book in me somewhere." That was my standard answer. *I know there is a book in me somewhere.* They thought this was cool, but there was something in their faces that said they doubted it, that it was just an old man's crazy dream, and that maybe I should stick to something more realistic like starting a nonprofit in a bitchin' city on another continent.

Time evaporated that summer and I began to think those kids were right. The late night writing I'd envisioned never happened. I told myself I would wake up early and write for an hour. It would be the first thing I did; I would sit with a tin cup of instant coffee and write into the sunrise, then I would clean the KYBOs. This didn't happen, either, except for the KYBO cleaning.

Weeks passed and the summer turned into September. I was off the island and back in my apartment where there was clean, running water and lights that turned on at the flick of a switch; there was a toilet I didn't have to stir. I made drip coffee by the pot. I had carpet between my toes, and on my thirtieth birthday, September 8, 1998, Mark McGwire hit his sixty-second home run in Busch Stadium to break Roger Maris's long-standing record of sixty-one. Mom and I were celebrating my birthday in an Italian restaurant a half-mile from Stuccoville, and we listened to the game on the radio in my pickup as we drove through the old neighborhood. The fig trees were all gone. I parked across the street from both our Stuccoville houses. We sat and stared at these old places against a backdrop of ballgame noise. I saw the shadows of my former selves, but there was one memory that emerged above every other. Maybe it was the ballgame that triggered it, but there it was, as lucid for me then as the day it happened more than twenty-two years before, the summer my father left in the cooling dusk.

I am standing shoeless in the front yard wearing a blue tank top and cutoffs and a maroon baseball cap. There are two white letters on the cap, FW, for Food World, my pee-wee league team. I am playing catch with my mother, who is in her bathrobe. There is a cigarette between her lips and a small black dog at my feet chewing green grass. He is a cockapoo named Rocky, named for Rocky Balboa, because the movie was big then, this famous story of a Philadelphia fighter who overcomes great odds to win a title. Rocky is there to ease the transition for me. My mother thinks a dog will be a comfort and help me feel less lonely.

That's it. That's the full memory. It is nothing more than a glimpse; it is a jagged little scrawl, but at the time, it meant everything, which is why it came back so clearly. Mom didn't say so that night, but I believe she saw it, too, the same thing, right before her eyes.

24

There Are Low Points and There Are Nadirs

"Despite all of your afflictions, your spirit to keep me on the right path continues to pay off. Your life, whether you think so or not, has been a tremendous success."

—Birthday letter to my mother, June 19, 1999

BEFORE MY BIRTHDAY, SOMETIME IN AUGUST, I LANDED two part-time teaching jobs at Fresno State, which not only paid the bills but also gave me time to write. These weren't career-type jobs. They were more like scheduled gigs, but they did just enough for my ego to make me feel like I was moving in the right direction. I was on a university campus, and I pressed myself into the stereotype. I wore whalebone cords and leather boat shoes and carried a faux-leather satchel I'd picked up for five dollars at a Gap closeout sale.

Three afternoons a week, I taught a class called "Upper Division Writing," which because it had "Upper" in the name, I presumed was *way more* advanced than Freshman Comp. I had an office on the edge of campus—as far out as you could go—where in the mornings I worked with a federal grant offering reading and writing services for nonnative speakers. I shared the space with a woman from NYU who loved turtles and popped Xanax and experienced frequent memory loss, mostly when it came to her car keys. She called in sick a lot because she was "ideating," she said, so I wound up most days with the office to myself. When I didn't have students in the space, I tried to write, but the stories would not come.

At home and at work, I sat before my computer in perpetual distraction. I must have started forty different stories and two or three different novels. I wrote spasmodically until I got frustrated. I had dozens of first paragraphs, each housed on a floppy disk on which I'd written the words "Fits and Starts." All of my words languished there, in those files on that disk. I tried to visit them occasionally and build on what I'd started, but they became for me like old girlfriends with whom I'd behaved disgracefully. I was ashamed to see them again because they reminded me of how awful I was. Eventually, my shame morphed into terror because I knew I had lost something fundamental, something much bigger than the ability to write.

Six years of graduate school and suddenly I had no voice.

In an effort to rediscover it, I became derivative. I tried to imitate success because I had heard somewhere that good writers borrow, but great writers steal. I was desperate, so I stole, which is what desperate people do. This is what my students did. The nights before assignments were due, they stole papers from the Internet and submitted the work as their own. I was chafed by their audacity in thinking I wouldn't notice. My theft wasn't a copy and paste job, which is how I rationalized my crime. Rather, it was an arduous process of imitation.

Here's how it worked: I pulled books from my shelves and read the first lines of stories to mimic language that might trigger a start. I might read a line like "I used to spend a lot of time with Mr. Aaron," then go to my computer and write, "I once hung out with a boy named Nathan Beagle." Then I moved to the next line: "He had a bench you could pass out on by the stove and that's where I was one day." Now, me: "He lived near a park by the railroad tracks and that's where I saw his scars." On to the next line, then the next.

Imagine it: One excruciating sentence at a time imitating structure and cadence and tone until I eventually grew weary and sad because I knew it was going nowhere. I did this deep into the night and I often drank through the process, thinking wine might knock loose the fear and free up my creativity. It did not. Drinking just made me sadder, and the reality that my stories were going nowhere translated to every other area of my life. I became short-tempered with my mother. Sometimes, I took care of her while drunk. This is what my Uncle Jack used to do with Marzelle, and this realization—that I was becoming my uncle—terrified me even more than my inability to write.

One night, late, Mom tried to get in bed but slipped to the floor. She had a button around her neck that she could push to call me. "I'm not hurt," she said. "But I missed the bed." She said I needed to come pick her up. It was one of those nights I had been not-writing and drinking, so I was in a bad place in my head. I marched like a child from my apartment, stumbled to her door, and rattled the key in the deadbolt. Inside, Sammy barked. Even after he saw me, he still barked. He yapped, actually, right up at me, and as I passed him, he nipped at my heel, like I was some kind of stranger. Maybe that was what he saw in me, someone strange and foreign and not all there. *Yap, yap, yap, yap, yap, yap.* It was loud and annoying and late, and he persisted all the way into Mom's bedroom, where she sat with her back to her bed, a sheepish but sad little smile on her face, and because I was drunk and Sammy was irritating and still at my heel, I gave him a donkey kick into the hall. He was resilient. He rolled like a stunt dog and came back at me. Mom glowered. "Say you're sorry," she said.

"To the dog?" I was apoplectic. "He *bit* me!" I was the injured party here. That's how I felt, anyway, like I was trying to make progress, but I kept getting donkey-kicked out the door.

Mom would not take no for an answer. She ordered me to apologize. "Say you're sorry to Sammy," she said. "Get on the floor and give him some love."

When I refused, she said, "I am *still* your mother."

There are low points and there are nadirs. You can have a bunch of low points in life, but the nadir is the lowest. It is rock bottom. It is at this point when all seems lost. When you have been drinking alone and it is late at night and you kick your disabled mother's tiny dog while she sits helpless after falling to the floor, this qualifies as a nadir. That's what I call it, at least in this story, at this point in my life, this moment in which I never felt lower.

Mom was right: She was still my mother. So, I knelt and reached out to Sammy. He had every reason to bite me. Instead, he submitted. He waggled his small black body and licked my hand. He tucked his docked tail between his legs. I was forgiven.

"Now," Mom said. "Get me up." I submitted. I did what I had been trained to do: I knelt before my mother and wrapped my arms around her middle. I had one hand on the small of her back, the other between her shoulder blades. I kept one knee in contact with the carpet. With the bed as support and on the count of three, I rose straight up on that knee. I lifted my mother's body. Her thighs came even with the bed and she shifted backward into a sitting position. I kept one arm around her back, and I used the other as a kind of lever. I reached behind her knees and slid her into bed. My mother did the rest. She pushed her heels against the footboard. She walked her shoulders back until her body found the part of the mattress that fit her. Then, she used an able finger to press the up arrow on the mechanism that raised and lowered her head. There was a metallic hum as her torso came up gently, buckling her in the middle. I covered her in a quilt, and Sammy scampered up his doggie staircase into bed. He curled against Mom's hip.

"Go home," my mother said. "You can come back when your head is right."

The morning after I kicked Sammy, I was headed out of my apartment for work. I felt lousy, and not just because I had been drinking late the night before. I had acted despicably and I didn't know how and when I could face my mother again. My shame was deep and painful, as was my headache, which had settled like a pickaxe behind my eyes.

It was December of 1999, about three weeks before Y2K didn't happen. The air was cold and drippy, and as I closed my door and walked toward the staircase, I saw Lisa, the girl next door, through her open blinds. She was a graphic designer for a downtown business weekly. That morning, she was standing at the sink. Sometimes, she sat at her table in that window reading the paper and I waved on my way out. She was a quiet, single girl who did not like noise, but she was always cordial, even though she rarely smiled. She also had a full-time job with benefits, and she was able to buy decent clothes. I also knew she was saving to buy a house. Given where I was in life, and given where I thought she was, I wondered if maybe I should just surrender, if maybe I ought to ask her out and see where things went. I wasn't attracted to her, but I figured I was at an age where I needed to think practically. I had always wanted to marry the girl-next-door anyway.

I made it down the stairs to the sidewalk, past Mom's apartment and into the parking lot, where I stood at the door of my pickup. Actually, I *found myself* standing there. It was as though my body was operating independently of my brain. Sometimes that still happens. Sometimes, I wind up at the mailbox, but I cannot remember taking steps to get there. My son says I teleport. Because I am a child of the seventies, I think of it more like *I Dream of Jeannie*. I blink and disappear, then reappear elsewhere, like magic.

That morning in the parking lot, I teleported; I blinked. Once I realized where I was, I stood and watched my breath in the cold air. Something wasn't right. Maybe it was just a brief blackout, but when I came to, something was nudging my conscience. That something told me to turn around and take the sidewalk back to the stairs, walk back up, and knock on Lisa's door. My wife Karen says this whole episode was God. I don't doubt it. There was certainly a palpable presence within me that morning, more than just the wicked headache, and at its urging, I turned around. I took the sidewalk to the staircase and when I reached the top, I turned left. I saw Lisa, still at the sink, and I stood a moment before her door. I knocked. I heard her footsteps pad softly on the carpet. Then she answered, wearing a terry cloth robe, its lapels gathered modestly in her fist.

I had been thinking about Lisa for some time. What I had been thinking about most—and what I was thinking about that morning—was asking her to put in a good word for me at the business weekly, even though she only knew *of* me. I said, "Can you see if there's a need for a writer?" Lisa said she would see. She said she would let me know later, and sure enough—about nine hours later—Lisa knocked on my door. She said the managing editor was eager to talk to me. She said the editor knew me from graduate school at Fresno State, knew that I was a fine writer, one of the better student writers she had known. There was a place for someone at the weekly. She was looking for someone to fill that place, the sooner the better.

From the nadir, there is no place to go but up.

25

See What the Page Gives You in Return

"Dear Son . . .

I'll start this little history back prior to your birth. Your request will be fulfilled to the extent that my memory allows me to tell it."

—Letter from my father, December 12, 2003

NOW OVER FIFTY, I HAVE LIVED LONG ENOUGH TO UNDER-stand trajectory. I can see the way events have knitted together to construct my life and how following the still, small voice in my head has had world-changing implications. There are people who would not be here had I neglected the spirit that urged me to turn around at seemingly innocuous places, like the parking lot of my apartment complex. What if I had ignored that spirit? Suppose I had zigged instead of zagged? Quite possibly, my present reality would vanish, supplanted by an entirely new, unfathomable one. My three children? All gone. In their places, other kids, or perhaps none at all.

We make hundreds of decisions every day that impact human history, yet we will never know how much. Think of it: What if, on the day after Thanksgiving 1988, Ramon had gone home for the holiday. Suppose his mom, on a whim, had called the frat house pay phone and said, "Ramon, I'm making that stuffing you like." Because Ramon hated more than anything to disappoint his mother, he goes home, and on that rainy Black Friday in 1988, there is no one to stop me as I head out to work on my motorcycle, helmetless. Because Ramon decided to leave, which happened because his mother decided to call him, I die from traumatic brain injury at the age of twenty. I have Ramon's mom to thank for this.

Or do I? What could have caused Ramon's mom to call in the first place? Maybe Ramon's little sister. She might have said, "I wish Ramon were coming home for Thanksgiving," after she saw a photograph of Ramon in a kitchen junk drawer where she was rummaging in search of a pen to scribble a phone message from a doctor's office. The previous week, Ramon's father had, say, become worried over the presence of some pearly bumps on his feet, so he'd made an appointment with a dermatologist. The bumps turn out to be an allergic reaction to a change in laundry soap, a *decision* Ramon's mom made because the new soap was on sale and she had thought, "What could be the harm in saving a few bucks?" How could she have known that there would indeed be harm, that her decision to change laundry soap to save some money would ultimately lead to my death?

Some call this Chaos Theory: A butterfly flaps its wings in Texas and that triggers a series of events that starts a deadly tornado in Burma six weeks later. Others see it as Grand Design; our decisions are not decisions at all. They are predetermined outcomes. Every event has been willed by God, so who are we to control things? Why even bother?

I have heard that if you want to make God laugh, tell Him your plans.

In May of 2012, when he was near death from throat cancer, I visited my father in Palm Springs. He and Loose-Wheel lived in the Thunderbird Mobile Estates Park, where they owned a triple-wide. This was high-end at Thunderbird, the place people strolled past at sunset to gawk, as though it were a parade float. Lucille had the outside all done up in river rocks and fake flowers. There were two bird baths and a few plastic flamingos among a dozen real cacti. Every night, Lucille sat perched on her elevated patio with a cigarette in her fingers and a Chablis on the side table. She waved to neighbors walking small dogs in sweaters. In Palm Springs.

By this time, I had been married to Karen for eleven years. We met through my job at the business weekly, which may have never happened had I not turned around on that cold morning in December 1999 and knocked on Lisa's door. We had three kids under ten. I'd had a four-year stint as a journalist with hundreds of bylines, and I'd had another year as a writer for a glossy monthly that covered trends in the construction industry.

At that point, I was nine years into a university career at Fresno State, helping graduate students refine and publish their research and creative work. My father had gotten the idea that I was a dean, but by then his mind was so addled with cancer drugs and booze that it was no use telling him any different; Loose-Wheel, I found out, had been spiking his feeding tube with cheap whiskey.

At the time I saw him, my father and I had been talking for years, but only through cards and letters and an annual phone call. I was with his sister Ginny, and that spring day in Palm Springs was our planned farewell to him. We knew we would not return for a funeral for reasons that were complicated and deeply personal. There were others he'd chosen to surround him who had become so embedded that his blood relatives were now outsiders. Loose-Wheel had become toxic to what was left of Dad's family. She had, with intention and with my father too sick to fight it, wrestled control of an account my Grandpa Leo left for Dad—all that *money in paper bags*—resources intended for things other than the booze and cigarettes and curios she squandered it on. In our minds, she had lost control, spent foolishly, and self-medicated constantly.

With Grandpa Leo's money, she bought a new laptop computer neither she nor my father could figure out how to use. She then spent hundreds more on a desk for it. Aunt Ginny was beside herself: "Why do you buy a desk for a *lap*top? It's supposed to go on your *lap*!" The whole monument sat against a wall in the triple-wide, two thousand dollars of Leo's money wasted on a thing that would wind up with Lucille's son after my dad's passing, the computer itself buried amongst a menagerie of Polynesian whatnots. We felt she was storing up treasures for her own offspring, using money she had no business touching. She said it took money to care for Dad, and she had every right to it.

There were mean, hurtful things said during our time there, things that no one could repair, and on our last day, Lucille threw her hands up and left us alone with Dad. She had been drinking Chablis all morning. She told us both to go to Hell, and Ginny said we would see her there.

We would learn by that evening that Lucille spent her afternoon at an Elks Lodge bar drinking until she couldn't stand. It was dusk, in the gloaming, and someone we didn't know, someone from their inner circle, delivered her home; under the carport, Lucille propped herself against the outside wall of the trailer, a cigarette dangling from her mouth.

I don't remember the words and their order. That's because there was such a blind flurry of them. I remember, though, that Ginny and I took turns attacking Lucille's weak will and the fact that she continued to smoke those damned cigarettes one after the other within feet of a man who needed an oxygen tank to breathe. I know we said it didn't take a genius to figure out that thousands of cigarettes and all of those years of her blowing smoke in his face were the cause of all this. Ginny called her a murderer; I called her a drunk and a thief. We were our ugliest, most inhumane selves. I wondered where it all came from.

For her part, Lucille slurred about how ungrateful we were for the effort she'd put into caring for my father and how we weren't around to do any of the dirty work and how no one in Dad's family ever liked her, especially his parents. She went on about how everything she'd bought she deserved because she was doing the work now and she was his wife goddammit and she had earned the right to spend whatever goddamned money she wanted on things that brought her the slightest joy, even Connie Francis's goddamned seagull if that's what she wanted. Since we'd been there, we'd done nothing but mock that porcelain seagull as an emblem of Lucille's foolishness.

"How do you know?" I yelled. "How do you know it ever belonged to Connie Francis?"

Lucille pushed herself away from the wall that held her up. She began to pitch forward like a tower of falling blocks. I stepped in to catch her. She smelled of cheap wine and smoke; she weighed little more than a bird. "How do you not know?" she said. "How do you *not know!*"

All over the trailer park, people emerged from metal screen doors. I saw their silhouettes in porch lights. I saw cigarette embers glow. Then there came a moment of heavy quiet, and in this moment, from inside the triple-wide, my father mustered enough wind in his lungs to wail: "Just shut the hell up!" He coughed and barked up phlegm. "Shut up!"

"Now look what you've done," Lucille said. "You've upset him." I held her as she teetered in place, barely able to keep her eyes open.

"I can't take it anymore," Ginny said. She said the whole thing was pathetic.

My aunt went inside and said her goodbyes to her only brother and reminisced one last time over their mutual past. I stood right outside the door, looking through the screen into the kitchen, and listened. I released Lucille into a sitting position on the stair. I secured her against a safety rail, wedging her upright into a corner where she closed her eyes. A pot-bellied neighbor appeared and asked me if everything was all right.

"What do you think?" I said. "Does any of this look like it's all right?"

Then I apologized. I said we'd keep it down. He nodded and left.

Inside, Dad and Ginny shared a story about my father hating green peas so much that to avoid eating them in the school cafeteria, he would shove them in his pockets and forget about them, only to get a tongue-lashing later from Margaret, who would find them as she checked for coins or army men before she did his laundry.

"I still hate peas," Dad said, and Ginny laughed. She has always had a beautiful, hearty laugh, even in bad times. They shared other anecdotes and said they loved each other. Ginny stood crying and hugged him around the neck before she walked out, stepping through the screen door and navigating around Lucille, who by this time was slumping with her head between her shoulders as the ash from her cigarette grew longer and more precarious. My aunt rolled her wet, swollen eyes and said she'd be waiting for me in the rental car. My job for the rest of that night was to ensure my father got to bed safely and that Lucille had been deposited inside, at the very least on a sofa, cigarette extinguished.

My own goodbye had come earlier that afternoon, when Lucille was at the Elks Lodge. I had traveled to Palm Springs with two goals in mind: forgive my father while he was alive, and help him straighten out his eternal address. This is what he had asked from me: forgiveness and a path to salvation. I had a book with me, Lee Stroebel's *The Case for Christ,* the story of a skeptical journalist turned Christ-follower after a season of calculated, primary research. I thought, of all books, this would be the one that might hit home with my father, who thought of himself as a writer.

About seven years before he died, Dad had self-published an overwritten novel called *The Felon.* He sent it off to a binding service, which also designed a simple cover. He needed an editor, because that wasn't part of the package, so he called on me, thinking perhaps it might be one last thing to bring us together. He wasn't getting along well, but despite illness, he was enjoying the experience of writing because it took him away from his reality. I went ahead and read *The Felon,* every page, and later, when Dad asked for my opinion, I told him it was great work, a great story, and he should keep going. I said this: "Enjoy the process." I said, "Go to the page each day expecting nothing and see what the page gives you in return." Somewhere along the line, I had gotten that same advice.

Had he been in a better place health-wise, had he been one of my own writing students, I might have told my father something more useful and pragmatic. I might have told him, for example, that when describing his heroine—a bright young attorney—something like, "She was a smart and capable lawyer" was much easier on the reader than what he had chosen: "She was a veritable walking encyclopedia of jurisprudence." But there was so much of that happening, I lacked the time and energy to slog through it all. It was also fundamentally flawed: Points of view shifted erratically, without purpose. Verb tense did, too; there were usage errors, comma splices, sentence fragments. I couldn't bring myself to fix it. I was a young father trying to figure out on my own how to be a good dad and husband while also tending to Mom, who at the time was still living on her own in an apartment she couldn't clean and using a bedside commode I didn't trust her to empty. Either Karen or I handled this chore daily to keep her apartment from reeking of urine.

The harder truth about it was that I didn't *want* to make the time. My investment in his book was equivalent, I felt, to his investment in me, which is to say, nominal.

That afternoon in May, Dad and I talked for some time about what awaited him on the other side. We talked about Lee Stroebel's story, and where Dad thought he would go after he died.

"God has no place for a man like me," he said.

I expected this. He'd had lots of time to reflect on his life, and for him, there was nothing to see but sin and bad decisions; it was pretty easy to conclude for himself where he might end up. But I told him it didn't have to be that way. We talked about the most famous verse in the Bible, John 3:16, the one the guy in the rainbow wig holds up for the camera during football games. "Whosoever believes in Him," I read, "shall have everlasting life." I told Dad that included everybody, even him. I told him about Pascal's wager, though I didn't call it that. Live out your days believing God is real, I said; put all your chips on infinite gain, because at this point, you have nothing to lose. Sure, it was a deathbed conversion, maybe a longshot, but if John Wayne could do it, so could Dad. I held his liver-spotted hand and prayed for him, then I told him to read the Gospel of John, which he said he would do before he died. I don't know if this ever happened. This was the last day we spoke.

I'd like to say that he looked lighter and less burdened after this, but that would be a lie. His head hung just as it had before; he labored for breath, and his eyes were still full of heartbreak and self-reproach. His breathing was ragged, and his voice ratcheted down to a whisper as he asked me a hard question I could not answer.

"What did I do?"

Never in my life have I seen a man so ensnared by his circumstances, so harnessed and un-caribou-like, so ready to die, as my father was then.

"The biggest regret of my life," he said, "is leaving you and your mother for that *bitch*." He was talking about Patty, the woman he drove to Montana with right after he left us. He could barely get the final word from his throat to his lips without gagging on sputum. Then, he surprised me: "The second worst thing was marrying her." He hooked his thumb toward a picture of him and Lucille, standing in a side hug near Dana Point, the Pacific Ocean glistening and sun-spackled behind them. I had snapped that picture. We'd eaten brunch that morning at a tiny, crowded restaurant overlooking the coast. Karen and I were newly married and she was pregnant with our twin girls. Lucille held her coffee mug with two hands and told us she knew a woman who had identical twins born three months apart. My father rolled his eyes.

"She had the first one in July," Lucille said. "Then the next one came in October." Her head bobbed like her neck was a spring.

Karen gave my leg a squeeze under the table. "Crazy," we said.

Later that same day, we stood with Lucille in the triple-wide's guest bathroom as she showed off a long line of rocks on a curio shelf, a rock from every state she had visited.

She went through each rock for us. "I got this one in Oregon," she said. "And this one on the side of the road in Idaho." Lucille turned Idaho Rock over in her small hand. It was a gray oval, about the size of her thumb.

"So neat," Karen said.

"Amazing," I said. "All the way from Idaho?"

Lucille nodded. She set the rock up on the shelf. "Yep," she said. "That one's my favorite."

The call came in the mid-morning, July 29, 2012. I had just finished running the San Francisco half-marathon. I showered quickly in the hotel and made my way on foot to the end of the full marathon course, where I'd hoped to cheer The Monk across the finish line. We were and still are friends, after all these years.

Three hours earlier, I'd set out along the Embarcadero in the cool San Francisco predawn. The pack had yet to break up, so I was working my way ahead through elbows and knees, quick-cutting around slower runners and yielding to those who wanted to move faster. I was running alone that morning, even though I was surrounded by thousands of others doing the same thing. It would be my own thoughts and muscles and resolve that would carry me through the next thirteen miles. On my right, amongst several others, I took mental note of a seafood restaurant, a place called Alioto's, where Dad had once taken me when I was a boy. I remembered it because he handed me a gold matchbox afterward to keep as a memento of our day. I kept that matchbox for years, never opening it. I turned the image of it over and over in my brain for miles, across the Golden Gate Bridge and back, cutting through cold fog both ways.

Soon, by mile nine or so, I forgot about the matchbox, focusing instead on the grit it would take me to climb a hill in the Presidio, a gut-crunching, calf-burning, mentally aggravating ascent I attacked with my head down, looking up occasionally at forest and ocean because I didn't want my memory of these moments to be marked only by images of asphalt passing beneath me. I made it to the top, my knees complaining the entire way, then down the other side, through a neighborhood of multistory walkups, then finally to the end, never stopping, crossing the finish line in two hours-four minutes, feeling strong and accomplished and euphoric even though I'd just missed my sub-two-hour goal. I was in the best shape of my life. The sun was out and the fog had cleared. The city was glorious with activity and alive with the smell of fresh fish and brewing coffee. I walked comfortably on warm leg muscles and cushioned shoes, my finisher's medal around my neck.

That was when my cell phone rang. It was Lucille's son, calling to tell me that Dad had passed earlier that morning, about three hours earlier, just around the time I would have been running along the Embarcadero, past Alioto's in the cold darkness, and thinking of him and the time he took me there, thinking of how he pressed into my palm his gift of a gold matchbox.

26

Elvis, by This Time, Was Living With Me

"For your birthday, we'll spend some quality time together and go to dinner, and yes, if you like, I'll wheel you around the mall."

—Birthday card to my mother, June 19, 2005

WHEN MOM WAS SIXTY-SEVEN, KAREN AND OUR THREE-year-old daughters went for a visit. There was to be a shopping trip to the local mall. At that point, Mom could still walk with a cane from her apartment to the car. She walked around her apartment, too—from bedroom to kitchen to bathroom—and when she was feeling bold, she walked all the way to the mailbox. It was important for her to walk, she said, because it kept the blood flowing. It kept her legs from atrophy.

She was in high spirits that day because she loved the mall. It was sunny and the girls wore matching dresses and shoes. Mom cooed over them. "We need to have their picture done," she said. "My treat." Karen said that sounded like a good idea. There was a photo studio at Penney's. It was a weekday and they wouldn't need an appointment. They would visit the food court for lunch, and the girls would crawl through the big rubber forest. Karen took Mom's pocketbook and apartment key. She put Sammy in his little kennel, then the four of them moved toward the front door.

I knew my mother had been having trouble with her left foot. She said it had been feeling prickly and asleep. Often, she'd ask to sit down, ask someone to loosen the Velcro strap on her shoe. But that morning, though her foot was tingling, she didn't stop to fix it; there was momentum she didn't want to lose. Plus, she didn't want to be a bother. So, she braved it and kept walking. She followed the energy to the door, and in the midst of the happy commotion stirred by two, three-year-old girls in matching clothes, she failed to pick up her foot. She tripped on the carpet and once she started going down, there was nothing she could do to stop herself. Karen said it looked like my mother's feet never moved, like she was bound at the ankles. Mom's head hit the door jamb, which decelerated her enough for Karen to grab a shirttail with her fingertips. This slowed her descent. For all we know, this saved her life. Still, Mom hit hard. It's a miracle she did not break every frail bone in her ossified body.

Beyond the threshold, there was a welcome mat and a pad of concrete that led to the sidewalk. When Mom went down, her head cracked against that concrete; her body wound up across her cane and over the threshold, her bottom half inside the apartment, her top half outside. Then, from beneath my mother, came a pool of blood. It bloomed crimson on the concrete. Mom lay on her cheek, both arms folded beneath her.

I don't know if Karen remained composed, because she doesn't remember. What she remembers is telling the girls to turn on the television, to find *Arthur* or *Clifford* or something animated and cheery that might separate them from the trauma. She remembers reaching beneath my mother to push the button on her pendant and she remembers the voice through the speaker near the phone: "911, what's your emergency?" Karen explained the emergency and the voice on the other side said to keep my mother calm, that the ambulance was on its way.

Karen took a pillow from the sofa and put it under Mom's head. She knelt next to her and whispered *shhhh* and rubbed her back. The voice said again to keep her calm. My mother wailed. She cried and blamed herself and Karen said, "No, no, no." It wasn't anyone's fault, she said. The ambulance was on its way. She heard its siren drawing close. The driver would know just where to go.

I have asked my daughters if they remember this day, and almost fifteen years later, they remember it all. The scene for them has not detached itself. There was to be a shopping trip, but there was an accident, and a bad sound, and crying, and blood from Nana's head on the sidewalk. They thought she was dead, and they remember what they felt at the time as they stood behind Karen in their matching dresses and shoes. They were scared, they said. Then they were sad.

They have both told me that this is their first memory. They have both told me they remember nothing in their lives before this.

The doctor said there was only one way Mom was getting out of his ER. There was an express recovery unit in a local nursing home, he said. I cringed: *the poor house.* Mom would get therapy there and Medicare would pick up the tab for six weeks. "I won't discharge her to her apartment," he told me. "Not until she gets therapy."

"Fair enough," I said. "Then she can go home? After six weeks?"

"After six weeks," he said. Then we would see. She would have to make progress there; she would have to prove she could do things on her own.

Before I left, the doctor told me I needed to seriously consider twenty-four-hour care. "Skilled nursing," he called it. Waiting lists could be long, though, so I'd better start looking now. I must have made a face. I must have looked at him in shock. He said the only way to bypass the wait was to have Mom admitted straight from the ER. He said if she came back with "as much as a sniffle," she could go from the ER into skilled nursing straightaway. "That's the secret," he said. "That's how you have to navigate the system." He whispered this last part from the side of his mouth. If I didn't learn this, he told me, I could find myself with nowhere for my mother to go. I never told my mother this. I never told her that the next time she went to the ER could be the last time she saw her apartment. Instead, I just let her live her life, and I let the worry strangle me.

While Mom was in rehab, the girls were in charge of Sammy, who was small and compliant and let them dress him in doll clothes. It was a big thrill for them to have a dog in the house. A couple times a week we took him for visits to the rehab hospital, where Mom was making great progress. She was motivated to do well and she worked hard, learned skills to take home with her, and qualified for a power wheelchair. Medicare picked up the tab on this, too. Mom liked the idea of driving herself places again; she liked the idea of independence, though she often lived in fear of it.

For a while, she did drive herself places. She drove herself to the grocery store next to her apartment; she drove herself to the salon and the bagel shop. She drove herself to the mailbox. When she did this, Sammy jumped on her lap like a tiny hood ornament and they navigated the meandering sidewalk through her complex. She grew attached to her power chair. She scuffed her apartment walls with it; she took the paint off corners. All the while, we looked in on her. We took her to church on Sundays. I pushed her through the narthex, and she told folks she was getting along okay, and they took her bony fingers in theirs and said she was an amazing woman, what with all she'd been through. Mom loved this kind of attention; she loved hearing from others that she was courageous and strong.

I took on some hours from the county again, but Karen did most of the work. She took the girls over to Mom's and they watched TV on the sofa while Karen ran the vacuum and unloaded the dishwasher and washed the clothes. She made meals and sealed them in bowls Mom could open; she sorted pills by days of the week. There were other helpers, women who came from the county, but Mom didn't want them around. At night, Mom called me to complain: They were stealing her pills, she said. They were stealing her socks and her stamps and her dog food. She could not trust them to be in her apartment. Her treasures were in danger. Elvis, by this time, was living with me.

"He's not safe here," Mom had said. "You have to take him. He's better off with you."

So, I went to Mom's apartment and got Elvis. He was in the back of her closet covered in a black trash bag. "Let me see him one last time," Mom said.

"It's not like I'm throwing him away," I told her. "You can visit him at my house whenever you're there."

Still, Mom wanted to see Elvis. I lifted the trash bag to unveil his snarl. He was young in the picture; his face was thin and he wore a red jacket, the collar turned up. He looked over his left shoulder, his eyes piercing and blue. "Bring him closer," Mom said. She leaned over in her wheelchair to get a better look. Her finger, light as a moth, pointed to his handwritten message: "To Lynn, my best to you always, Elvis Presley."

"I went by Lynn, then," she said. She was wistful.

"It's a nice picture," I said.

"Your dad hated it," Mom said. "He always thought there was something between us."

"Was there?" I asked, and Mom grinned. It was a might-have-been grin. But then she told me no. She told me she never had a love affair with Elvis Presley.

I wondered, though. I let myself fantasize that I was Elvis Presley's illegitimate son. I, too, had a snarl; I could swivel my hips. My renditions of "Teddy Bear" and "Blue Christmas" were spot-on. It was not impossible for there to be a little Elvis in me.

"Take him," Mom said. "Put him somewhere safe."

I did this. I put Elvis in a safe place, in the back of my closet, still in the trash bag. He rested there against a wall, next to a box that held Karen's wedding dress.

Over time, other treasures made their way to my place. I brought home Marzelle's family photo albums, Mom's autographed glossies of movie stars, and Sinatra's *Come Fly With Me* on vinyl. I wound up with the September 13, 1968 issue of *The Hollywood Reporter* and all twenty volumes of *Uncle Arthur's Bedtime Stories,* gifts to my mother and Uncle Jack in 1944. Mom thought my kids might like them. She entrusted me with love letters and gifts from old boyfriends, too: a gold Cameo compact from a boy named Bill Magraft, and a Phinney-Walker boudoir alarm clock from Jim Muren, given in 1957.

Slowly, her closet emptied and mine filled. I absorbed Mom's treasured past in pieces until there was nothing left for her to give me.

In 2008, when our daughters were six and our son was one, Karen and I got a late-night call from 911 dispatch. Mom was transferring from the commode and she fell; she missed the bed and hit the floor. She told dispatch she thought her tailbone was broken. I got to her apartment before the ambulance did. When I found her, she was sitting on the carpet in a shaft of light from her closet. Her back was against the bed and Sammy was on her lap. But before that, when I was still home and on the phone, I told Mom that everything was going to be okay. "Try to be calm," I said. "Try not to move." We were on a three-way call: on one line, dispatch; on another, me; and on the third, my mother. "Mom," I said, "It's going to be okay. It's going to be fine." But Mom was inconsolable. At that moment, she could not be made to believe that everything would be fine. I handed Karen the phone and grabbed my car keys. "Tell her I'm on my way," I said, but Karen just held the receiver in her open hand. It remained there as I left her with my mother and her cries and her awful, dawning awareness: "No, no, no, no, no, no, no, no."

27

I Release You to This Next Great Adventure

"Resident has self-care deficits and requires extensive assistance in bathing, grooming, dressing, bed mobility, transfer, toileting, and ambulation, due to chronic disease/compromising functional ability, chronic pain, deformities of the hand/foot, impaired mobility, reduced activity tolerance, unsteady balance, and mood issues."

—K.O., MD, Progress Notes,
February 21, 2018

MOM WAS MAD FOR A FEW WEEKS. SHE DIDN'T TALK MUCH to me. She didn't talk much to her roommate, either, who was Armenian and spoke no English. In the nursing home, I sat next to her bed and defended myself.

"The ER doctor said he'd find me guilty of elder abuse," I said, and this was mostly true. He did use the words *elder abuse.* He said I could bring her home to live with me or look for a private facility. Costs varied, but they were generally in the neighborhood of five-thousand a month. We lived in fifteen-hundred square feet and were raising twin girls and a new son, and we didn't have money for what he called "Cadillac Care." A government-subsidized nursing home was the only option. For her to live alone, in her condition, was "no different than elder abuse."

That's what he said. If there was a threat to prosecute me in those words, it was veiled. I let myself believe in that possibility though, because it allowed me to shift the blame. It allowed me to say to my mother, "This nursing home thing is not my fault." That's what I needed to believe, and that's what I needed her to believe. I could not be the one to separate her from her independence, yet. I also knew that it was unconscionable to do otherwise. In the end, it came down to a question: Which guilt was easier to live with?

I signed to have her admitted to a nursing home.

"I know this is hard," the doctor said, "but it's the right thing to do. She couldn't survive on her own."

"What do you think she's been doing for the last fifty years?" I said.

Every Sunday, driven by guilt, I picked Mom up from the healthcare center. That's what she made us call it—all of us—even the kids. Sometimes, we let "nursing home" slip, but she corrected us, gently: "It's a *healthcare center*," she said. To her, it could not be a nursing home, because that was a place where forgotten people lived, and by now she knew she had not been forgotten.

Sundays became heavy days. I began to dread them as early as Monday. They were a process. Mom had to be transferred between chairs, wheeled to the medicine cart for her pills, then transferred again to our van. Each transfer was precarious; her legs twisted easily, and her knees buckled. Her body was fragile and unpredictable. Then there was her wheelchair; it was old and clunky and weighed forty pounds. It was ill-tempered and refused to fold easily—unless you weren't expecting it—at which point it would snap shut and pinch your fingers. There were some days this happened, and I got so mad, I just let it drop on the asphalt. I once kicked the manual wheelchair after it pinched me. I kicked it over and over again, and I did this in front of my children. Another time, I pushed it away from me through the parking lot, then chased after it before it rammed into a parked car. My mother was buckled in the passenger seat and because she could barely turn her head, I don't think she ever saw me during these fits, but Karen and the kids did, and it shames me.

At our house, we sat at the table and put food before her. We prayed and thanked God for food, for family. "For a house to live in and food to eat," was always how it went. Then we said "Amen." I forked small bites into Mom's mouth. I moved a straw near her lips, and she drank tiny sips of Pepsi. Afterward, we moved her to a comfortable chair, where she watched Sunday television until her head lolled back and she fell asleep with her mouth open. Most Sundays, she would wake after an hour and have to use the bathroom. Karen managed this. It took two of us to get her over the toilet, but once there, Karen handled the dirty work. I felt guilty over this. I resented my mother for having to urinate, but Karen said it was no big deal. She said there were things I should be excused from, and wiping my mother was one of those things. When it came time to re-dress her, I held Mom in a standing position with my eyes closed while Karen attached the diaper. I held her while Karen pulled up her pants, then the two of us pivoted her into the wheelchair. My mother said she was sorry, and we said it was okay, that it was nothing more than life coming full-circle.

By five o'clock, we took her back to the healthcare center, set her up for the week, and I did things for her that seemed inane and unnecessary. I refolded sweatpants in a drawer. I arranged blouses in her closet by color, long-sleeve on bottom, short-sleeve on top. I counted her cans of Pepsi to make sure no one had absconded with any during the afternoon. Mom lived in constant fear of this, of other residents stealing a can of Pepsi while she was away. She once told me she had me do these things so she could keep me around longer. "I'm sorry," she said. "I don't like it when you go," and that softened me. I told her I was sorry for always rushing, but I was tired, I wanted to be home, I had to work the next day.

"It's okay," she said. "You need to be with your family."

"*You* are my family," I said. "You are the strongest part."

One Sunday, as I wheeled her from her room into the hall, she made me stop. There was a woman in a wheelchair right outside her door. It was white-haired Wanda. At one point in their time there, Mom and Wanda had shared a room. They did not get along. Mom thought Wanda was a bully and a fake. That's because before Wanda wound up there, she was a preacher in some other state. When they were roommates, Wanda had animated, tearful colloquies with the Lord Almighty. Mom said Wanda was a Pentecostal. She entered ardent reveries and entreated angels. She sang spirited hymns until her cheeks jiggled. I knew all about Wanda, and I knew Mom did not care for her, so I stopped Mom's wheelchair and started to steer around her.

"Stop," Mom said. "Back up." I stopped. I backed up. I thought maybe Mom wanted to exchange pleasantries, but no; for her, it was a standoff. "Wanda steals." She said this as though Wanda weren't sitting right there in front of her. She made no effort to whisper this as an aside. Mom told me to back up into the room and block the doorway. Mom said Wanda was under surveillance for rolling into empty rooms and rummaging drawers.

"Wanda doesn't steal," I said. "C'mon."

"She steals," Mom said. "I'm telling you."

I told her that Wanda most likely did not know what she was doing. Wanda had dementia. "She probably just thinks your room is her room," I said.

"No," Mom said. "Wanda steals. She knows exactly what she is doing."

We had to wait in the doorway until Wanda had pulled herself along the chair rail and gotten far enough down the hall to turn a corner and disappear from sight. It was an excruciatingly slow journey and my mother watched every painful millisecond of it. In the meantime, I hid Mom's valuables; she made me do this. I put her television remote in her pillowcase, along with her zippered coin purse and her hearing aid batteries. I said, "Mom, who's the crazy one here?" and she did not find that funny at all, not one bit. I wound up doing this every Sunday before we left. I hid everything my mother thought had value, including postage stamps and bendy straws, which in the healthcare center were like cigarettes to inmates.

"Count my Pepsis before we go," she said. "Go ahead. Count them. You'll see. Wanda steals." I did this; I counted Mom's Pepsis, and when we got back, I counted them again. The count had not changed. "Happy?" I asked.

Mom said, "Hmph." She said that Wanda did not steal, not that day, anyway. But in general, Mom said, "Wanda steals."

There were other Wandas.

There was Bendta, the woman Mom lived with right after the Armenian who didn't speak English. Bendta was a hoarder who had her daughter smuggle in cans of beer. She stashed her contraband amidst piles of books and magazines and threatened anyone who offered to organize her things. Bendta was known to fall asleep drunk in her chair, and the CNAs lived in fear of her. She growled at workers that she would have them fired. At Residents' Council, Bendta complained that the food was crap, the CNAs were rough and lazy, the showers were cold. On the Sundays I took Mom out, we'd return to find that her things had been shoved farther into the corner. "Every time I come back," Mom said, "I have less space than I did before I left."

It seemed true. I kept an eye on this by counting floor tiles. I stepped them off from Mom's wall to the middle of the room. Sure enough, as weeks passed, Mom had fewer floor tiles than Bendta, whose space grew by increments each Sunday. I said something about this to the social services lady. "Look, my mother only has a third of the room!" Social services listened to my complaint and responded efficiently; they moved Mom from Bendta's room into the dementia ward. This is what happens when you lodge a complaint in a nursing home; the complaining party gets moved to the first open space, even if it's in the dementia ward, even if the complaining party is not demented.

Despite Wanda, despite Bendta, and despite Sooki—the woman in Station 2 who once bit a CNA and threw her feces at the curtain separating her bed from Mom's—the healthcare center wasn't so bad. In fact, there was one roommate she actually *liked*. Her name was Wilma, and she helped Mom retrieve things she dropped. She held the phone to Mom's ear when she needed to call and ask me for things. We were cheered by this; we thought Mom and Wilma would be friends to the end. We knew Wilma would not bite anybody or throw her feces.

Then Wilma moved out; she went home to the place she had once shared with her dearly departed husband. Mom got sad. She wanted to live on her own, too. Wilma made her believe this was possible. "If Wilma can do it, why can't I?" she asked me, but we both knew the answer here: Wilma could still do things. Wilma could walk and use her hands and brush her teeth and use the toilet. We did not know why Wilma was there in the first place. Mom grieved Wilma's loss, which in so many ways was our loss, too. Mom said that living in the healthcare center was a death sentence.

Later, when I was sad and frustrated, I did an awful, unthinkable thing. I wish I could take it back. What my mother had said about living a death sentence stuck with me. I was thinking about it while walking from the healthcare center with my children. My girls were fifteen by then; my boy was ten. As we slipped through the hall, I said to the three of them that if Karen died first, if for some reason I was left alone, I did not want to be a burden. I did not want them to feel the guilt that I had lived with every day for a decade, the guilt of putting your parent in a nursing home, or a healthcare center, or whatever name it went by.

"Put a gun in my mouth," I told them, "and pull the trigger." They were horrified at the thought. "Daddy," they said, and then said nothing. All three of them stood in the chill of it. "Really," I said. "You cannot let me live like this." They swore they would not. They all said they would take care of me, that they would take turns. I felt even more guilty because I had just shamed my kids into caring for me. That, or they would have to shoot me in the mouth. I hadn't even considered that this would make them feel worse—killing me, that is—but my head still wasn't right, hadn't been for a long time. For a solid decade while Mom was in the healthcare center—and who knows how long before that—I was a tangled mess between the ears.

In May of 2019, I met with a hospice nurse named Debbie in the healthcare center lobby. She had short blonde hair, a deep tan, a husky smoker's voice, and bleached teeth. In a folder on her lap, she had Mom's progress notes, and she read me bullet points: no circulation in the right leg; blockage of four arteries; gangrene in the toes. Mom had already been to the hospital; we had hoped for revascularization there, which would open those arteries and restore blood flow. Instead, the doctor said she was not a candidate. That's what doctors say when they believe a patient might die on their table.

Next option, amputation: lop off the gangrened toes, so Mom would not have to suffer the pain of dying appendages. "It could be quick, it could be slow," Debbie said. But amputation was dicey, because there was no oxygenated blood flowing to her toes; the wound left behind might never heal. She would likely die during the procedure anyway, so Mom was not a candidate for amputation either.

So, that's how I wound up in the lobby of the healthcare center with Debbie. Hospice was Mom's final option: maximum comfort with morphine while her toes rotted, then fell off. Mom was a suitable candidate for that. I had a social worker tell me that hospice was not a death sentence: She'd had patients graduate from it, she said. "One woman spent last weekend with her family at the coast," this social worker told me. I imagined my mother in a tasseled cap and gown, a hospice grad. I imagined her sitting in her wheelchair at Moonstone Beach, on the boardwalk, overlooking the water. I thought she would float through an oblivious, narcotic haze while her toes dropped off, and she would be brought back from it when the deed was done. She would open her eyes to seven toes, maybe eight. That's what she believed, too. She said she would "bear and grin it" and we got a chuckle from that. "My mind these days," she said.

At some point I asked Debbie how long she thought my mother had to live. Were we talking months or weeks? Debbie broke my heart. She said six weeks. I had anticipated this news for more than thirty years, so I held it lightly. In my head, I grew defensive. Also in my head, I told Debbie she had no idea who she was dealing with. My mother had spent her life defying expectations, so why should this be any different? I figured Mom would mend. She always had. She had never failed to get better.

Debbie began to go through a standard-issue hospice brochure with me, then she flipped it aside. "I hate this book," she said. "I can do much better when I freelance." So, that's what she did; she freelanced. She told me what to expect when a person is dying. She called it "actively dying," which struck me at the time as contrary, but I see it now. I can look back on the last few months of Mom's life and I can actually see the ways her body was letting go of her, and nobody seemed to notice. I am sure Mom did, though. I am sure she knew her body well enough to feel it releasing its grip on her. Then again, it could have been the other way around.

Here's what Debbie told me: The body in its dying looks for things to eliminate, and taste buds are the first to go. The body will say, "I don't need to taste things," and that part of the body will just shut down. This had been happening to my mother for several weeks. She no longer cared for the sweet treats we delivered; they remained in her drawers, unopened.

Then there was the blood flow. My mother hadn't been able to sit up or walk for a month because her body convinced itself it no longer needed to pump blood to certain places. Mom hadn't been using her legs, so her body said, "Why bother?" The body seeks economy in its final weeks. It looks for ways to operate efficiently, much like other organisms and systems. What isn't needed is eliminated. So, in Mom's case, it was things like appetite and blood flow. Over the course of weeks, we watched her pinkie toe shrivel and blacken. We watched necrosis creep into the rest of her foot, and up her ankle. We watched my mother's body die in pieces.

Debbie and I talked about making Mom as comfortable as possible while this necrosis persisted. There would be drops of concentrated morphine, four at a time every six hours, placed inside her mouth. A nurse would turn her every two hours. All the while, Mom would have vivid, morphine-induced dreams. She might dream about a time when she was seven years old, and I might walk into the room and say hello, and she might wonder who I was. She might wonder how it was that she, at seven years old, could be a mom. Imperceptibly, she would come out of this; she would come around to the reality of her situation. "Oh, yes, hello," she would say. "I must have been dreaming." And in these dreams,

Mom would talk with the unseen. She would talk with those who went before her: Lloyd, Marzelle, Jack. She would reattach herself to them, to her history, and this experience would be lucid and happy for her. This might happen with me in the room, and I would need to affirm her reality. I would need to act as though we were all there together, in whatever setting happened to be unfurling in Mom's present tense: her sixteenth birthday party back home in Joliet; Wayne Newton with her parents in the Hollywood Bowl; clutching Marzelle's hand during Lloyd's funeral in Clinton, Indiana.

Finally, Debbie told me to identify myself by name before I spoke, rather than leaving my mother to guess who I was. I could not fathom a reality where my mother did not know who I was, but then again, I did not understand the ways the mind prepares the body for its final moments. Like the body, the mind seeks efficiency. It seeks to offload things it does not need, like old memories. Debbie said Mom might make out-of-character statements, which may indicate she was ready to say goodbye. "It's a test," Debbie said, "to see if you are ready to let her go." I would have to accept these moments when offered. Debbie said to kiss, hold, hug, cry, and say whatever I needed to say. The greatest gift I could give my mother, Debbie said, was permission to leave.

A week later, with her well into morphine, I went to my mother's room. I sat next to her bed. She was awake and we smiled at each other. There were locks of wet hair stuck to her forehead, and I pushed them out of the way. There were whiskers sprouting from her chin, and I knew how much she hated this. She said they made her look like a shrew. This was one of the things she was able to do on her own, even near the end. She was able to shave the whiskers from her chin. There would be visitors. There would be people who came to wish her well and say goodbye, and I knew she would not want to look like a shrew. So, I looked through her drawer and found a razor. She saw it appear in my fingers, and she lifted her chin to me.

"You're an angel," she said.

She pursed her lips so her skin stretched tight, and I ran the razor over the whiskers. I took great care in this. I left behind a tiny swath of smooth skin on her knobby chin, and when I was done, my mother looked relieved.

"That's better," I said. "Wouldn't want people thinking you're a shrew."

She nodded and there was a tiny grin that turned up one corner of her mouth. Her body still permitted a tiny grin.

I spent the rest of the afternoon in her room, fussing about the place. By then, I had lost faith that she'd recover. I tidied her closet and her drawers. I fluffed her stuffed animals. I looked for a ballgame on the television. I put headphones over her ears and looped an Elvis gospel CD, because that was her favorite. Mostly, I waited for the dreams and hoped I would have a part in them. I waited for her to welcome her family into that space and share a final bit of joy. But there were no dreams, at least not for me. I saw my mother's lips moving periodically, and I saw the tiny grin, and I imagined that she was with someone who preceded her. It could have been anyone in her remarkable history. It could have been her dad or mom or brother or a dear friend who left too soon. It could have been Elvis Presley. It could have been God.

Mom's breathing was labored and her body was wracked with fever. It was eleven p.m. and I had already gone through the ritual of preparing to leave, telling her I would see her bright and early the next morning. I bent and spoke into my mother's ear. Her nurse, Eleanor, told me to do this. Eleanor told me my mother was leaving, but she could still hear me. Hearing, she said, is the last thing to go in the dying. Mom would hear me until the very end. I have taken comfort in this. I believe my mother heard what I had to say, what I had written on a tablet I found in her tidy drawer: "I give you permission to let go and you don't need to feel guilty for leaving me. I will be all right. My family will be all right. I release you to this next great adventure."

That was it.

That was the last thing I said to my mother.

Epilogue
Ich Liebe Dich

"Make sure to check the wind direction and do not scatter against the wind. The cremains can be sticky and not only will it blow back in your face, it will stick to your skin and clothes, making for a messy and embarrassing situation."

—Cremation Institute, *Scattering Ashes Guide, 2019*

O N June 19, 2019—THE DAY MY MOTHER WOULD HAVE turned eighty-one—I released her ashes over the side of a boat in a small, quiet cove on Huntington Lake. It was like spilling a bag of sugar. Her remains left the box quickly, then vanished into the inky water. She was gone in a matter of seconds. The Monk was with me, driving the boat.

"Hmph," he said.

"That wasn't how I pictured it," I said. I slumped down in the bow of the boat. I looked at the blue sky, the white clouds, at airplane vapor trails, crossing. I told The Monk that the whole thing looked different in my mind, the whole *scattering-of-ashes* thing. I had planned on surface tension, for one, followed by a period of absorption, and then a kind of gossamer, downward cascade. I didn't actually say the words "gossamer, downward cascade." I said something else. I said, "I thought she would float first, then sink kind of slowly." It was to have been a beautiful and liberating exit, fitting for a woman who for so long had been weighed down by all the ways a body can fail. But of the many things I learned from my mother, perhaps the most indisputable is this: The body promises nothing.

"If you would have tossed them from the back of the boat," The Monk said. He seemed to be thinking about the science of it all, considering my missteps. "Probably would have been better if we were moving."

"Maybe that would have been better," I said. We thought about this. The key would have been tossing Mom's ashes *with* the wind while moving, as opposed to *into* it, but at that point, the whole thing was a non-issue; it was neither here nor there. My mother was gone, and her final exit, for the moment, was a massive letdown.

"At least you will always know exactly where she is," The Monk said.

I sighed. "It's a good spot," I said. "Couldn't be better."

And it is a good spot. It is a spot in the cove I have floated over in a canoe almost every summer for twenty-nine years. It is a spot I will continue to visit, likely, until I die, which now that my mother is gone, seems strangely imminent. Part of this feeling comes from my own body's slow failings. I can feel myself degrading. My lungs lack the capacity they once had, and deep breaths are now often accompanied by a whistle; my left hip has grown cranky, as has my right shoulder, each joint wearing thin on what *Gray's Anatomy* calls "the articulating surfaces"; and then there's the inflammation in my fingers, which can only take so much typing before I slather them in menthol. These are mild complaints I accept as part of my own glacial transformation, no different than crows' feet or liver spots or the beginnings of a wattle.

Then there's the company I keep: Karen, The Monk, The Monk's wife, three people with six parents, all living. Within this company, there are conversations about their parents, about guilt and needs and maladies. There are grim foreshadowings: minor falls that inflict major wounds, memories gone blank, bladders and bowels run amok. There is talk of private, in-home care and visits to ERs and long waits for specialists, and I sit quietly, having earned my release from it, empathetic and relieved and all the while thinking, *I am no longer a son.*

On a cold morning in February, seven months after I committed my mother to Huntington Lake, I returned with my family to the Sierra National Forest. We were in the woods just east of Mom's final resting place. From where we stood, I could see her cove through a stand of pines, mostly unrecognizable in the snow, but there, nonetheless. We were there for Karen, who for her father's past few birthdays has chosen to give him the gifts of time and bucket-list experiences, rather than sweaters and ties.

That day, we were making good on one such promise: a snowshoe trek to a frozen waterfall, five miles round-trip, which at one precarious point triggered his vertigo and required Karen's calm encouragement to put one foot in front of the other. Our daughters were there—older now, still dramatic but helpful—and like Karen they soothed their grandfather along the trail with their own brand of comfort. My son was there, too, but he was twelve and still learning about things like warmth and consolation and generosity of spirit. These things have not come naturally to him, unlike bouts of impertinence and exasperation. I love my son, and though he has two parents committed to growing him, I feel especially responsible for him at times like that morning, when he set out with vigor, leaving the rest of us behind, despite me telling him to stay close.

It took him five minutes to lose us.

In the snowy mountains, even in drought years, there are dangers. I appraised them that morning, mostly the ragged cliff sides and deep, shady drifts over and into which snowshoed hikers could instantly vanish. My son had already pronounced the trail "lame" and stated his intention to go rogue and stray from it. His words were in my head as I trekked uphill, hoping to see him around one bend, then another. Minutes passed and there was no sign of him. Behind me, Karen and her dad and my daughters chugged uphill and began to grumble. I heard my father-in-law say the words "search party."

I tried not to let my fears get the best of me. He's fine, I told myself. Then, what if? I hiked to a sunny spot on the trail and stopped, and from there I called my son's name into the woods. Behind me, the others stopped; they leaned on their poles and listened for a return call, but nothing came, nothing except my own rebounding voice. In the mountains, the silence following such a moment is charged with fear. We all felt it, and even though I knew in my bones that my son was safe, probably bristling with defiance, there was still a frightening wonder.

After another five minutes and several more calls into the woods— all of us yelling now—my son emerged from behind a tree on the trail. He waved his poles crosswise over his head, and my heart grew light but angry. I stomped up to him as he complained about the rest of us taking so long. I complained right back at him about how he put us in crisis mode. "That was pretty stupid," I said. "You had all of us worried." He rolled his eyes and threw his head back and moaned over the absurdity of it all. How could I be so unreasonable?

"You told me to hike ahead," he said. "Those were your *exact* words."

"I did not," I said.

"Did, too."

"I never would have said that," I told him.

"But you did."

We went back-and-forth like this, me wondering exactly what I did say, him insisting I gave him sovereignty to roam the snowy woods alone.

Despite the ambiguity, I scolded my son because I felt it wholly necessary to remind him that I cared enough to do so. "When I don't get upset by this," I told him, "that's when you should worry." I pulled him close to kiss his head and bury my face in his hair, which smelled musty and damp, like I imagine gushing hormones might smell. It might also have been the smell of frustration or longing or self-doubt. "I love you," I said. Because my son still has a hard time with this—with saying *I love you*, I mean—he responded in German, which he has determined is the safest way to express himself.

"*Ich liebe dich,*" he grumbled.

It is not like the real thing for me, but with my son, I take what he gives me. I will not force him to say "I love you, too, Dad." I will not coerce him to such a place.

Soon, maybe midway through the second mile, my son's early enthusiasm for the snowshoe trek turned into something much different: utter, unequivocal torture. He had already shed his snowshoes, which I strapped to my pack, and had taken to navigating the terrain in scuffed Vans. At one point, with the two of us behind the others, he sat on a rock and complained of a sore knee. "I *literally* can't go on," he said.

I reached for him. "Come on," I said. "The waterfall is just around the corner." I told him I didn't come all this way to miss it, though to be honest, it wasn't much to see. A frozen waterfall in the High Sierra sounds much cooler than it really is. "It's just ice," he said when we got there.

"Yes," I said. "But look at the way it's just frozen there, waiting to move." I told him it was a metaphor for adolescence. My son moaned over this. He rolled his eyes at me. "I can't believe we have to walk *all the way back*," he said. "Ughhhhhh." He completely missed the metaphor.

By now, his shoes and socks were soaked through, his feet wet and bitterly cold. This was his choice, but I'd have moaned, too. I told Karen I would walk ahead with him, and she could take her time with her dad, who admitted at the turnaround to feeling tired and spent. My daughters, beleaguered by their brother, opted to stay behind with them.

"I'll go ahead then," I said. "I'm afraid if I stop too long, I'll stiffen up." This was true. My own body now radiated pain, mostly to my hip but also into my fingers, which had been curled around the grips of my walking poles for a couple of hours. There was also the matter of my surgically repaired right forearm, which for the last thirty years—thanks to medical hardware—aches in the cold.

We started back well enough, my son and me. He walked alongside and I tried to keep his pace. The potential for connection was not lost on me; I had my boy all to myself on a snowy trail with at least an hour in front of us. I tried conversation, first about baseball, then about a girl he likes, but neither topic hit its mark. Because I was both talking and walking at altitude, I grew breathless quickly. My pace slowed. My son began to separate.

"I'll see you at the bottom," I said. "Just wait for me by the truck."

Meanwhile, on the trail behind us, Karen's father fell. He took a shortcut off the main path, and the way I heard it told later, both his feet sunk to his ankles and he pitched forward, face-down and, for a moment, lay breathless. But my father-in-law is resilient; he is also humble and self-effacing. After Karen helped him up, the four of them had a good laugh over the whole thing, my father-in-law chuckling, his face covered in snow.

"It was so funny, Dad," my daughters both said. "You should have seen it." They said my father-in-law was a snow-angel, face-down.

"I wish I would have seen it," I said. "It sounds hilarious."

By this time, my son was in the truck, warming his feet. I looked through the window at the back of his head, his dirty blond hair so much like my own when I was his age. People have said he looks just like me, and I have thought this, too. In fact, I had been thinking this as I watched him walk down the hill, that from behind, the likeness was eerie, which is to be expected of a father and son, that the younger would by nature look something like the older. "I'll see you at the bottom," I had said, and my son turned and waved, and there it was, frozen for an instant, the young me in all of my possibility, a still photograph. Just as quickly, he turned away and became a boy walking ahead, his gaze forward, his spirit churning, his cold, wet feet shuffling over the resplendent snow.

Acknowledgements

I WROTE MOST OF *STUCCOVILLE: LIFE WITHOUT A NET* between January and May of 2019, the final five months of my mother's remarkable and unexpectedly long life. I was fifty and she was eighty, and I had been caring for her in a variety of ways through forty-two years of illness. The book began as a challenge from a friend, Audrey Monke, who vowed to bully me until I wrote it all down, all forty-two years and then some, because she had faith in the story and in the teller.

It was Audrey who sent me to Author Accelerator and Michele Orwin, a careful and thoughtful reader who helped me work through my chapters, forty-plus pages a month for six months, until I had a workable rough draft. Michele was a perfect fit because she understood the story I needed to share. She was patient, responsive, and honest. Like Audrey, Michele also had faith in the story.

Turns out, so did the generous teacher and fiction writer John Dufresne, who mentored me at Florida International University from 1996–1998. I knew John was gracious with his time, but I still was surprised when he agreed to read my book since I hadn't been in touch for twenty years. That's the kind of man John is. He never refuses an opportunity to help a writer in need, and he never forgets a student. I was even more surprised when he told me how much he liked *Stuccoville*, how much he believed in it, how I had finally become the writer he always knew I could be.

Faithfully, then, I sent out my draft. I pitched my story to book agents and editors and university presses, and like most anonymous authors,

I got a lot of passes; worse, though, were the nonresponses. I would have rather heard "no, thank you," than nothing at all.

Then came Jay Christopher at WiDo Publishing/E. L. Marker, a small Utah press. I pitched Jay and he asked for twenty pages; later, he asked for more. Jay wound up reading the whole book multiple times, and he gave me sharp, insightful feedback. Jay was tireless in his work, and he became a trusted, diligent editor. He read my book on evenings and Saturdays, and Jay's transformative efforts have helped make *Stuccoville* a book I am proud of.

Thanks abound to so many others who helped build this book, but in particular those who read my early, clumsy writing: Eugene Zumwalt, Liza Wieland, Steve Yarbrough, John and Connie Hales, Linnea Alexander, Tom DeMarchi, Lynne Barrett, Les Standiford, and Campbell McGrath.

Thank you as well to friends Steve Monke and Scott Wong, who lived through most of my mother's afflictions and were there with me at the end.

Thank you to my children, Caroline, Katherine, and William, who are living testimonies to my mother's grit and courage, and who love me even though they've watched me at my worst.

Thank you to my wife Karen, who navigated the most difficult years of my mother's illness with me and provided quiet, heroic support on days I could not muster an ounce of peace in my heart.

And, of course, thank you to my mother, Barbara Radke, who crammed her life into files labeled "important papers" she thought I might need someday.

Her efforts built a history.

About the Author

CHARLES LEWIS RADKE IS A GRADUATE OF CREATIVE writing programs at Fresno State (1992) and Florida International University (1996). He is the author of *Sierra Summers: A History of Gold Arrow Camp* (2017). His short stories have appeared in *The San Joaquin Review, Hayden's Ferry Review, Gulf Stream Magazine,* and *The South Dakota Review.* In graduate school, he was the recipient of an AWP Intro Award for fiction and the Estelle Campbell Prize for literature from the National Society of Arts and Letters. He lives in Fresno, California.

charleslewisradke.com

CPSIA information can be obtained
at www.ICGtesting.com
Printed in the USA
LVHW031715250121
677445LV00038B/832

9 781947 966437